Security Planning and Design

A Guide for Architects and Building Design Professionals

The American Institute of Architects

Security Planning and Design
A Guide for Architects and Building Design Professionals

Joseph A. Demkin, AIA, Editor

WILEY

John Wiley & Sons, Inc.

This book is printed on acid-free paper. ∞

Copyright © 2004 by The American Institute of Architects. All rights reserved.

AIA, The American Institute of Architects, and the AIA logo are registered trademarks and service marks of The American Institute of Architects.

Published by John Wiley & Sons, Inc., Hoboken, New Jersey.
Published simultaneously in Canada.

No part of this publication may be reproduced, stored in a retrieval system, or transmitted in any form or by any means, electronic, mechanical, photocopying, recording, scanning, or otherwise, except as permitted under Section 107 or 108 of the 1976 United States Copyright Act, without either the prior written permission of the Publisher, or authorization through payment of the appropriate per-copy fee to the Copyright Clearance Center, Inc., 222 Rosewood Drive, Danvers, MA 01923, (978) 750-8400, fax (978) 750-4470, or on the web at www.copyright.com. Requests to the Publisher for permission should be addressed to the Permissions Department, John Wiley & Sons, Inc., 111 River Street, Hoboken, NJ 07030, (201) 748-6011, fax (201) 748-6008, e-mail: permcoordinator@wiley.com.

Limit of Liability/Disclaimer of Warranty: While the publisher and author have used their best efforts in preparing this book, they make no representations or warranties with respect to the accuracy or completeness of the contents of this book and specifically disclaim any implied warranties of merchantability or fitness for a particular purpose. No warranty may be created or extended by sales representatives or written sales materials. The advice and strategies contained herein may not be suitable for your situation. You should consult with a professional where appropriate. Neither the publisher nor author shall be liable for any loss of profit or any other commercial damages, including but not limited to special, incidental, consequential, or other damages.

For general information on our other products and services or for technical support, please contact our Customer Care Department within the United States at (800) 762-2974, outside the United States at (317) 572-3993 or fax (317) 572-4002.

Wiley also publishes its books in a variety of electronic formats. Some content that appears in print may not be available in electronic books. For more information about Wiley products, visit our web site at www.wiley.com.

Library of Congress Cataloging-in-Publication Data:

Security planning and design : a guide for architects and building design professionals / by the American Institute of Architects.
    p. cm.
Includes bibliographical references and index.
    ISBN 0-471-27156-X (Cloth)
    1. Buildings—Security measures. I. American Institute of Architects.

TH9705.S4 2003
720'.4—dc22

                                                2003014859

PRINTED IN THE UNITED STATES OF AMERICA
10 9 8 7 6 5 4

Contents

Preface

Building security and safety took on new meaning on September 11, 2001. Unprecedented terrorist actions that day at the World Trade Center in New York City and the Pentagon in Washington, D.C., made building owners and users think as they had never thought before about how secure and safe they are—or aren't—in the buildings they use every day.

In the wake of these tragic events, the American Institute of Architects launched initiatives to explore the relationship between security and building design and to define the architect's role in that relationship. These efforts included a virtual conference; a Web-based security resource center; the booklet *Building Security through Design: A Primer for Architects, Design Professionals, and Their Clients*; several forums involving public and private sector participants; and a national conference cosponsored with the office of Architectural Surety at Sandia Laboratories.

Security Planning and Design adds to these initiatives. As a guide for architects and building design professionals, *Security Planning and Design* presents concepts, principles, and processes, rather than a "cookbook" of recipes or prescriptive solutions. The following bird's-eye view of the material contained in each chapter offers a quick idea of what is covered:

Chapter 1, Security in the Built Environment, explores contextual issues for security at regional, community, and local levels. Emerging issues facing design professionals are discussed, including existing versus new building design, security and aesthetics, and designing for security in an open society.

Chapter 2, Understanding Threats, examines threats that drive the need for security planning and design in buildings. The focus is on criminal and terrorist threats with respect to their nature, how they are carried out, and how their effectiveness can be reduced.

Chapter 3, Security Design Concepts, describes the basic components of security, presents a framework to help designers think about security in a comprehensive way, and identifies approaches for incorporating security concepts, strategies, and measures into the design process.

Chapter 4, Security Planning and Evaluation, highlights the assessment process used to define security needs. Methods are described for analyzing assets, threats, and vulnerabilities, and for defining acceptable risk levels from which functional security design requirements and design strategies can be developed.

Chapter 5, Building Hardening, explains concepts for making buildings more resistant to the effects of ballistic attacks, forced entry, and explosions. Blast mitigation structural design methods, tools, and techniques are covered, as well as issues concerning the selection of hardened building materials and components.

Chapter 6, Building Security Technologies, profiles available security equipment and systems for surveillance, detection, and access control functions in buildings. Issues such as functionality, operation, spatial requirements, aesthetic implications, and cost are addressed, along with other design and selection considerations.

Chapter 7, Biochemical and Radiological Building Protection, presents concepts and technologies for protecting people in buildings from the effects of chemical, biological, and radiological contamination, including response strategies for HVAC and potable water systems.

Chapter 8, Security and Emergency Operations, looks at both security and emergency preparedness in building operations so that design professionals can better anticipate the implications of design decisions on these aspects of building use.

Chapter 9, Putting Security into Practice, provides practical advice about security considerations in both the business operations and project delivery aspects of architecture practice. Hypothetical design examples are presented to demonstrate the application of security strategies and measures to selected building functions.

A sequential reading of the chapters is preferable due to their general flow. Also, some readers may find it helpful to review the definitions in the glossary before delving into chapter material. Like most specialized areas, the world of security has its own vocabulary.

The architecture profession has worked closely with its professional allies in the past to address issues of national scope and prominence. In response to the energy crisis of the 1970s, multidisciplinary efforts enabled architects to design buildings with higher levels of energy efficiency. In the 1980s and 1990s, cooperative environmental research and informational initiatives provided pathways to help architects create "greener" building environments.

In a similar spirit, the AIA is collaborating with security and other allied professionals to help bring security knowledge into the mainstream of architecture practice. As this occurs, architects and building professionals can be increasingly effective in addressing their clients' security concerns.

Joseph A. Demkin, AIA
The American Institute of Architects
Washington, D.C.

Acknowledgments

The American Institute of Architects appreciates the efforts of those who participated in the creation of *Security Planning and Design*. When architects and security experts collaborate to bring information and knowledge together about security design in buildings, both the profession and the public benefit.

The AIA extends a special note of thanks to Richard P. Grassie. Besides being a contributing author, Mr. Grassie served as technical advisor for the book. His assistance and advice in this capacity were invaluable and his efforts are deeply appreciated.

Other contributing authors willingly and graciously shared their knowledge and experience on varied aspects of the subject. The AIA extends expressions of thanks to Randall I. Atlas, Joseph Brancato, Peter D. DiMaggio, Behrooz (Ben) Emam, Michael C. Janus, Stuart L. Knoop, Thomas L. Norman, and Robert C. Rudolph. Biographical profiles of the contributing authors follow these acknowledgments.

Contributors Stuart L. Knoop, Peter D. DiMaggio, and Thomas L. Norman also merit additional thanks for their insight and suggestions during the editorial planning that helped define the scope of the book.

Those participating in other ways are also thanked for their help: Ramon Ferreira of Weidlinger Associates, Inc., specially prepared the graphics for the chapter on building hardening. The chapter on putting security into practice was prepared and reviewed by Gensler staff members Benjamin Fisher, FAIA; Donald Ghent, AIA; John Gunn, AIA; David Koren, Assoc. AIA; Gene Lee; Jean Lee; and Barbara McCarthy, along with Michael Peragine of Costas, Kondylis & Partners.

Suggestions and advice from AIA general counsel Jay Stephens, Esq., and AIA Government Affairs managing director Rodney Clark were most helpful. The editorial and research assistance efforts of AIA staff editor Pamela James Blumgart were indispensable, as was the copyediting work of Mary Anderson.

On a final note, the AIA would like to thank Amanda Miller, associate publisher for professional and trade publications with John Wiley & Sons, Inc. Amanda encouraged and supported the publishing effort, and provided ongoing advice and assistance.

Contributor Profiles

Randall I. Atlas, Ph.D., AIA, CPP, is president of Counter Terror Design, Inc., Coral Gables, Florida. Dr. Atlas is a nationally recognized trainer and author on crime prevention through environmental design (CPTED) for the National Crime Prevention Institute, ASIS International, and the American Institute of Architects. He is a consultant to the Department of Housing and Urban Development and has conducted numerous CPTED surveys. Dr. Atlas has contributed to the *Protection of Assets Manual* and is a regular contributor to *Access Control & Security Systems, Security Technology & Design*, and *Security Management* magazines.

Joseph Brancato, AIA, is vice president and managing principal in Gensler's New York City office. Mr. Brancato focuses on client development and global account leadership, provides oversight to the firm's practice areas, and participates in projects that include architecture, interiors, and strategic consulting. He is a frequent presenter and panelist on topics such as disaster planning, workplace best practices, and strategic alliances. Mr. Brancato is a member of Gensler's executive council.

Peter D. DiMaggio, PE, is a structural engineer and senior associate with Weidlinger Associates, Inc., in New York City. He has been project manager and lead blast design engineer for numerous projects for the Department of State, the General Services Administration, and the Department of Defense. Mr. DiMaggio has lectured and written extensively on the capability of structures to withstand high-explosive attacks.

Behrooz (Ben) Emam, AIA, PE, CFM, is senior manager for global facilities planning and engineering at Amazon.com. A registered architect, professional civil engineer, and certified facility manager, Mr. Emam has extensive experience in architectural and structural engineering; facility design, construction and project management, and emergency preparedness. He regularly teaches classes in construction and facility management and conducts seminars on seismic preparedness and disaster planning.

Richard P. Grassie, CPP, is president of TECHMARK Security Integration, Inc., a Boston-based firm providing security design and technology integration services. Mr. Grassie has served as consultant to Fortune 500, institutional, and government clients in the United States and abroad. He is a board member of the International Association of Security Consultants and is past chair of the ASIS International Security Architecture and Engineering Council. He has written numerous articles and conducts workshops and training seminars on security for public agencies and private industry.

Michael C. Janus, PE, is the director of Building Protection Programs for the Battelle Memorial Institute, a nationally recognized leader in the field of CBR defense. Mr. Janus has conducted protection assessments for more than 75 buildings throughout the country and has led building protection programs for Battelle. Clients for these projects include the Department of Defense, the Federal Emergency Management Agency, the Department of Energy, the Department of Justice, the Department of Transportation, the Internal Revenue Service, the International Monetary Fund, the National Archives, and the National Basketball Association. Mr. Janus holds several U.S. patents, including one for an expedient CB collective protection device.

Stuart L. Knoop, FAIA, is president of Oudens and Knoop Architects, PC, of Chevy Chase, Maryland. He has 25 years of security design experience on numerous facility types, including 60 embassies and consulates worldwide. Mr. Knoop chaired the National Research Council (NRC) review of security design criteria for the Federal Interagency Security Committee, served as a member of the NRC committee on security of future U.S. embassy buildings, was vice-chair of the NRC committee that produced *Protecting Buildings from Bomb Damage*, and served on the NRC committee for oversight and assessment of blast effects and related research.

1 Security in the Built Environment

Stuart L. Knoop, FAIA

People can achieve security through their actions, such as when they band into groups for mutual protection or conduct diplomacy to avert war. Generally, these actions are accomplished by political, military, law enforcement, and operational means. Security is also achieved through physical features in the natural and built environments. Choosing a mountain site for human settlement or a cave for human habitation is a basic way of achieving physical protection. For the purposes of this discussion, this form of protection will be called *physical security*.

> Protection and security are only valuable if they do not cramp life excessively.
> —Carl Jung

Throughout the course of human history, architects, designers, and builders have addressed security of all kinds. Often, the most visible security components of a building, such as doors, gates, fenestration, and window grilles, have been raised to levels of high art through architectural design. The inclusion of physical security in the design of a building or other structure is not antithetical to design that inspires.

At the most fundamental level, we shape our built environment to provide shelter from natural phenomena such as precipitation, temperature extremes, and sun. Beyond these basic needs, building design also encompasses the two distinct—yet closely related—issues of safety and security.

Building safety issues deal with natural and unintentional threats such as earthquakes, hurricanes, floods, and accidental spills. *Building security issues* are about the prevention and detection of intentional, humanly motivated threats such as criminal, terrorist, and other malevolent acts directed toward buildings and their occupants.

Natural threats can result in the same hazards, such as fire, structural failure, toxic releases, and other abnormal conditions. Sometimes, designing for one can address the other. For example, redundancy for electrical power simultaneously addresses emergencies caused by a thunderstorm or a terrorist attack.

The safety aspect of buildings is addressed by building codes that establish *minimal* standards for the design of building systems and components. In contrast, decisions about building security are left to the discretion of building owners and their managers and operators. However, planning for building safety should not compromise security readiness.

Code requirements are intended to minimize the effects of fire, but architects also plan for safe refuge or escape if a fire occurs. In other words, physical security design may provide a level of protection from a terrorist's bomb, but safety design is aimed at ensuring that occupants can escape from the resulting fire and smoke. Security and safety are complementary, rather than contradictory, requirements.

A Contextual Perspective

Physical security for a particular facility considers the context of the surrounding environment. Regional and community issues can directly or indirectly affect security considerations for a project. Such broader issues may encompass matters of site selection and location, site access, availability of utilities, and adjacent threats, among others.

REGIONAL ISSUES

Whether selecting a site for a community or an individual building, the first consideration has always been its location with respect to the natural environment. Historically, this may have meant selecting a site isolated from potential enemies, on an island or in a remote aerie on a mountaintop. In modern times, the location of a commercial facility may be dictated primarily by economic considerations, such as availability of labor and material resources and access to transportation. Nonetheless, security continues to be a factor when a site is chosen.

In an era when any geographic area can be reached by aircraft, missiles, or satellites, deciding whether to locate, say, a major data processing facility in a potential target area such as midtown Manhattan or downtown Washington, D.C., certainly requires security information on a regional scale. Other considerations of a regional nature have traditionally included access to food, water, fuel, and other necessities for survival under siege or during a disaster. Although many of these essentials can be stockpiled for longer periods than in the past, their availability is still a concern. For example, the potential vulnerability of power plants and oil pipelines to terrorist bombs, and of water and food supplies to chemical and biological terrorism, have become topics of national concern.

Another regional concern has traditionally been control of approach and escape routes to and from a location affected by a disaster or attack. The virtual sealing of river crossings from Manhattan Island following the September 11, 2001, attack on the World Trade Center demonstrates the modern equivalent of this ancient security concern.

COMMUNITY AND LOCAL ISSUES

Some security considerations are tied more closely to the immediate surroundings of a building. For example, when selecting a site in a particular community or neighborhood, security must be balanced against such matters as access to transportation, availability of utilities, convenience to occupants and visitors, and symbolic significance in society. Often, the factors that make a site desirable can complicate physical security.

In addition, a site that is otherwise appealing could be a problem from a security standpoint if it was adjacent to a property involving hazardous use, such as an oil refinery or a weapons plant. Other, less obvious adjacencies may be of greater concern. For example, it may not be possible to control neighboring parking areas, and some government agencies offer unpopular or controversial services.

Another important consideration in selecting a building site is how easy it would be for law enforcement and emergency fire and rescue services to access the site. Congested central urban areas may be convenient and desirable for many purposes, but traffic congestion—especially in an emergency—may critically delay police, fire, and ambulance arrival. Similarly, a remote site in a rural area may be too far from adequately trained and equipped response personnel.

CONCENTRIC BARRIERS

The most obvious protection from the effects of a hostile act is any barrier that can prevent or delay an adversary from reaching a target. In the past, natural geographic features such as rivers, mountains, and dense forests were used to introduce physical barriers between people and the outside world. However, human ingenuity overcame most of these long ago, so we designed and constructed other barriers instead. More recently, we have had to devise defensive mechanisms to combat technological threats such as electronic eavesdropping and wiretapping.

❖ First Level of Defense

Walls, fences, and revetments of various kinds have long served as the first line of defense for a specific site. The historically famous walls of ancient cities such as Troy, Jerusalem, and Jericho are classic examples. In fact, relics of such ancient walls survive in many cities, including London and Rome. Early European settlements in North America, such as Québec City and Jamestown, Virginia, often had walls as well. Walls were sometimes augmented by other elements—most famously, moats or even the tidal waters of the sea as at Mont-St-Michel and St. Michael's Mount on opposite sides of the English Channel (see Figure 1.1).

FIGURE 1.1
Cliff Village, Mediterranean Coast, Spain. Civilizations throughout history have used natural geographic features such as mountains, rivers, and dense forests to provide protection from the outside world.

Today, although city walls serve only as reminders of history, perimeter protection of individual buildings or sites is a familiar sight. For example, the walls around the colleges at Oxford and Cambridge (or Harvard Yard) are venerable, architectural parts of their respective urban fabric (as well as the subject of many anecdotes and limericks). The entrance features—gates—are themselves significant architectural accomplishments. Tom Tower, Christopher Wren's entrance to Christ Church College in Oxford, is a splendid example (see Figure 1.2). Such entrances are known in modern security parlance as *access control* elements or measures.

Beyond the miles of chain-link fencing topped with concertina wire that enclose military and other national security installations, more benign fences are a common device to establish territorial limits. Around the world, we use barriers—whether a white picket fence or a neatly trimmed hedge—to define what is ours. When someone trespasses (literally, "crosses over" a barrier), we know our property has been violated and we may be threatened. Thus, even an easily breached perimeter barrier has a security function, setting limits that, once breached, entitle the owner to

FIGURE 1.2

*Tom Tower, Christ Church, Oxford.
In the past, entrance portals and
gates controlling access to cities and
prominent structures were often
developed as magnificent examples
of architectural form.*

FIGURE 1.3
*Acropolis, Athens.
Escarpments were used
in many historical appli-
cations to provide for
perimeter defense.*

some reaction. More elaborate fences around houses are also familiar, and not necessarily repugnant.

Other perimeter defense features include escarpments. Perhaps best known are those at the Acropolis in Athens (Figure 1.3). Escarpments also appear at the Getty Museum in Los Angeles, although perhaps less for security than for the spectacular view.

In modern practice, site perimeters are secured with many types and combinations of barriers, but for all the objective is the same: Keep intruders out, stall them, and/or keep them at a safe distance. This latter function, known in security parlance as *standoff,* was a function of the moat and wall combination in medieval castles. Siege engines could be kept far enough away to minimize their effectiveness in delivering invaders or projectiles over the castle walls. Achieving standoff in modern design may require a barrier that can keep a bomb-laden vehicle at a distance sufficient to mitigate the effects of a blast.

With sufficient time and effort, however, any barrier can be breached. Thus, a major function of a barrier is to allow time for a response, such as arrival of law enforcement or escape of occupants from a facility under attack. History is replete with examples of perimeter barriers that failed because they were destroyed, surmounted, or compromised by the gatekeepers. The effectiveness of a perimeter barrier of any kind is only as good as its weakest part, which is often a human weakness.

❖ Second Level of Defense

The next physical barrier—the next ring in a concentric system of defenses—is the *envelope* of the building. The envelope of a building—comprising walls, roofs, and openings for doors and windows—primarily protects the building and its occupants from the natural elements, precipitation, sun, and wind. In a security context, however, the building envelope serves the same functions—and has the same vulnerabilities—as the site perimeter barriers. In other words, it is intended to keep enemies out, delay enemy penetration, and buy time for response. As with a perimeter barrier system, the enemy will seek the weakest portions, often the openings required for access, light, and ventilation.

The building envelope must be able to withstand assaults by an intruder who has overcome the perimeter barriers, whether by forced or surreptitious means or following a blast pressure wave. For centuries, windows and doors have been designed to protect against battering and prying using relatively simple tools and damage from fire and other means. Less common in nonmilitary buildings are openings designed to resist the effects of a blast or a ballistic attack. Protection from both types of assault is possible and, depending on the threat and risk analyses for a building, may be necessary.

The architecture of the envelope presents an enduring image of a building and its function. For the designer, then, the most challenging task is to design an envelope that doesn't leak and doesn't admit the enemy, yet represents the building's status architecturally. This is what architects have done for centuries.

A common fear is that buildings designed with security in mind may become fortresslike as windows and other openings are sacrificed to greater expanses of wall. Despite this concern, our culture is comfortable with many buildings that are essentially windowless—theaters, shopping malls, and museums, to name but a few. Even chapels can be essentially windowless but inviting. These buildings are familiar, open to public use, and can be architecturally pleasing.

❖ Third Level of Defense

A designer must include barriers on the interior of a building as well, as warranted by the nature of potential threats and to ensure safe escape for the building occupants. This may mean constructing walls and doors strong enough to further delay the progress of an intruder. An extreme example of this is a bank vault with a massive door as the most physically protected core of a particular building type.

Emerging Security Needs

Traditional security threats are familiar from personal experiences and stories in the news media. They include individuals acting alone and using the most common tools (e.g., hammers, screwdrivers, and lock picks) and weapons (e.g., knives and handguns). They also include violent spontaneous mobs such as sometimes develop following a sports event or organized mass demonstration. Other familiar threats include state or institutionally sponsored individuals such as spies, assassins, and terrorists; organized mobs; and professional armed forces using a full range of ordnance.

Historically, for protection from traditional threats, we depended on traditional building materials applied in varying ways, most of which achieved effectiveness through sheer size and mass. These materials included earthworks for revetments; stone and brick masonry walls and floors; and iron and steel gates, fences, and grillwork. Use of these materials was enhanced by judicious site selection and incorporation of natural features such as water in moats and open fields for good visibility.

In the not-too-distant past, some nations, including the United States, were separated and protected from their rivals by natural barriers, especially oceans and mountains. Today, as the world grows smaller, such barriers are no longer effective except for the time that distance may buy in a supersonic age. Moreover, our economy is inextricably linked with the economies of other nations and, increasingly, traditional borders are crossed based on supply and demand for goods and labor. National boundaries are increasingly porous, if not yet altogether transparent.

Modern weapons, even those available outside the military establishment, can overcome most of the building materials traditionally relied on for physical protection. Small arms and weapons can penetrate construction materials commonly used to build doors and windows. Hand-held power tools from drills to jacks and bolt-cutters can easily breach a typical steel fence or window grill. Personally transported explosives can destroy masonry walls and other common assemblies. Larger explosive charges, including those made from commonly available materials such as fuel oil and fertilizer, can be transported in vehicles. Military-grade weapons are increasingly deployed (especially in troubled areas of the Middle East), including armor-piercing rocket-propelled grenades and plastic explosives.

Modern research and technology have provided means to counter some of these new threats. Blast-mitigating structural design, new materials that reduce glass and masonry fragmentation, and solid and transparent materials resistant to ballistics and forced entry are some examples. But these new materials and methods of construction have led terrorists to more imaginative and increasingly violent means to make their statements. For example, the use of fuel-laden commercial jetliners as weapons of destruction debuted in 2001 as though in retaliation for the failure of the 1993 vehicle bomb attack on the World Trade Center in New York City.

In 2001 the possibility of biological terrorism also became a reality with the discovery of anthrax-tainted mail. The federal government is funding research in both civilian and military agencies for development of antitoxins. Although use of chemical agents in war was nominally banned after World War II, the potential for use of chemical agents by terrorists became apparent with the Sarin gas attack on the Tokyo subway, and fears of repeat incidents remain. Even the use of small nuclear weapons by terrorists, and larger ones by rogue states, has attracted the attention of the media and Congress with the realization that existing stocks, especially in the former Soviet Union, are poorly secured and even unaccounted for.

Meanwhile, our increasing cultural and economic dependence on electronic communications and data transfer has introduced new threats to businesses and governments. These threats include eavesdropping on hard-wired as well as radio-transmitted communications and computer hacking by both amateurs and professionals, including introduction of worldwide computer viruses. Such threats have spawned a growth industry in communications and data security, which encompasses physical security designed to prevent entry by unauthorized persons and electronic access from outside the building.

There is little doubt, experts agree, that the need for physical security design will continue as long as there are conflicting social, religious, and political agendas in the world. Terrorists—that is, persons seeking to inflict harm and make statements through violence against civilian targets—may act individually or in small groups that are difficult to detect, infiltrate, and neutralize before they act. Unlike established states with governments and armed forces, terrorists may or may not be part of an organization that can be defeated in a geographically centered war, such as that conducted against al Qaeda and its Taliban protectors in Afghanistan. Such groups may be global with covert support from numerous states or groups within states.

So great is the threat of terrorist actions against buildings even in the continental United States (once thought immune from such attacks) that insurers are excluding terrorism from their coverage and the federal government is developing ways to mitigate claims.

The nature of the national response to an ongoing terrorist threat is, at this writing, under intense debate. It may eventually comprise increased border security, more federal funding of security measures, more surveillance of users and visitors in selected facilities, and more sophisticated airport security measures.

Research and development of construction materials and technologies with respect to security seems on the rise in both the government and the private sector. New markets have been developing for products with security applications: Biometric technologies such as retinal scans may move out of the high-security field into more widespread applications, and fragment-retention fabrics, films, and coatings are increasingly available and applied.

Design Professionals and Security

Architects and engineers have designed for security in buildings from prosaic warehouses to the most extraordinary palaces. The designs have ranged from the utilitarian, for weapons bunkers, to the sublime, such as museums like the National Gallery of Art in Washington, D.C., a nearly windowless, finely articulated façade.

Some of the most renowned Western architects, engineers, and artists have addressed physical security. Examples range from Michelangelo's grilled window for the Medici Palace in Florence (ca. 1517–1520) to Pier Luigi Nervi's design for underground gasoline reservoirs in Palerno (1938–1940). In the United States, security has been a subtler part of the architectural program, although it has been used iconically, as when Skidmore, Owings & Merrill, in 1954, placed a bank vault door facing Fifth Avenue through a vast glass wall in the midtown branch of Manufacturer's Trust Company (Figure 1.4).

Since the United States became a dominant world power after World War II, it has drawn the attention of protesters overseas. As a result, U.S. foreign service buildings have been under escalating assault worldwide, forcing the architects of new U.S. embassy buildings to create designs that simultaneously represent the values of an open society and defend the facilities from attack.

The 1970s saw the introduction of the now-familiar walk-through metal detectors and parcel checks under the scrutiny of Marine security guards behind ballistic- and forced entry-resistant barriers. As opposition to U.S. policies escalated, especially in the Middle East, the use of high

FIGURE 1.4
Manufacturer's Trust Bank, New York City. The vault door of this bank, which is visible from the sidewalk, serves as an icon of security and a central design feature.

explosives against U.S. installations emerged. The 1983 attacks on the U.S. embassies in Kuwait and Beirut and the U.S. Marine barracks in Beirut resulted in the Omnibus Diplomatic Security and Anti-Terrorism Act of 1985. This, with the 1986 National Research Council study "The Embassy of the Future," began an official program of security design that has addressed many forms of belligerence directed against buildings.

Design professionals are as well-equipped to address design for security as for any other building program requirement, given knowledge of the issues and an adequate statement of the problems by the owner and security consultants. Most architects and engineers, however, do not have the knowledge or access to data needed to develop programmatic security requirements themselves. The owner, using either its own experience or that of specialized consultants, must determine the threats to which a facility may have to respond. Government agencies and some corporations have in-house resources or access to the intelligence information needed to make these judgments. The probability that one or more threats will occur is based on historical data extrapolated to the future and considerable probabilistic acumen applied to the time and place of the project in question.

Once the building owner has established the potential threats to a project, an analysis of the vulnerability of the project site (whether existing or contemplated) to such threats can be performed. A design professional might be involved in this assessment, depending on the nature of the threat and the knowledge and experience of the designer. Typically, a specialized security consultant is needed to perform this analysis, especially for complex facilities or special threats.

For example, an architect may be able to judge vulnerabilities for some common criminal threats but may not know enough to evaluate vulnerability to damage from ballistics or explosives. The behavior of materials and assemblies under these kinds of attack may or may not be reliably available in the general literature or manufacturers' product information. Certainly, the impact on building elements of a blast of a given charge weight, discharged at a particular distance, can be calculated. In some instances, however, the actual behavior of a particular building material assembly, such as a curtain wall, may be ascertained only from testing.

With a vulnerability analysis completed, an owner can better determine the level of acceptable risk, considering the resources available. There is no such thing as no risk, and no owners, even federal agencies, have unlimited financial or human resources to mitigate all risk. Therefore, a balance between physical security measures and budget must be struck; the owner alone can determine that balance.

The assessment of risk involves a complex series of judgments that consider the potential consequences of a threatened action in terms of human casualties and potential property loss and in terms of the criticality of a facility to the owner's or society's structure and mission. Finally, the susceptibility of a facility to various threats may reside in its symbolic value to an assailant, as has been seen in attacks on the World Trade Center and the Pentagon.

Once a threat assessment, vulnerability assessment, and risk assessment have been completed, and the owner has articulated the resources it is prepared to devote to mitigating the threats to an acceptable level, a programmatic statement can be developed. The design professional then uses this to begin the physical design for security.

The architect must be equipped to bring resources and skills to bear on a security problem in the same way as any other design problem. To accomplish this may require engaging specialists in areas in which the architect is not trained or experienced, such as blast mitigation, communications security, or the use of electronic hardware and software to augment physical and operational security measures.

Security Design Issues and Challenges

In many instances, designing for physical security also addresses fire and life safety requirements. In any case, all threats to a building—from storm, earthquake, terrorist bomb, or accidental fire—require protection of the occupants from the immediate, direct effects of the event, such as flying debris or structural collapse. After that, it is the designer's task to design for safe evacuation of a facility and safe entry by emergency personnel.

While we may wish to restrict entry by unauthorized persons as a security consideration, doing so must not impair access by fire and rescue teams. As with other emergency evacuation planning, multiple means of egress and redundant systems for power and light, communications, and fire detection and extinguishment must be provided. However, strategies for ensuring these redundancies in physical security design may be different from planning for other emergencies. For example, when bomb threats are a consideration, it is important to place utility services as far as possible from one another and from uncontrolled vehicles.

Generally, physical security may be seen as a means of providing more time to ensure safety. For example, installation of systems that detect and warn of an event or construction of a wall, door, or window assembly to resist forced entry can buy valuable time. Fifteen minutes to an hour of forced-entry or fire resistance provides that much time for protective forces to arrive, defend a facility, or apprehend assailants, as well as for occupants to escape and perform necessary security chores before a building is breached, such as destroying sensitive documents or locking up valuables.

Examples of building systems that can serve the dual functions of security and safety are intrusion detection and smoke and fire detection systems and alarm and communication systems that warn occupants of an event and guide evacuation and safety actions. Egress systems, including corridors, stairs, and safe havens, are vital to any emergency event planning.

Some threats allow for detailed advance planning and security measures. For example, measures against electronic data and communications eavesdropping and disruption can be planned, even though the persistence of hackers has shown the difficulty of planning for all contingencies. For other threats, no detection or advance warning may be possible, especially in the case of a terrorist incident.

All threats—natural or humanly motivated—require a plan for response. Who will do what when an armed intruder has gained access to a building? What is the policy for dealing with hostage situations? What will be done if a mob has formed and is threatening to breach the perimeter;

will firearms be used? What internal organization is there to respond to fire or blast situations; will there be periodic practice evacuation drills? Will each floor or department have a trained fire safety marshal? What arrangements have been made with public fire, law enforcement, and rescue organizations? The facility design must accommodate the expected response actions and provide for their implementation.

After protecting the occupants and contents of a building from the results of a natural or human assault, the final goal of physical security design is to minimize damage to a building and its systems so recovery may be possible. This is, of course, a challenging task because the effects of earthquakes, windstorms, floods, and explosions are difficult to predict. For example, the heating, ventilating, and air conditioning systems in a London building (St. Mary Axe) that structurally survived a terrorist bomb had to be replaced because of the glass fragmentation that permeated them.

PHYSICAL SECURITY FOR EXISTING VERSUS NEW BUILDINGS

Designing a new building to mitigate threats is simpler and more cost-effective than retrofitting an existing building. Adding security measures as an afterthought, even during construction of a new facility, is rarely as successful or as cost-effective as planning security from the earliest phases of design. Important security benefits are achieved not by hardware and electronic devices but by shrewd site selection, proper placement of the building on the site, and careful location of building occupants and functions to minimize exposure to threats. These factors also have the benefit of reducing operating expenses over the lifetime of the building. An obvious example of this is planning for a minimum number of entrances to a site or building that must be highly monitored, staffed, and protected.

Although existing buildings can be retrofitted to improve security, the cost may be prohibitive if it means significant disruption or loss of operations and revenue. Entrances can be consolidated, walls and structural systems reinforced against blast, and electronic surveillance and alarm systems added. In some cases, however, it may be more economical and operationally more prudent to relocate a facility or build a new building.

The vulnerabilities of an existing building can be evaluated against a threat analysis for the structure. Methods for retrofitting the building to address these vulnerabilities are then examined. Technology has provided many materials and techniques that make it possible, though not always economical, to protect existing buildings against extreme duress such as bomb damage. The bottom line is that the owner must determine the level of resources that will be spent on security design. For example, an owner may easily mitigate a threat of surreptitious and forced entry to a warehouse by strengthening doors and windows and improving detection and alarm systems. If the threat is a blast against a historic masonry structure in a dense urban setting, however, the cost of reinforcing the masonry and installing redundant structural materials may be prohibitive and so disruptive that the building cannot be occupied during renovation. In this case, a related issue would be the difficulty and cost of maintaining the architectural and historical character of the building.

■ PHYSICAL SECURITY AND AESTHETICS

As asserted earlier, architects and other designers for centuries have incorporated security responses into the aesthetics of buildings. For example, Italian Renaissance palaces have massive street façades on the ground floor with stylized, effective security grilles over windows and massive gates that typically lead to a central courtyard, exemplified by the Pitti Palace in Florence (Figure 1.5). Utilitarian service spaces were usually on the ground floor, and the owners' quarters and main rooms on the floor above. The fenestration of the ground floor is smaller and more closed than that on the upper floors, where the windows and doors are grander and more open. This arrangement has security as well as status implications and is

FIGURE 1.5
Pitti Palace, Florence. The façade of this Renaissance palace embodies features that reflect many functional considerations, including security.

part of the aesthetics of the buildings. Even religious buildings have had their security considerations, and some of the most beautiful and ornate wrought-iron gates and enclosures can be found on openings to churches and chapels.

The most basic elements of architecture are themselves part of the security systems for buildings: walls, windows, doors, and roofs are all basic parts of the architect's palette of design. Similarly, the walls, fences, gates, landscaping, elevated terraces, and monumental stairs enclosing a site may serve security functions. Architects have made these architectural features magnificent at the same time they protect buildings.

Glass is one of the most fragile materials from a security standpoint. However, glass contributes significantly to the spatial and environmental quality of buildings and symbolizes openness in a democratic society. When blast mitigation is a concern, glass may have to be used in moderation and positioned more creatively. But even modern curtain walls can be designed to accommodate blast effects. Blast-mitigation design does not have to result in a windowless or fortresslike solution. It is interesting to note that some well-known, essentially windowless, buildings do not look like bunkers. Examples include John Russell Pope's National Gallery of Art in Washington, D.C.; Ali Mardan Khan's Taj Mahal in Agra, India; and Le Corbusier's Chapel at Ronchamp in France (the latter shown in Figure 1.6).

■ SECURITY IN AN OPEN SOCIETY

An open, democratic society can and does function with varying levels of security, including restricted accessibility by an unscreened public. However, in light of recent concerns over terrorism in public places, the number of public venues with no control over access is dwindling. Protecting buildings that house the functions of a democratic, free, and open society in many ways ensures that society's continuance. For example, for the safety of the untrained and unwary visitor, access must be limited to research laboratories containing highly infectious or toxic substances, clean rooms requiring immaculate environments, or manufacturing plants that use hazardous processes. Privacy is also important to the freedom expected by U.S. citizens, so protection of records and access to information and communications are both essential.

Restricting access is one way to protect public buildings that house legislatures, courts, public services, and places of learning and worship. Restricted access to private sector buildings is a tenet of U.S. society, which recognizes the right of businesses in a market economy to protect their

FIGURE 1.6
Notre Dame du Haut, Ronchamp. Buildings designed with little or no fenestration do not have to appear fortresslike.

information and processes from competitors. While it is reasonable to protect both public and private places from destruction for the safety of those who use them, it is important that provision of that protection not convey an image of secrecy and fear. This is the task of the architect.

CONFIDENTIALITY OF SECURITY SOLUTIONS

The floor plans of a building can reveal the security strengths and weaknesses of that building. For this reason, it is only sensible to limit distribution of building plans and other related documents. This is probably one of the most difficult security precautions to maintain during design, bidding, and construction of a facility. Except for high-security government installations, control over drawings is next to impossible. Beginning with the staff in the design firm, the bidders, contractors, subcontractors, workers, and manufacturers involved in a project all must access the drawings in whole or in part. For high-security government facilities, drawings can be classified under a system of procedures governed by law with state-inflicted penalties for breaching the system. Even then, leaks occur.

To limit the damage caused by unintended release of building drawings, one technique is to compartmentalize the information so that very few have access to the entire picture. However, if one of the select few to know the entire project is an adversary, as has happened in some high-profile cases involving persons at the CIA or FBI, the system will fail.

In any case, some level of control over distribution and access to important physical security design information can be observed by protecting storage of the documents, limiting access to data on computers, maintaining records of distribution, and recovering all distributed copies after completion of a project. In an era of easy reproduction of nearly anything, this is easier said than done, but that is no reason to be careless. Architects should be alert to inquiries about a building design that seem unwarranted or come from persons with no need to know. It may be necessary to refuse requests for copies of documents until reasons for a request are known.

COSTS OF SECURITY

As with every program requirement for design of a building, initial and long-term costs for security are directly related to each other. Every security decision involves long-term cost considerations with respect to operating personnel and systems, as well as maintenance and repair. Obsolescence is especially important in security systems subject to rapid technological advances. As with systems for medical care, manufacturing, or research, flexibility is the key to minimizing unnecessary costs in future system upgrades.

After completion of threat and risk assessments, the building owner determines what resources will be applied to physical and operational security in relation to the facility's core mission costs. If it costs so much to construct and operate the security for a building that basic functions are starved of resources, this is obviously a poor trade-off.

The most effective way to maintain an acceptable balance of costs is to consider security from the beginning of the building planning and design process. Security requirements should be integral to the decision-making process from the outset.

▊ LEGAL MATTERS

Design professionals are under constant scrutiny for the performance of the buildings they design. Owners and the public in general expect architects and engineers to provide safe and serviceable buildings that function as intended. Architects taken to task for their designs are judged on whether they have acted within a standard of care exercised by their peers for the same kinds of service. Professional liability insurance providers warn architects not to undertake services they are not competent or legally licensed to perform.

▊ ONE OF MANY FUNCTIONS

Physical security is only one of many functions of building design. While any project has some element of security in its program, security must take its place among numerous competing demands. While the architect and consultant help the owner understand the trade-offs in those demands, it is for the owner to assess security threats, determine risks, and set final priorities for the security aspects of a project. With those requirements and judgments in hand, the architect applies professional knowledge and skills to creatively blend security with other project requirements in a balanced manner.

2 Understanding Threats

Thomas Norman

To develop effective security responses for a facility, it is essential to first determine what the threats are to the people who occupy and use it. Otherwise, security responses may be either insufficient or more than is necessary to address the likely threats to a given environment.

This chapter provides in-depth background information on threats, as they are the core reason for developing security measures. Threats against people, property, and buildings are looked at from several perspectives, including types and sources of threats, ways threats are carried out, and methods for reducing the effectiveness of threats. Although both safety and security threats are touched upon, the focus here is on the latter. The next chapter addresses threats as part of the security assessment process.

A danger foreseen is half avoided.
—Thomas Fuller

Threats in Perspective

A threat is an adverse event that has the potential to harm or destroy an asset. The earliest humans constructed shelters for protection from inclement weather and predators. As architecture and technology evolved, building design addressed a host of other threats. Some of these arose from natural causes (safety threats), while others were caused by human actions (security threats). The distinction between these types of threats is important and worth repeating: Safety threats arise from natural or accidental conditions, whereas security threats result from actions planned and carried out by people.

Safety threats to buildings are addressed by building codes. By law, architects and other designers must conform to design and construction standards applicable to the jurisdiction in which a project is located. Mandated requirements in building codes are intended to protect the health and safety of building occupants, firefighters, and emergency personnel, and to maintain the structural integrity of buildings in the event of fire and other adverse conditions. Although safety threats relate to security threats, building codes do not contain security requirements. Decisions about the level of physical protection in a facility fall to building owners and users.

Safety threats, which are *unintentional*, result from natural phenomena (e.g., lighting, floods, hurricanes, and tornadoes) or through human negligence and ignorance (e.g., improper use, accidents, equipment failure, and system flaws). Security threats are *intentional* and originate in human actions. Angry individuals, vandals, criminals, and terrorists can carry out intentional threats. The threats addressed in this book are, for the most part, security threats. However, whether threats are intentional or unintentional, they may have similar outcomes, ranging from nuisances to disasters of major scale.

■ SAFETY THREATS

Safety threats come from either internal or external sources. Internal threats result from fires, accidental injury, or deferred or improper maintenance and neglect. Outside sources include natural and accidental events. Fires are the most common form of substantial financial loss for most businesses and private individuals. The National Fire Protection Association issued the following estimates in its report "Fire Loss in the U.S. During 2000":

- ◆ The United States has one of the highest fire death rates in the industrialized world, at 14.5 deaths per million of population.
- ◆ Fires in the United States killed 4,045 people and injured another 22,350.
- ◆ Duty-related incidents killed 102 firefighters.
- ◆ Fire killed more people in the United States than all natural disasters combined.

✦ Fire deaths in the home accounted for 85 percent of all fire fatalities.

✦ Public fire departments attended 1.7 million fires, which caused an estimated $11.2 billion in property damage.

✦ An estimated 75,000 incendiary or suspicious fires resulted in 505 civilian deaths and $1.3 billion in property damage.

Many organizations discontinue their fire safety programs after many years without incident, and consider sprinklers to be sufficient protection. But sprinklers, at best, save buildings—not lives, equipment, or documents. Sometimes the damage caused by sprinklers is more costly than the fire they suppressed.

The most cost-effective approach is always prevention. Fire prevention takes two forms: *reduction of combustibles* and *avoidance of fire hazards*. Establishing no-smoking environments is a good step, as is strictly following procedures for use of coffee machines and other electrical appliances. Deferred maintenance of electrical equipment is very high on the list of fire causes.

Similarly, accidental injury is often associated with poorly maintained environments. Environments that can cause injury should be marked and protected. Simple neglect is at the root of most safety claims against organizations. An uncovered well or an unfenced third rail or reservoir can kill. Some threats are obvious, but, tragically, the victims are often innocent and unaware children.

Natural disasters and major accidents can also result in high-value losses. However, these events, although perhaps inevitable over a long period, fall into the "important but not highly probable" category—not less certain, just less urgent. Therefore, many organizations defer emergency planning and disaster recovery planning, sometimes indefinitely.

The absence of a crisis management plan *is* a crisis. The absence of a disaster recovery plan *is* a disaster. Natural disasters and industrial accidents happen all the time—not in the same place every day, but as surely as the days go by, they happen.

▊SECURITY THREATS

Security threats associated with buildings and the people in and around buildings cover a fairly wide range of acts, carried out by individuals acting alone or by groups, whether loosely or highly organized. Individuals or groups that commit criminal and terrorist acts have varying motivations and frequently employ characteristic methods related to those motivations.

❖ Acts by Angry Individuals

When angry individuals vent their wrath on people and property, the potential for harm is in the extent and duration of their emotion. While we normally think of anger as momentary, it can also ferment over years, eventually erupting into violent rage. While any angry individual can be lethal, the longer anger stews, the more likely death can result. An offender need not even be angry at others; he or she may be angry only at him- or herself.

Chapter 8 addresses issues associated with building security operations and emergency preparedness.

Workplace violence is a leading cause of high-value losses to organizations, despite the fact it is so foreseeable. When workplace violence occurs, coworkers commonly express no surprise at who the perpetrator was. Training programs on workplace violence are among the most effective and least expensive security measures to implement. Although short-term anger is difficult to predict on an individual basis, certain environments are more vulnerable to violent outbursts of short-term anger. Short-term violence almost always involves either individuals known to have "short fuses" (e.g., domestic violence cases) or environments in which anyone can enter at any time in an uncontrolled fashion (such as a late-night convenience store tended by a single employee behind an unprotected counter). In any event, the vulnerabilities are often obvious to informed individuals. Characteristically, angry individuals vent their fury as part of a cycle; afterward they typically experience remorse and sadness until the next outburst. This is not true of criminals and terrorists.

❖ Criminal Acts

Criminals commit crimes against persons, property, information, and business reputation with the intent to gain advantage, do harm, or both. Law-abiding people often find it surprising that criminals can evaluate the risk of a crime and still commit it, that these perpetrators do not see the possibility of spending years behind bars as too high a price to pay for illicit gain. Criminals universally see risk differently. They do not fully comprehend the price of crime until the moment that judgment is passed. Some analysis indicates that convicted criminals usually do not spend their time behind bars contemplating the cost of their crime but, rather, how to succeed next time.

Criminal acts are also issues of scale. Nuisance acts (e.g., graffiti, illustrated in Figure 2.1, or public urination) and petty offenses account for most crime. It is relatively easy to develop effective security measures against such acts. Designing environments that create an impression that

FIGURE 2.1

Vandalism and nuisance acts such as graffiti account for a large portion of criminal acts against buildings.

the risk of capture is too high can effectively deter many criminal acts of this scale. Chapter 3 describes the nature of these environments.

In contrast, major crimes against persons can be more difficult to deter and resist, depending on whether the act is *planned* or *impulsive*. Planned crimes are generally carried out against a specific individual because of what he or she represents to the offender. Impulsive crimes are carried out randomly against persons who meet the criminal's target criteria and who are in the wrong place at the wrong time.

The potential for planned crimes against property, information, and business reputation calls for the strategic, cost-effective development of countermeasures (see Figure 2.2). Failure to plan may save a few dollars in the short term, but will cost far more in long-term spending on ineffective security measures or in security losses that cannot be recovered.

❖ Terrorist Acts

Terrorism results from violent, long-term stewing rage directed toward a nation, a political system, an individual, a building, or an icon that represents something important to the terrorist. The terrorist rarely acts alone

FIGURE 2.2
The rate of burglary and property theft has declined over the past several decades in the United States. However, these offenses still represent the largest sector of all crime.

and instead is almost always part of a group of similarly angry individuals. All terrorists focus on a single purpose and are patient in the extreme. They are willing to learn, plan, and sacrifice themselves for a "greater cause" at any cost—whether the intended target is an individual who symbolizes the cause of their rage or a building and its occupants, as in the 1983 bombing of the U.S. embassy in Beirut, Lebanon, shown in Figure 2.3.

The extent to which a terrorist's actions and their effects become a media event, the number of lives lost, and the magnitude of the horror inflicted on an entire population are the measures terrorists use to determine their success. A terrorist will adopt any lifestyle; deceive, betray, and sacrifice any friend or love relationship; and triumph in the loss of life and tragedy of others. A terrorist would be entirely capable of detonating a nuclear bomb, killing millions in the heart of an international city.

Because any organization can be a target of terrorism, all organizations would be wise to track their public profiles to identify potential threats. Recently, for example, more than 300 U.S. companies doing busi-

FIGURE 2.3
The 1983 bombing of the U.S. embassy in Beirut, Lebanon, is one of a string of terrorist attacks on U.S. buildings throughout the world resulting in property destruction, death, and injury.

ness with Israel were targeted for a boycott of their goods, unbeknownst to many of the companies. In fact, many of these firms had no such connection to Israel, meaning the information on the boycott list was inaccurate. Such lists, however, have historically led to malevolent direct action by individuals or groups related to the cause being espoused, as well as actions by others with no direct connection at all.

Threats of Adjacency

Many business owners inadvertently place their companies in harm's way because of who their neighbors are. Few organizations know what all of their neighbors do. Against the advice of security consultants, the New York City Office of Emergency Management placed its Emergency Operations Center (EOC) in 7 World Trade Center, next door to the highest-profile terrorist target of all time: a target that had already been hit, a target to which terrorists swore to return. Ultimately, they did. The EOC was destroyed during the very kind of emergency it was built to handle.

Is the client's facility next door to a company that stores toxic chemicals? Is it next to a highway where a toxic chemical spill or toxic fire could shut down everything around it? If a facility is located in a flood zone or earthquake zone, does it have multiple ways in and out? In real estate, an old saying tells us that "location is everything." That holds true in security and safety matters as well.

How Threats Are Carried Out

The methods and tactics angry individuals, criminals, extremists, or terrorists choose to carry out their threats depend on the sophistication and logistics of the individual or group. Commonly employed tactics are described in the following subsections.

BALLISTIC ATTACKS

To carry out assaults, aggressors can use small arms (e.g., pistols, rifles, and machine guns) or standoff weapons (e.g., antitank weapons and mortars). Both types are used worldwide, but standoff weapons have not gained widespread use in the United States. High-powered rifles are commonly fired from a distance (e.g., from a concealed position, the roofs of adjacent buildings, within adjacent buildings, or other vantage points). Other small arms are more likely to be used at close range. Antitank weapons require a direct line of sight to the target. Mortars and variants of this weapon do not require a direct line of sight; they can be fired over obstacles or through roofs and often carry a significant quantity of explosives.

BOMBS

Bombs are used extensively by terrorists and extremists. Methods of delivering them include throwing hand grenades, Molotov cocktails, and similar small bombs; placing small bombs by hand in strategic locations; placing larger bombs for detonation in parked or moving vehicles; and sending bombs through the mail.

Chapter 5 presents methods for hardening buildings against bombs and other modes of attack.

Buildings that might be exposed to conventional explosives can be protected to some extent by understanding the capabilities of explosive charges and the size of the containers required to deliver them. While small satchel or backpack charges can severely damage the interior of a building and cause great bodily harm, such charges are unlikely to cause the destruction of the building itself.

CBR CONTAMINATION

Chemical, biological, and radiological (CBR) threats have become a concern in building design. Contamination tactics involve the release of chemical, biological, or radiological agents into the air or water supply. Biological agents include organisms that cause serious diseases such as anthrax and smallpox. Radiological agents may include radioactive isotopes from medical sources and nuclear power applications, among others.

Effects of Bomb Blasts

The high-speed projectiles and overpressure that result from bomb blasts cause injury and death. Of particular concern are the glass shards formed when glass explodes. Even safety glass, which normally breaks into noninjurious "pellets," does not behave so well during a blast. Instead, it breaks into thousands of pellets, each with sharp edges flying at near-supersonic speed.

Overpressure is a less commonly known but equally deadly result of bomb blasts. When a bomb detonates, an immediate chemical change takes place. A nearly instantaneous conversion of chemical matter to heat and energy causes a heat wave, an atmospheric overpressure blast wave created by a supersonic expansion of gases, and a seismic event (transmission of a blast wave into the ground and outward). Compared to the blast wave, the heat is transmitted a fairly short distance, but it can ignite combustibles close to the blast, resulting in fires. The front of the blast wave, however, forms a wall of highly compressed air that can travel as fast as 1,150 feet per second, or 784 miles per hour.

When a blast wave meets a structure, it wraps around all surfaces of the structure for less than a second. The forces are very great, and the larger the building, the greater the effect. Whereas a smokestack might survive a blast because the blast wave wraps around it so quickly, an adjacent building might be destroyed because the blast wave exerts pressure on the building for a far longer time. Another factor affecting damage is distance; the closer the blast is to a structure, the greater the damage. The initial period of extreme overpressure is followed by a reverse blast wave of almost equal intensity as air rushes back into the vacuum created when the initial blast blew the air away from its point of origin. This process of air compression and resumption of equilibrium creates two blast waves, both highly destructive.

Following is a list of vehicles and their general delivery capabilities in pounds of TNT and the amount of atmospheric overpressure at 30 feet and 100 feet from the blast's point of origin.[1]

Vehicle Type	Lbs Charge	At 30 ft	At 100 ft
Compact Car Trunk	250	182 psi	9.5 psi
Large Car Trunk	500	367 psi	15 psi
Panel Vans	1,500	1,063 psi	33 psi
Box Trucks	5,000	2,900 psi	100 psi
Single-Tractor/Trailers	30,000	9,290 psi	593 psi
Double-Tractor/Trailers	60,000	13,760 psi	1,150 psi

Adult humans can withstand only about 30 psi to 40 psi of overpressure before their lungs collapse. Death is certain at 100 psi to 120 psi. However, death can occur at pressures as low as 10 psi with infants and the elderly.[2]

A person on the opposite side of a building from a blast is not protected from the blast wave. There is no shadow for a blast wave as there is for heat, as the blast wave wraps entirely around the building. The blast can be mitigated to the extent the building surfaces collapse (e.g., glass breakage), and the forces of the blast are dissipated by the interior building surfaces.

Total disintegration of a human can occur at pressures above 2,000 psi. Above 5,000 psi, sometimes not even a trace of the person remains. Obviously, it is best to be as far away from a blast as possible. This is why *standoff distance* is important when blast is a consideration.

---

[1] Charge capacity overpressure information supplied by Hinman Consulting Engineers, Inc., San Francisco, California, a leading blast effects consulting firm.

[2] Ibid.

Terrorist Tactics and Weapons

Tactics
- Direct assaults
- Surreptitious attack (e.g., placed explosive)
- Hostage taking
- Suicide assaults

Weapons

Small Arms
- Rifles
- Pistols
- Submachine guns
- Other small arms

Standoff Weapons
- Rocket-propelled grenades
- Mortars

Explosives
- Hand grenades
- Pipe bombs
- Incendiary devices
- Explosives (by type)

Vehicle Bombs
- Stationary vehicle
- Moving vehicle

Mail Bombs

Contamination
- Chemical
- Biological
- Radiological

Chapter 7 discusses CBR protection approaches and strategies for buildings.

Although CBR attacks are difficult to deal with, and vary in intensity and duration, there are strategies and measures to protect building occupants from CBR agents, whether released outside or inside a building. General countermeasures include reducing the possibility that chemical and biological agents could enter a building interior through air and water intakes.

CYBERTERRORISM AND CYBERCRIME

Only a few years ago it was unimaginable that a computer hacker in a foreign country could skillfully alter construction drawings showing the steel structure of a building in a way to make the building more sensitive to blast

The Cyberthreat Is Real

The threat of cyberterrorism and cybercrime is both real and profound. Riptech, an Internet security company, stated in the "Internet Security Threat Report" it released in January 2002 that the number of cyberattacks in the last half of 2001 increased 79 percent over the number during the previous six months.

The report also stated that more than 43 percent of the companies studied experienced at least one attack during that period that would have resulted in severe loss of assets if defensive security measures had not been taken. Of the attacks, 39 percent appeared to be deliberate attempts to compromise a specific system or company; and 61 percent appeared to be opportunistic, that is, the attacker was broadly searching for any vulnerable system on the Internet. The rate of targeted attacks was 42 percent for companies with more than 1,000 employees, suggesting that larger, higher-profile companies may be victimized by deliberate attacks more frequently than lower-profile companies.

More than 30 percent of the attacks targeted U.S. companies—more than for the next nine countries combined. The most severe attacks were against energy, financial, and high-technology businesses, in that order. It is not only likely but virtually certain that in the future terrorists will attempt a major attack on U.S. infrastructure via the Internet.

damage. With this form of invasion, the architect or engineer might never know that such a change had, in fact, been made. It is terrifying to imagine that some so-called Trojan horses may lie sleeping in an architect's own drawings, but there is evidence that such tactics have been discussed by terrorists. Anyone who relies on unencrypted data files is at risk.

To respond to various types of cyberthreat, architects may need to consider the access and control of spaces that accommodate more sensitive information technology (IT) and data systems. From identity theft to intentionally derailment of trains and shutdown of electrical grids, the same computers that have enabled higher efficiency in business are exposing government and industry to entirely new threats. More occurrences of cyberterrorism and cybercrime are undoubtedly on the horizon.

Crimes and terrorist events can be thought of as markers on a road that leads from cause or intent to action to outcome. Any terrorist or criminal action requires motive, means, and opportunity. If any of these can be short-circuited, no outcome occurs. The "Threat Realization Sequence" sidebar outlines the sequence of steps from motive to success. At specific places along that line, a motive can be derailed or opportunities removed.

Threat Realization Sequence

Intent Phase

1. Bad person (called the "Threat" here) develops an intention.
2. Threat becomes aware of existence and value of intended target's asset(s):
   + Impulsively, or
   + With long-term intention to find and target assets.
3. Threat feels no loyalty to the asset owner or affected parties.

Assessment Phase

1. Threat surveils and assesses the asset.
   + Determines asset location and value.
   + Determines vulnerabilities.
   + Determines existence and effectiveness of any security measures, including:
     - Security personnel
     - Employees or concerned persons
     - Physical barriers
     - Electronic barriers
     - Access control systems (although these can also be a vulnerability)
     - Detection systems (alarms)
     - Assessment systems (CCTV and intercoms)
     - Likely response time and force effectiveness
     - Facility security procedures
2. Threat assesses the likely price to be paid for capture.
3. Threat assesses overall risk versus reward of carrying out the intended threat.

Planning Phase[1]

1. Threat assesses ability to disable or bypass any security measures.
2. Threat assesses ability to enlist inside help.
3. Threat gathers additional intelligence about the asset, its vulnerabilities, and security features.
4. Threat develops methods and timing:
   a. Best time to carry out the threat.
   b. How best to infiltrate and exfiltrate.
   c. How best to avoid detection during the act.
   d. How to respond to detection.[2]
   e. Determines how to avoid detection after the fact.[2]

Action Phase[3]

1. Threat encounters and overcomes barriers and delaying methodologies.
2. Threat carries out the attack:
   a. Infiltrates
     - From outside
     - From inside
     - From outside with help from inside
   b. Avoids detection, if possible and for as long as possible.
   c. Takes assets or damages or destroys assets (whatever the intent is).
   d. Damages or infects assets transmitted by target assets (e.g., poisons water supply, sabotages food product line).
   e. Deals with any response mounted by the asset owner.
3. Threat leaves the property unnoticed if possible.
4. Threat takes planned measures to avoid detection after the act.

---

[1]The planning phase may take years, but in the case of an impulsive threat may be accomplished in seconds.

[2]These steps are generally ignored by all but the most skilled criminals; terrorists typically make a claim of the act. This sometimes results in the murder of witnesses, both co-conspirators and the innocent.

[3]The action phase is when a threat makes a last-minute go/no go decision based on environmental changes.

Virtually every criminal and terrorist follows this process, either consciously or intuitively. To the extent it is followed consciously, the perpetrator is more likely to succeed; to the extent it is followed intuitively, the perpetrator is less likely to succeed. The more time, detail, and accuracy criminals or terrorists invest in assessment and planning, the more likely their efforts will be successful.

Reducing Threat Effectiveness

The possibility of threats being carried out can be reduced in several ways, each of which short-circuits the threat realization sequence:

- Improve the organization's public image and increase employee morale.
- Institute employee screening and workplace violence programs.
- Reduce vulnerabilities by protecting, offsetting, or transferring risk.
- Detect and neutralize the threat in the planning phase (requires a good intelligence program or an informant—this rarely occurs).
- Detect and neutralize the threat in the act (sometimes occurs with well-designed security procedures and systems and well-trained security staff).
- Recapture the asset after the threat has been carried out (rarely occurs).

Of these ways for reducing threats, the first three are the most effective and are likely to be the least costly. They are also the methods over which the architect, manager, and security practitioner have the most control. To the extent a threat can be interrupted in the intent or assessment phases, success is highest. The following principles also apply to this model:

- If the perpetrator feels loyal to the asset owner or affected parties, the intent is less likely to reach the assessment phase.
- If the perpetrator believes the risk is greater than the reward, the intent is less likely to reach the planning or action phase.
- To the extent that security measures are effectively designed and security staff is well trained, the attack is less likely to be successful.

Many of these principles also apply indirectly to safety threats and unintentional threats. Awareness programs and facility safety tours are among the best defenses against safety threats. Most of the best security programs are not capital-intensive, nor do they require huge outlays in operating costs. They do, however, require effective assessment and planning—ironically the two steps most organizations are least willing to spend money on.

Security can be likened to accounting or financial auditing in that both identify and minimize losses. But whereas no business would operate without accounting and auditing processes, threat assessment and security measures often fall out of the financial loop because they do not directly generate revenue and because security- and safety-related losses are unpredictable expenses. This is a mistake, however, because a coordinated process of security accounting and auditing—assessing assets, threats, vulnerabilities, and security measures, as well as ranking risks and security measures—is the only reliable way to ensure that losses can be identified and prevented.

Threats have the greatest chance of success in a "threat-friendly" environment.

Vulnerable environments can facilitate bad behavior, so to the extent that an architect, manager, or security practitioner can design or manipulate an environment subject to threats through operational, physical, and detection/assessment/response measures, it is possible to reduce the likelihood that threats will be successful.

A Basis for Security Planning

Identifying potential threats that an organization or enterprise may face is a critical part of security assessment and programming. These efforts determine the desired levels of protection and functional design requirements for a facility.

Many threats are obvious to the skilled observer, some even to the casual observer; others, however, are not apparent to anyone. If a threat analysis does not uncover less obvious threats, it does not mean they do not exist. It is statistically probable that many large enterprises have ongoing security threats that they are unaware of. The security assessment process works from more obvious to less obvious threats. Threat analysis may also include forensic accounting to uncover undetected business losses. Such losses often bring the discovery of serious threats that might otherwise have remained unknown.

Some obvious threats can be checked against standardized lists. Others require more rigorous analysis, involving use of historical data and evaluation of current conditions. Threats, of course, do not exist in a vacuum. They exist because an asset exists: no asset, no threat. Obviously, some assets are more critical than others, and threats to the highest-value assets are ranked as the most significant.

In addition to asset criticality, threat analysis also considers probabilities (a circus elephant stampede is possible but not probable) and ranks threats from most to least probable. The probability of many threats can be established using private statistical sources, as well as government crime and demographic data. City police departments also keep track of such records in accordance with FBI standards.

We are all in the same boat. It is important for all government and private organizations to recognize that the tide of terrorist threats has risen and that the cost of doing business has risen with it. Security measures that were not financially practical in early 2001 may now be necessities.

Given enough time, almost every business, government entity, or private organization will be subjected to some form of violence. The fact that an organization or enterprise has existed for 100 years without occurrence of such an event is actually a probability reduction toward an unhappy outcome, not proof of security. Almost nothing can remove a target from a terrorist's list once that target has been identified. Identifying threats and their potential outcomes is thus a key and critical part of the process of developing security plans and programs from which effective security design solutions can be prepared.

Chapter 4 describes the major increments and steps in the security evaluation and planning process.

One should assume that all threats are unknown in the analysis and assessment phases.

3

Security Design Concepts

Randall I. Atlas, Ph.D., AIA, CPP

Building design is based on specific functional criteria. From the function, the design evolves. Examples of building functions include encouraging efficient job performance, supporting user needs, keeping users safe from hazardous conditions, and protecting occupants from crime and other violent acts.

While designing buildings to be secure is sometimes viewed as Orwellian or "over the top" by many in the design community, there is hardly any building type that does not require some level of security. For example, convenience stores and gas stations are considered high-risk facilities. Schools and apartment buildings have significant security concerns. Shopping centers and parking garages are continual targets for crime. Hospitals and hotels are at great risk from sabotage, theft, and robbery. Military and government buildings have been designed with security in mind for years.

Concerns about security in the built environment have grown because of the increase in terrorism in the United States and abroad. The destruction of the Murrah Building in Oklahoma City brought sweeping changes in security design criteria, including new standards for federal buildings and their leased spaces. In addition, court decisions on premise liability have significantly increased the demand for enhanced building security. Property owners, managers, and design professionals are being held responsible for the consequences of security-related incidents in facil-

To keep oneself safe does not mean to bury oneself.
—Marcus Annaeus Seneca

ities. Monetary awards have been made on the basis of actual and punitive damages. The security factor in buildings is becoming a risk management decision long before it becomes an architectural decision.

As crime, sabotage, terrorism, and other acts of violence increase against buildings and people in buildings, architects and other building design professionals are called upon to address building security more vigorously. This demand poses challenges to design professionals, particularly understanding security fundamentals, determining security requirements, employing appropriate security technologies, and realizing the security implications of design decisions. Figure 3.1 summarizes proper design and use of the built environment.

The Purpose of Security

Safety in buildings is mandated by building codes and standards that establish how buildings are to perform during abnormal conditions (e.g., fires, hurricanes, floods, and earthquakes). Building security, on the other hand, is about how assets (people, information, and property) can be protected from the effects of malevolent acts carried out by individuals or groups of individuals (e.g., violent people, criminals, extremists, and terrorists).

BASIC COMPONENTS OF SECURITY

The primary components of security are detection and deterrence of malevolent threats before they can be carried out. In the event they are car-

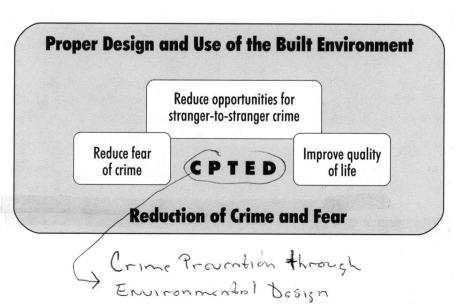

FIGURE 3.1
Goals and objectives for the proper design and use of the built environment

Crime Prevention through Environmental Design

ried out, an additional critical component involves provision of appropriate response and recovery actions.

- ◆ *Detection.* Before a threat can be delayed or responded to, it must
  be detected or perceived. A security system should be able to identify the presence of a threat, but detection ultimately relies on
  observation by building users or security personnel. Observation
  methods can be direct—that is, without the use of equipment—or
  they can employ monitoring and detection devices to extend and
  enhance human capabilities to observe activities and conditions.

- ◆ *Deterrence.* Once a threat has been detected, a security system can
  delay its occurrence by physical or operational methods or a
  combination of both. The intent of the security delay function is
  to extend the time before a threat can be carried out and to maintain distance between a threat and the target.

- ◆ *Response.* The ability to respond to or intervene in a threat stems
  from what occurs in the detection phase and the amount of time
  created for apprehension or neutralization in the deterrence
  phase. Response actions can be official or unofficial. An official
  response may involve law enforcement or private security forces.
  Unofficial responses may involve building users such as door-
  men, neighborhood watch patrols, and so on.

Detection and deterrence are worthless if there is no one to respond
to a threat or an emergency. Comprehensive security plans integrate
detection, deterrence, and response components. In the absence of deterrence or delaying measures such as barriers or guard stations, an intruder
can commit a crime and leave before a response can be made. Conversely,
deterrent measures without a detection component give no advance warning of a problem.

SECURITY FUNCTIONS

The security functions of *access control* and *surveillance* are used to achieve
the objectives of the detection and deterrence components of security.

- ◆ *Access control* refers to controlling individuals, vehicles, property,
  and materials as they enter, exit, and move about in designated
  areas of a facility.

- ◆ *Surveillance* involves monitoring, observing, and sometimes
  recording events and conditions in and around a facility.

Architects and designers can address security planning and design
more effectively when they have a comprehensive context in which to view

security. The remainder of this chapter describes a conceptual framework that offers this context. In addition, several techniques and approaches for developing and applying security design strategies are presented.

A Framework for Security Design

Crime prevention through environmental design (CPTED, pronounced sep-ted) is an environment-behavior theory and methodology based on the proposition that enlightened architecture and site design deters criminal behavior and reduces fear of crime. CPTED offers a comprehensive basis for approaching and developing security design solutions. It is based on the notion that effective design and use of the built environment can reduce predatory stranger-to-stranger crime while supporting all intended building functions and improving quality of life for building users.

CPTED theory draws on both social and physical sciences. Oscar Newman's 1971 work *Defensible Space*, as well as Tim Crowe's efforts in the early 1990s, developed CPTED theory by integrating behavioral psychology, the sociology of human behavior, and architectural design to create safer environments. (Crowe's published work on CPTED is cited in Appendix B, Publications.)

CPTED STRATEGIES

The goal of the CPTED model is to reduce opportunities for individuals to engage in unwanted or criminal behavior. The model supports fundamental security objectives and functions through use of the strategies for natural access control, natural surveillance, and natural territorial reinforcement as supported by the principles of management/maintenance and encouragement of legitimate activities. Although CPTED strategies are distinct, they overlap and are interrelated. (Their "natural" prefix refers to the fact that once their functions have been incorporated into the spatial and physical elements of a facility, those functions become an inherent, or *natural,* part of the design.)

◆ *Natural access control.* Built and natural obstacles such as doors, fences, or shrubbery can limit access to a building or a defined space (see Figure 3.2). For example, protection from break-ins through lower-story windows can be accomplished by planting a row of dense, thorny bushes near the windows and using locking devices and possibly an alarm system. The deterrent methods chosen depend on the risks associated with a particular facility.

FIGURE 3.2

Gated entrance for access control as a design feature

♦ *Natural surveillance.* Enhancing the ability of occupants and casual observers (police, others) in a facility to see what is happening around them increases the detection of trespass or other misconduct. For instance, a loading dock enclosed with a high, solid fence that blocks the view of the area may attract potential thieves. An alternative would be the use of see-through fencing, which permits an unobstructed view of the area by workers or passersby. Figure 3.3 demonstrates placement of a security guard station to enable effective surveillance of the immediate area.

♦ *Natural territorial reinforcement.* Territorial reinforcement theory holds that people will pay more attention to a particular space if they have a sense of "psychological ownership" of it. This feeling can increase the vigilance of users, sending the message that trespassers will be identified. For example, small shrubbery edging sidewalks in an apartment complex can be used to discourage potential trespassers from cutting through the territory of individual apartments (see Figure 3.4).

In a hierarchical context, natural territorial reinforcement is the overarching and broadest of the CPTED strategies. Territorial reinforcement encompasses surveillance strategies, which in turn encompass access control strategies. All of these strategies are supported by the following principles:

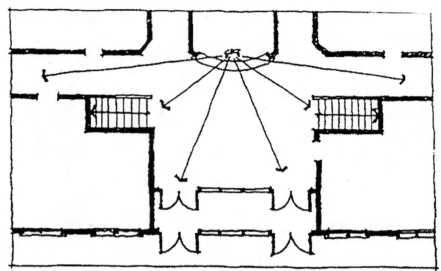

FIGURE 3.3
A security guard or concierge station located and configured to permit effective natural surveillance of stairs and entrances

FIGURE 3.4
Design and placement of landscaping, walks, walls, and fences to achieve territorial reinforcement objectives

◆ *Management and maintenance.* For spaces to look well cared for and crime-free, they must be maintained at acceptable levels. The broken window theory suggests that once a window has been broken, an abandoned building or car will be vandalized quickly. Maintaining facility elements such as lighting, paint, signage, fencing, and walkways is critical for communicating that some-one cares and is responsible for upkeep. Effective management of properties is essential to ensure proper maintenance.

◆ *Legitimate activity support.* Criminal activity may thrive in spaces if residents and management do not claim them by encouraging legitimate activities. A crime prevention program for a space will be effective only if residents and users engage in the activities for which the space has been designed. (This concept, called the *3-D approach,* is described later.)

CPTED DESIGN CONCEPTS

The CPTED process employs three types of security concepts to achieve the objective of creating physical space that considers the needs of legitimate users, the normal and expected (or intended) functions for the space, and the predictable behavior of illegitimate users and intruders.

◆ *Mechanical concepts.* Sometimes referred to as *target hardening*, mechanical concepts and measures emphasize hardware and technological systems, such as locks, security screens on windows, fencing and gating, key control systems, closed-circuit television (CCTV), and other security technologies. Mechanical measures should not be relied on as the sole means for creating a secure environment. They should be used in conjunction with organizational and natural measures.

◆ *Organizational concepts.* These concepts rely on people (e.g., individuals and vested groups) to provide surveillance and access control functions in the spaces they occupy at home or at work. Organizational measures may use concierges, security guards, designated guardians, residents in block and neighborhood watch programs, police officer patrols, and other individuals with the ability to observe, report, and intervene in undesirable or illegitimate actions.

◆ *Natural concepts.* These concepts employ physical and spatial features such as site and architectural elements to ensure that a setting is designed to deter crime while supporting the intended use of the space. Natural measures are also used to reduce conflicts between user and use. Examples of natural features include landscaping, outdoor seating and planters, fences, gates, walls, doors, windows, stairs, and so on.

Security Layering and Zoning

Security layering and zoning provide tools that can be used in conjunction with CPTED concepts and strategies to incorporate security measures into building design. Security layering defines the defensive elements of a facility in three primary elements: the site and its perimeter, the building envelope, and the building interior, each of which can be visualized as a series of concentric defensive rings and zones. Each layer contains spaces that go from public to semipublic to private zones. Combinations of various physical, technological, and operational security measures can be applied to these primary lines of defense as well as to the areas between them.

■ SITE PERIMETER

The site provides the first and greatest opportunity for achieving a secure facility. Site security analysis considers the site perimeters and grounds of a facility, elements that serve as the first level of security defense planning. A security site analysis begins with an assessment of conditions both on and off the site. Factors to be studied include topography, vegetation, adjacent land uses, vehicular and pedestrian circulation patterns, neighborhood crime patterns, police patrol patterns, sight lines, areas for concealment, location of utilities, and existing and proposed lighting. Other factors for site security planning are access points for service vehicles and personnel, employee access and circulation, and visitor access and circulation.

Whenever possible, security evaluation and planning should begin during the site selection process.

A site that has high security risks may not be automatically disqualified if the location is desirable for other reasons. The owner may choose the site, but acknowledge the security threats and vulnerabilities and address them through a combination of physical, technological, and operational strategies and measures.

A well-designed security solution should detect intrusion as far away from the asset to be protected as practical.

■ BUILDING ENVELOPE

After the site perimeter and grounds, the building envelope is the next line of defense against intrusion and forced entry. The building envelope or shell should be thought of as having four sides, a top, and a bottom. The principal points of entry to be considered include doors, windows, skylights, roof, floor and crawl spaces, fire escapes, and storm sewers.

Situational Crime Prevention

Situational crime prevention is a concept related to CPTED, and the two approaches to preventing crime can be used to complement each other. The goals of situational crime prevention are to increase the effort required to commit crime, increase the risks associated with crime, reduce the rewards of crime, and remove excuses for illegal behavior by inducing shame or guilt in criminals. Following are techniques and methods that can be used to achieve these goals.

Increasing the Effort Required to Commit Crime

+ Target hardening measures such as use of locks, screens, steel doors, fences, and shatterproof glass
+ Access control measures to limit access to vulnerable areas
+ Removal or deflection of offenders from the target area
+ Control of crime facilitators (e.g., remove access to cans of spray paint, install collect-call-only public telephones, remove shopping carts, tow abandoned cars, institute weapons-screening policies, etc.)

Increasing Perceived Risks Associated with Crime

+ Entry and exit screening to monitor who enters an area and who, and what, leaves
+ Formal surveillance by CCTV and security guards
+ Surveillance by employees, concierge, parking attendants, security guard stations
+ Natural surveillance, such as placing windows strategically, installing external lighting, limiting blind spots, and cutting hedges

Reducing Anticipated Rewards of Crime

+ Target removal strategies, such as instituting a no-cash policy, issuing direct deposit checks, and using removable car radios
+ Identification of valuable assets to make them more difficult for criminals to sell and easier for owners to retrieve
+ Reduction in temptation (e.g., rapid repair of damage caused by vandalism and quick removal of graffiti)

Removing Excuses for Noncompliant Behavior

+ Clear rules and boundaries to remove ambiguity that allows otherwise law-abiding persons to commit offenses and excuse their crimes with claims of ignorance or misunderstanding
+ Policies that openly forbid shoplifting, speeding, smoking, drug use, littering, and so on
+ Facilitation of compliance by actions such as designating trash sites to stop illegal dumping or conveniently placing trash bins for litter control

By nature, doors and windows are some of the weakest links in a building and inherently provide poor resistance to penetration. Attention must be paid to the doorframe, latches, locks, hinges, and panic hardware, as well as the surrounding wall and the door leaf. Window features to be considered for secure design include the type of glazing material, the window frame, the window hardware, and the size of the opening.

The architect's challenge, and the security consultant's task, is to provide solutions that are attractive and unobtrusive while they deter unauthorized access.

The exterior wall construction is also a security consideration. The structural characteristics and materials of the building shell determine the level of security the building offers. Most stud walls and metal deck roof assemblies can be compromised with hand tools in less than two minutes. Nonreinforced concrete block walls can be broken quickly with a sledge-hammer or a car driven through them. Thieves have broken into retail stores by driving cars through the front of the buildings.

BUILDING INTERIOR

The third level of security comprises specific security measures at points inside a facility. For example, sensitive areas may warrant special protection using a combination of security technology, manpower, and restricted travel paths. The level of protection may be achieved by using security zoning (discussed later) with access limited to persons having proper clearances.

In public lobby areas, a receptionist or concierge can screen visitors and give them badges that allow them to enter interior spaces, elevators, stairs, and so on. Employees can have identification badges and access cards to enter secured areas of the building. Within a building, computer facilities and other sensitive areas may be accessible only to those with special clearances. Other designated spaces (e.g., the CEO office) may be restricted and screened by an assistant. Restricted access may also be used for support spaces such as mechanical areas, mailrooms, telephone closets, power and utility areas.

SECURITY ZONING

Closely related to security layering, security zoning allows building users (employees, visitors, vendors, and others) to reach their destinations, but prevents them from entering areas where they have no reason to be. Controlling access to specific departments or areas of a building, when appropriate, can screen out unwanted visitors, reduce congestion, and help employees identify and challenge unauthorized persons. Security zoning can be established using three zone types: unrestricted, controlled, and restricted.

◆ *Unrestricted zones.* Some areas of a facility may be unrestricted during hours of designated use. The design of unrestricted zones should encourage persons to conduct their business and leave the area without having to enter controlled or restricted zones. Unrestricted zones might include spaces such as lobbies, reception areas, snack bars, certain personnel and administrative offices, and public meeting rooms.

◆ *Controlled zones.* These zones require a valid purpose for entry. Once admitted, individuals may travel from one department to another within the controlled area without severe restriction. Controlled zones might include such spaces as administrative offices, staff dining rooms, security offices, office working areas, and loading docks.

◆ *Restricted zones.* These are sensitive areas limited to staff and individuals assigned to spaces within those areas. Some sections within restricted zones may require additional access control. Functions and departments often located in restricted zones include vaults, sensitive records storage, chemicals and drugs, food preparation, mechanical areas, telephone equipment, electrical equipment, control rooms, laboratories, laundry, sterile supply, special equipment, and other sensitive work areas.

Security zoning can be used effectively in the design of office buildings, schools, hospitals, jails, courthouses, laboratories, industrial plants, and other facilities. The first design decision in employing security zoning is successful resolution of circulation patterns. Once this has been solved, attention can be given to physical and organizational security systems (e.g., mechanical and operational strategies and measures).

3-D APPROACH

Traditional security design often relies on denying access to assets that are likely targets. This is usually achieved with fortress- and bunkerlike designs employing measures such as reinforced concrete walls, high-security locks, alarms, and similar measures. While warranted in some situations, this approach tends to overlook opportunities offered by "natural" access control and surveillance strategies. With appropriate site and architectural design, natural strategies may be able to offer results equivalent to "mechanical" hardening and surveillance.

Security Design Strategies

The 3-D process and/or a detailed security assessment provides a basis for determining security design strategies. Such strategies combine organizational, mechanical, and natural measures to support the security functions of access control, surveillance, and territorial reinforcement. Sample strategies for each of these functions follow:

Access Control

Access control might be considered at all entrances and exits to a site, in the building at internal access points to restricted or controlled areas, and at features that may be used to gain access to a property (e.g., trees, ledges, skylights, balconies, windows, tunnels). Organizational methods of access control may include security guard forces. Mechanical strategies for access control include target hardening through use of locks, card key systems, and windows that may have protective grilles or glazing that withstand blows. Door and window hardware may be made of special material and mountings to make them difficult to remove or tamper with. In high-security areas, walls, floors, or doors may be reinforced with materials that are difficult to penetrate. Natural access control strategies make use of spatial definition and circulation patterns, as well as security zoning concepts.

Surveillance

Organizational surveillance strategies may use assigned guardians such as police and guard patrols; individuals who have a vested interest in protecting the assets (e.g., grandparents sitting on the porch, block watch captains, residents, or business owners), are being paid to watch assets (off-duty police, security guards, secretaries or receptionists, information station attendants), or are occupying and using the space (employees and visitors). Lighting and CCTV are some of the mechanical measures for improving surveillance. Natural strategies might include elements such as windows overlooking the property, glazing in doors, low-height plantings and high canopy trees, raised entrances, balconies, and porches.

Territorial Reinforcement

A sense of territorial influence can alert potential offenders that they do not belong in a space, they are at risk of being seen and identified, and their behavior will not go unreported. Natural access control and surveillance contributes to a sense of territoriality and boosts security by encouraging users to protect their turf. Organizational territorial reinforcement programs may be carried out by neighborhood crime watch groups, receptionists, roving patrols, and guards. Mechanical territorial reinforcement measures may include perimeter detection systems, guard tour security systems, and so on. Natural measures include the design and layout of a site and architectural elements such as landscaping, fences, walls, and signage.

These natural strategies can be developed with what is called the *3-D approach*, a process that defines security needs through consideration of three aspects of space: designation, definition, and design. Basic questions that could help define each of these aspects for a particular space include the following:

+ *Designation:* What is the purpose or intended use of the space?
+ *Definition:* How is the space defined? What are the social, cultural, legal, and psychological ways in which the space is defined?
+ *Design:* Does the space support the prescribed or intended behaviors?

The 3-D approach can be used in conjunction with more comprehensive and detailed security assessment approaches, which are covered in Chapter 4.

Bringing Security into Design

Architects and other building designers are challenged to stay current with rapid and substantial advances in security technology. As a result, even routine projects may involve security system specialists to bring security knowledge to the project team. However, as with other areas of specialization, architects need a basic understanding of security principles and the processes security specialists use and apply. This knowledge will help architects evaluate, engage, and work with security specialists and security equipment manufacturers.

The building design process often integrates the complicated and sometimes conflicting goals of security, life safety, and accessibility, along with other project variables and requirements. Space, function, and people must ultimately support security objectives.

Despite increased interest in security issues and the value offered by early planning, security is too often treated as an "after-the-fact" issue. The budget assigned to security is frequently what is left over in the construction or operations budget. But designing without security in mind can lead to expensive retrofitting and higher operating costs for security personnel. If not planned for, security equipment can also distort or conflict with key design elements and possibly hinder primary building functions.

More importantly, overlooking security can lead to increased exposure to liability. Case law is abundant with successful claims for insufficient security against owners, architects, and building managers. The need for security is clear and present. The most effective time, and least expensive way, to provide security is as part of the programming and design processes.

OPPORTUNITIES FOR ENHANCING SECURITY

The greatest opportunities for achieving effective security lie in selection of the site and in proper identification of the security requirements to be included in the architectural programming process. Finding a site that meets project requirements and provides security advantages requires consideration of both on-site and off-site conditions. These may include adjacent land uses, neighborhood crime patterns, police patrol patterns, pedestrian and vehicular circulation, topography and vegetation, sight lines, areas for concealment, location of utilities, and existing and proposed lighting.

Chapter 4 describes the security assessment process, which can be described as security programming that is usually conducted by physical security specialists.

The problem definition stage, when security parameters are determined, can include analyzing the cultural and legal implications of how spaces in the building will be used to identify which user behaviors will be prescribed, desired, and acceptable. In addition, owner or user policies and practices can be identified. Such research is part of the security evaluation and planning process in which threats, assets, vulnerabilities, and risks are analyzed to arrive at functional security design criteria (see Figure 3.5). With this information, spaces can be designed to support desired legal or legitimate behaviors and intended functions at the same time they provide the desired levels of asset protection.

INCREASING VALUE AND FUNCTIONALITY

Balancing physical, technological, and operational security measures with aesthetics, other building functions, and cost is a problem-solving challenge that designers continually confront. Design criteria for project considerations such as accessibility, acoustics, ergonomics, lighting, and security, all become part of the programming requirements. In the past, however, security was often not included during programming and security design criteria were added as an afterthought. Deliberately integrating security into the design methodology can increase both building value and functionality (see Figure 3.6).

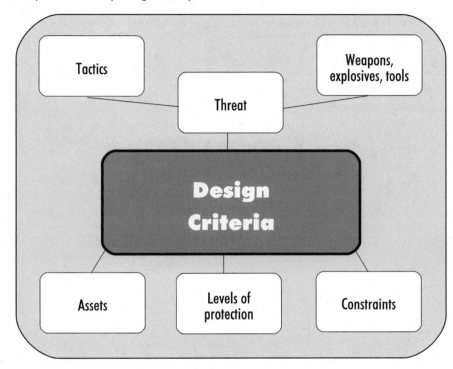

FIGURE 3.5
Functional security design criteria derived from the security assessment process define the level of security required to protect assets from potential threats.

GAINING MARKET ADVANTAGE THROUGH SECURITY

Building security involves more than bars on windows, a guard in a booth, a camera on the ceiling, or locked doors and gates. Effective security solutions call for systematic integration of design, technology, and facility operation and management. By understanding building use and operation, recognizing relationships between architecture and human behavior, and applying a mix of technologies that can enhance operational functions, architects and building design professionals can create environments that meet the security requirements of their clients.

As the scope of architectural services evolves, and as responsibilities and liabilities increase, the importance of designing for security grows. Beyond secure, stable, and safe environments in which to live, work, and play, we need environments that are resistant to criminal or terrorist behavior. Over time, such needs may become as important as having electrical and telecommunications services in our buildings.

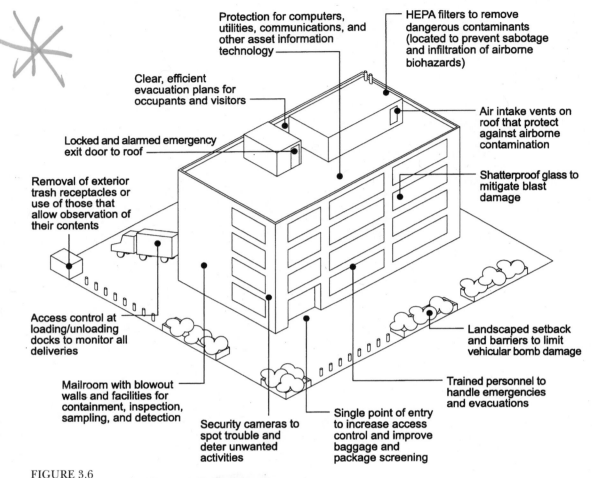

Protection for computers, utilities, communications, and other asset information technology

HEPA filters to remove dangerous contaminants (located to prevent sabotage and infiltration of airborne biohazards)

Clear, efficient evacuation plans for occupants and visitors

Air intake vents on roof that protect against airborne contamination

Locked and alarmed emergency exit door to roof

Shatterproof glass to mitigate blast damage

Removal of exterior trash receptacles or use of those that allow observation of their contents

Access control at loading/unloading docks to monitor all deliveries

Landscaped setback and barriers to limit vehicular bomb damage

Mailroom with blowout walls and facilities for containment, inspection, sampling, and detection

Trained personnel to handle emergencies and evacuations

Security cameras to spot trouble and deter unwanted activities

Single point of entry to increase access control and improve baggage and package screening

FIGURE 3.6

Natural, mechanical, and organizational concepts, features, and measures combined in an overall building security design

If security elements are carefully considered during programming and design, overall building functionality and aesthetics need not be compromised. Banks, courthouses, and schools have been designed with security criteria for years with no detrimental effects to their operation and image. It is now time to design our office buildings, multifamily residential housing, shopping centers, neighborhood parks, and even Main Street, USA, with security in mind.

Security in the built environment is another issue for the architecture community to address just as it does interior, acoustical, structural, telecommunications, and mechanical design. Firms and design professionals who acquire security knowledge, skills, and resources can apply those expanded capabilities to gain marketing advantage. In the end, everyone wins. Building users and occupants can have safer environments, and building owners and design professionals can be less subject to litigation. We either pay now or we pay later. Designing with security in mind makes good architectural and business sense.

4 Security Planning and Evaluation

Richard P. Grassie, CPP

Architects and other building designers need a starting point for incorporating security functions into building design. A security assessment and plan provides such a basis. Without them, architects may find their designs fall short of their clients' security requirements through either insufficient or inadequate protective measures.

This chapter describes the approach, methods, and steps that security consultants and specialists generally use to determine security requirements and strategies. Following an overview of basic security assessment issues, the chapter walks readers through the increments and steps of the assessment process. It concludes by discussing the development of security requirements and strategic options.

Overview of Security Assessment

Security assessment is an analysis of assets or things to be protected, potential threats to those assets, and the vulnerabilities that put those assets at risk. As Chapter 2 explains, threats make security responses necessary. Security threats come from angry individuals, unsophisticated common criminals, relatively sophisticated professional career criminals, extremist groups, or terrorist cells.

Security threats may target and attack human, physical, and informational assets. Any adversary, regardless of sophistication, who targets a client asset usually weighs the potential success and fruits of the attack against the risk of detection and apprehension (see Figure 4.1). While building owners and occupants rely on security assessment and risk analysis to determine asset exposures, adversaries conduct their own risk analysis to determine their targets' vulnerabilities and the feasibility of successfully attacking, harming, or destroying particular assets.

The most beneficial, meaningful security assessments consider the points of view of both the building owner and the adversary, so the approaches and methodologies presented in this chapter do just that. Properly conducted security assessments can help a client decrease asset exposure. Security designs emanating from such assessments should incorporate proven strategies and measures for protecting and preserving assets through deterrence, detection, control, and response strategies.

RISK MANAGEMENT AND RISK CONTROL

Risk is the key factor in accurately assessing the potential for damage or loss of a client's assets. Risk management is the overall process by which security specialists identify a building's assets and vulnerabilities in order to identify and implement prevention and mitigation measures that will result in an acceptable level of risk.

Clients face many kinds of risks, depending on the nature of a business or enterprise—for example, operational, product, financial, legal, tax, and regulatory risks, as diagrammed in Figure 4.2. Operational risk

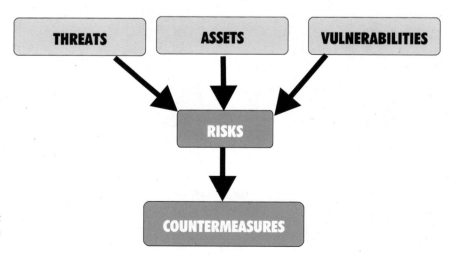

FIGURE 4.1
*Security assessment
elements*

Principal Security Assessment Questions

The client should address the following key questions in a security assessment:

- ✦ What do we want to protect?
- ✦ What are we protecting against?
- ✦ What are the current or expected asset vulnerabilities?
- ✦ What are the consequences of loss?
- ✦ What specific level of protection do we wish to achieve?
- ✦ What types of protection measures are appropriate?
- ✦ What are our protection constraints?
- ✦ What are the specific security design requirements?
- ✦ How do the integrated systems of personnel, technologies, and procedures respond to security incidents?

primarily concerns external or physical threats, and many businesses jump at the opportunity to assess how they can cost-effectively protect critical assets. While a client's investment of time and money in a security assessment can reduce the likelihood of harm or loss in its operating environment, the assessment process also helps align the client's security objectives more effectively with other organizational objectives, thus reinforcing them.

Risk management and control are central to the security assessment process. Whereas both engage the elements mentioned previously to determine risk, the scope in which they address risk differs. Because risk cannot be eliminated, *risk control* aims to minimize or mitigate each identified risk through applied security strategies or measures. *Risk management*, on the other hand, evaluates and quantifies identified risks, then prioritizes security requirements based on the criticality and vulnerability of the assets. In the security assessment process, some risks may be targeted for control, while others may be accepted, transferred, or avoided if security measures to reduce or eliminate them do not appear cost-effective.

Once potential risks have been identified and quantified, the next step in the assessment process is development of functional security design requirements. This critical step is sometimes overlooked, but without it the quantum leap from identifying risks to designing solutions is more difficult. Functional security design requirements allow designers to devise and justify the best-fitting solutions for a problem. Proposing changes in a design concept in the later stages of design and construction documentation

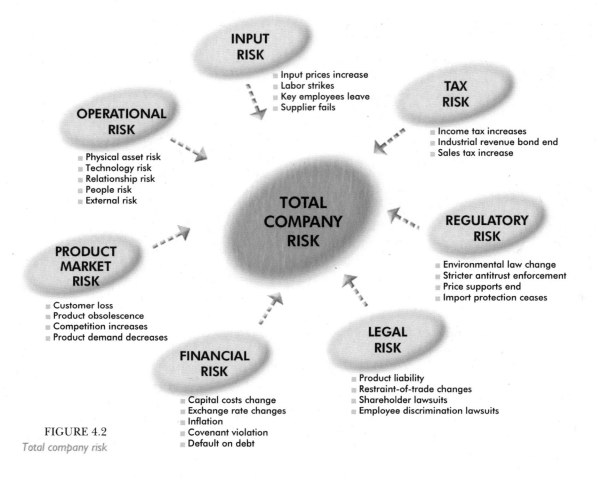

FIGURE 4.2

Total company risk

without such requirements is difficult. There is nothing to which the risk reduction or mitigation caused by the proposed changes can be compared.

TYPES OF SECURITY ASSESSMENT

Security assessments can take many forms, but most take into account the nature of the client organization and of the assets potentially at risk (e.g., personnel, physical resources, intellectual information, and computer resources). Related assessments may look at issues such as business continuity.

Assessments are rarely centered on a single class of assets (e.g., personnel or physical resources). Developers and designers of office buildings, however, typically focus security assessments on base building assets, which primarily include personnel and physical resources, and leave individual tenants to assess their own internal security needs (e.g., internal access control, protecting proprietary information and computer resources). Corporations, in contrast, usually take a more holistic view toward asset protection by incorporating all types of protection requirements into their assessments.

A security audit differs from a security assessment. The *security audit* is usually performed by an outside, objective party to determine whether the client organization measures up to certain standards, either self-imposed or set by an outside agency. A *security assessment,* conducted by the owner or an agent of the owner, is an open study of the security posture of a business or enterprise to determine areas of weakness and to make recommendations for improving an existing program or developing a new one. Building owners and developers often conduct comprehensive security assessments using their internal or contract security staff or a security consultant familiar with the client's security culture and standards.

▐ASSESSMENT TOOLS AND TECHNIQUES

Checklists are key tools in the security assessment process, whether they are completed manually on paper or by using a laptop computer. Checklists can be a quick way to identify and record information and data concerning critical assets, threats, vulnerabilities, existing crime prevention and security awareness initiatives, security operations, and implementation requirements and objectives.

Security specialists use a variety of sampling techniques for collecting demographic, socioeconomic, or crime data related to an assessment objective. In the case of crime and incident data, a consultant may seek to obtain local information and data about potential threats and previous victimizations to develop a risk profile for a particular site or building. With their records of past incidents, local law enforcement agencies are excellent sources of information about potential threats in a particular area. deleterious

When a client has a security department, the security staff should provide the source and victimization data necessary for a proper threat analysis. Private companies also offer computerized national risk data based on relationships between demographic characteristics and the amount of reported crime in a neighborhood.

Assessment Elements

Following are some of the elements to consider in assessing a client's security program.

+ Facility security control during and after hours
+ Personnel and contract security policies and procedures
+ Personnel screening
+ Access control
+ Video surveillance, assessment, and archiving
+ Natural surveillance opportunities
+ Protocols for responding to internal and external security incidents
+ Degree of integration of security and other building systems
+ Shipping and receiving security
+ Property identification and tracking
+ Proprietary information security
+ Computer network security
+ Workplace violence prevention
+ Mail screening operations, procedures, and recommendations
+ Parking lot and site security
+ Data center security
+ Communications security
+ Executive protection
+ Business continuity planning and evacuation procedures

The Security Assessment Process

Security assessment (diagrammed in Figure 4.3) is typically accomplished as a distinct activity during programming. For both new and retrofit building projects, security assessment findings affect the project delivery process from the start of preliminary design. From this point forward, the project team integrates selected security concepts, strategies, and measures into the documentation process for all disciplines (e.g., architectural, structural, mechanical, electrical) and into the subsequent project phases of bidding and negotiation, construction, and building operation.

Chapter 9 discusses security considerations in all phases of project delivery.

The assessment process encompasses distinct asset, threat, vulnerability, and risk analyses, and culminates with the determination of functional design requirements and recommended strategies for achieving

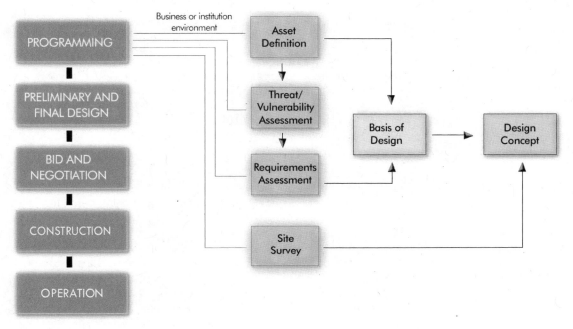

FIGURE 4.3
Security assessment in project delivery

desired levels of asset protection. The client is then able to select the strategies it deems most appropriate.

ASSET ANALYSIS

Assets, those things a client values and wants to protect, are the basis for a client's protection program. Therefore, security evaluation and planning usually begins with an asset analysis (diagrammed in Figure 4.4). This process includes identification of client assets, without initial categorization as critical or noncritical. A comprehensive asset list usually encompasses the following general asset types:

Some security specialists oversimplify or skew the security assessment process by favoring a specific solution (e.g., only hardware measures).

   ✦ *People,* including employees, contractors, and visitors
   ✦ *Physical assets,* including resources, property, and negotiable instruments
   ✦ *Information,* including proprietary, financial, and research information

Some clients require the assessment to cover all assets of the organization, while others concentrate on a single building or even a single asset within a building. Limiting the assessment scope in this manner does not

Assessment Scope of Work

The generally accepted assessment approach is to assess a client's ability to effectively and efficiently respond to a variety of security incidents, ranging from simple security violations to direct attacks on client assets, whether they occur locally or anywhere else. The following tasks, therefore, may be included in the scope of the assessment:

- ◆ Observe existing procedures at parking lots and the main facility entrances to control access and screen visitors. Assess external and internal access control procedures and measures for sensitive operations such as the data and communications centers.
- ◆ Observe and assess the vulnerabilities of existing traffic and parking plans, particularly relating to the safety and security of client personnel and visitors.
- ◆ Assess high-risk areas and operations to determine exposure and methods for protecting and monitoring critical internal operations. Evaluate the capabilities and effectiveness of the current security staff to "interface with," "monitor," or "manage" security operations in these areas.
- ◆ Assess and evaluate the effectiveness of existing and proposed security measures and systems included in any proposed security plans, including any recommendations regarding hardware, structures, staffing, and policies and procedures.
- ◆ Assess security lighting by conducting a night survey of lighting for video surveillance and personnel safety at main entrances, employee entrances, and in the parking lots.
- ◆ Conduct security surveys of the client site and facilities during normal operating hours, at night, and during daytime hours of reduced operation periods (such as on weekends).
- ◆ During night and other after-hours surveys, observe recurring events, such as delivery of material to the loading area, construction, and maintenance and cleaning service calls, to assess exposures, risks, and vulnerabilities to these after-hours operations.
- ◆ Review contract security reports of incidents at the client facilities, obtain local police crime and incident reports and area crime trends, and extrapolate local government threat assessments for the client environment. Factor all of these sources into the overall risk assessment.
- ◆ Evaluate the physical perimeters, parking lot security, and gates at the site and around the facility to determine how effective they are at controlling access and deterring intrusions.
- ◆ Evaluate the effectiveness of personnel security procedures, including personnel screening and facility operations related to security

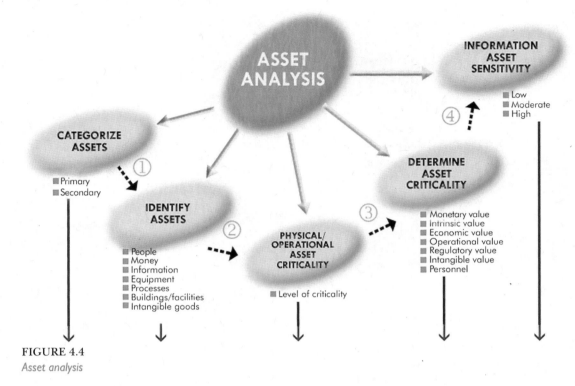

FIGURE 4.4
Asset analysis

necessarily create disadvantages for the analyst, but it could result in incompatible or redundant protection elements for different assets, unnecessarily increasing security costs.

In addition, even if an assessment is limited to a single client building, it must consider that building within the total asset protection scheme of the client in order to determine asset criticality and identify likely threats. Considering a building in context makes it possible to integrate that single building into a client's existing protection scheme.

In asset analysis, as further explained later, assets are first identified and categorized, then rated based on monetary value, intrinsic value, operational value, and other criteria. The evaluation of these ratings determines the criticality of the assets.

❖ Identify Assets

Client assets can be identified as primary (e.g., people, physical resources, information, and image) and secondary (support resources such as generators and fuel sources). If a secondary asset is later identified as critical to

Sample Client Assets and Responsibilities

+ People (employees, visitors)
+ Proprietary information and trade secrets
+ Finished products
+ Computer hardware and software
+ Maintenance equipment
+ Cafeteria and kitchen equipment
+ Employee records
+ Telephone and data equipment
+ Mechanical and electrical systems
+ Corporate image and competitive edge
+ Employee vehicles
+ Building structure and site
+ Employee property
+ Utility equipment

the survival of a primary asset, the secondary asset must receive the same level of protection as the primary asset.

The first attempt to list a client's assets should include as many types as possible. This process can be an enlightening because organizations are rarely required to develop comprehensive lists of assets. Initially, asset types are broadly classified, for example, as people, rather than managers or directors; or as information assets, rather than proprietary information, trade secrets, and so on. This approach helps the analyst view the breadth of personnel and information assets. In subsequent threat, vulnerability, and risk analyses, asset subclassifications will be used to determine specific asset criticality. Once an initial asset list has been completed, the next step is to determine asset criticality.

❖ Determine Asset Criticality

When considering asset criticality, security analysts tend to separate physical assets from information assets. Physical assets are viewed in terms of their *criticality* to the organization's mission. Informational assets are viewed more in terms of their *sensitivity* to the organization's operations. However, as our society increases its dependence on information and knowledge, information assets increase in importance because critical proprietary or trade-secret information can rarely, if ever, be effectively replaced. Conversely, an organization's physical assets usually can be replaced, although at a cost of time and money.

How critical a particular asset is to an organization will determine the level of protection it requires. When determining the criticality of a client's assets, a security analyst typically evaluates each asset in terms of the following:

◆ Monetary value

◆ Intrinsic value

◆ Economic value

◆ Operational value

◆ Regulatory value

◆ Intangible value

Assets are scored from 1 (for nonessential assets) to 5 (for essential assets). At this point, a decision must be made either to continue including an asset in the analysis process or to exclude it from further consideration. Information assets are also factored into the overall assessment; their level of sensitivity is based on a different set of factors, which are typically scored from 1 (very low) to 5 (very high).

Scoring a company's assets gives the analyst a means to create ranges—such as essential to moderate criticality or very high to moderate sensitivity—for deciding which assets will be analyzed further. Assets that fall outside the identified ranges are typically excluded from further analysis.

THREAT ANALYSIS

Unauthorized access or harm to a client's critical assets—including employees, information base, network communication channels, and products—can lead to a serious, possibly catastrophic, disruption of operations and devastating losses of resources and market position. A threat is defined as a source of unauthorized access or a *potential attack on a client asset*. A threat analysis (diagrammed in Figure 4.5), which identifies sources of harm or loss and estimates the likelihood of attack, is used to determine specific vulnerabilities. These vulnerabilities can then be used to prepare a conclusive risk assessment.

Major steps involved in a threat analysis include identifying threats to specific client assets and determining how attractive the assets are to an adversary, identifying adversary categories and capabilities, developing an adversary profile, and developing a design basis threat (DBT). The latter step involves distilling the capabilities of potential adversaries and the

CRITICAL ASSETS →

THREAT ANALYSIS

SECURITY BASIS OF DESIGN

ATTACK LIKELY?

DEVELOP ADVERSARY PROFILE

ADVERSARY CATEGORIES/ CAPABILITIES

DETERMINE ASSET ATTRACTIVENESS

- Asset value
- Similar events
- Relative exposure
- Relative opportunity

- Unsophisticated criminals
- Sophisticated criminals
- Disgruntled employees
- Disoriented persons
- Activists/protesters
- Extremists
- Terrorists
- Subversives

- Objectives
- Organization
- Operations
- Behavior
- Resources

FIGURE 4.5
Threat analysis

Chapter 2 addresses security threats in terms of types of adversaries, including how they think and the methods and tactics they use.

attack scenarios for each asset into a design basis threat, which is the threat most likely to inflict the greatest harm or loss on a client's assets. The DBT is used in the remaining assessment phases to determine asset vulnerability and potential risks before functional security requirements are formulated and a conceptual security design solution is recommended to the client.

❖ Determine Asset Attractiveness

Assets are analyzed and evaluated to determine their attractiveness as a threat target, based on the following criteria:

✦ How accessible the location of the asset is

✦ How the asset itself is controlled

✦ Whether an adversary would perceive visible security measures as a deterrent

✦ How probable it would be for an adversary to escape once an attack had been executed (e.g., via high-speed avenues of escape, concealed departure paths)

Threat Classifications

Threats to client assets can be classified in many ways. Following is one example of a classification system for security assessment and design purposes:

- ✦ *Crimes by outsiders,* such as rape, murder, robbery, assault, burglary, larceny, and vandalism. This category also includes external threats, up to and including terrorist attacks. These incidents can occur in parking garages, parking lots, or other semipublic spaces, including adjacent public areas. External threats are generally from an unknown perpetrator, either sophisticated or unsophisticated, seeking a potential victim or access to facilities to cause some degree of harm. External threats can come from disoriented persons, activists, extremists, subversives, or terrorists.

- ✦ *Crimes by insiders,* such as theft of products, supplies, and equipment; theft of employees' property; and equipment sabotage. The internal threat source is an organization's own disgruntled employee, a vendor, or a subversive who has gained unauthorized entry strictly to cause harm to the client organization. These persons usually familiarize themselves beforehand with building operations and security measures and are therefore in a position to exploit a company's or other employee's exposures. The external threat—of armed robbery, parking lot assault, or rape—instills the greatest fear among employees and visitors, and the internal threat poses the greatest risk to the organization's economic stability.

- ✦ *Drug dealing and associated violent crimes* by employees and non-employees, including acts of revenge or workplace violence by a disgruntled employee, employee-on-employee assaults, and sale and consumption of drugs in the workplace.

- ✦ *Intellectual property theft or compromise* involving proprietary data or research information. This type of action may be conducted by both employees and nonemployees, sometimes in collusion with each other. It includes fraud, compromise of trade secrets and client lists, communications eavesdropping, and computer information access crimes.

- ✦ *Sexual assaults and sexual harassment,* which can have a devastating effect on the organization as well as the victim. Sexual assaults and sexual harassment can occur in any work environment. Consequently, the potential for sexual assault is factored into the security assessment, particularly for open or enclosed parking areas and walkways.

An asset attractiveness analysis can help establish a potential adversary's interest in attacking an asset, the degree to which the asset would be valuable to an adversary, and an adversary's ability to initiate an attack on the asset. The attractiveness of an asset and its criticality are weighted according to their relative contribution to the likelihood of attack. Combined, these weighted factors indicate an asset's potential for attack, considering both the user's and the adversary's perspectives.

❖ Identify Adversary Categories and Capabilities

Another goal of threat analysis is identification of adversaries that would and could potentially mount an attack against specific client assets. This step involves compiling a list of potential adversaries by defined categories. These may range from unsophisticated criminals to extremists, terrorists, and subversives. The capabilities of adversaries in each category are identified with respect to their objectives, organization, operations, behavior, and resources.

❖ Develop the Adversary Profile

Once a list of potential threat sources has been compiled, profiles are developed for each threat category according to its capabilities, organization, operations behavior, and available logistical resources. This step both identifies adversary categories for further analysis and helps determine the likelihood of attack on attractive assets. The security analyst is careful to properly classify threat sources according to their perceived objectives because these play a vital role in shaping the DBT. For example, sabotage and damage/destruction of property may seem to be similar adversary objectives. However, an adversary's objective affects how he or she views a client's assets and thus the type of threat that adversary represents. For example, an insider saboteur is keen on destroying a business, whereas a vandal vents anger by disrupting or defacing property.

❖ Define the Design Basis Threat

The threat assessment concludes with the weighting of previously evaluated data to indicate whether an attack is highly likely, likely, probable, possible, or highly unlikely for each selected adversary category. The likelihood of an attack is a function of an asset's criticality to client operations and its attractiveness to each category of adversary under consideration.

For developing the DBT, a cutoff is established for the attack likelihood measurement—either at highly unlikely or possible, depending on what level of risk the client finds comfortable. The assessment then proceeds based on those threat sources deemed most possible. Later assessment phases may screen these unlikely threats again, more strenuously, to determine their potential effects before including them in the DBT.

VULNERABILITY ANALYSIS

After assigning likelihood ratings to each threat source or adversary in the DBT, the security analyst selects highly likely, likely, probable, and possible risk-causing events to move to the next assessment phase—vulnerability analysis. Vulnerabilities are physical or operational weaknesses in building facilities that adversaries could exploit to carry out malevolent acts. The main purpose of vulnerability analysis is to identify the exposure of assets to potential threats. Asset vulnerability information is also used to determine the adequacy of existing protective measures and to assess the extent to which additional protective measures may be necessary. The exposures and additional protective needs that are identified are then used to develop security design requirements.

Vulnerabilities are identified through surveys and plan reviews of existing buildings or discussions of proposed architectural designs for new buildings. Existing buildings typically have protection schemes in place; therefore, the designer concentrates on identifying asset exposures by viewing critical assets through the lens of the DBT to identify any that have weak or nonexistent protection strategies within the overall building protection scheme. The analysis of new buildings focuses on identifying vulnerabilities by using the DBT to assess planned protection for assets that will reside in the new facility.

Once what is to be protected, its value, its attractiveness to various adversary types, and potential modes and severity of attack has been determined, the next step in the vulnerability analysis is to analyze what is in place to deter, delay, deny, detect, assess, and respond to the potential risk of attack. This is where vulnerabilities or exposures are determined. (The graphic in Figure 4.6 summarizes the major assessment elements of a vulnerability analysis.)

❖ Identify Adversary Attack Modes

The vulnerability analysis begins by considering what modes potential adversaries might employ to attack individual assets, resulting in an assessment of attack severity. The attack modes may include moving or stationary vehicle bombs; exterior attack; standoff attack; forced or covert entry; insider compromise; visual surveillance and eavesdropping; attack via mail or package delivery; cyberattack; and chemical, biological, or radiological contamination. The identified mode is based on the particular characteristics and capabilities of potential adversaries who were previously identified.

FIGURE 4.6

Vulnerability analysis

❖ *Identify Protective Capabilities*

For an existing site or facility, a detailed site survey is used to record existing security measures and assess overall protective capabilities for addressing postulated attack scenarios (see Figure 4.7). Information is compiled about security force capabilities, barriers and structural integrity, access controls, detection systems, assessment systems, personnel capabilities, and the availability and effectiveness of policies and procedures. Existing measures are compared with the minimum requirements for protecting critical assets against the attack mode outcomes identified in the DBT. Shortfalls in existing protective measures are identified as vulnerabilities and documented in the security assessment.

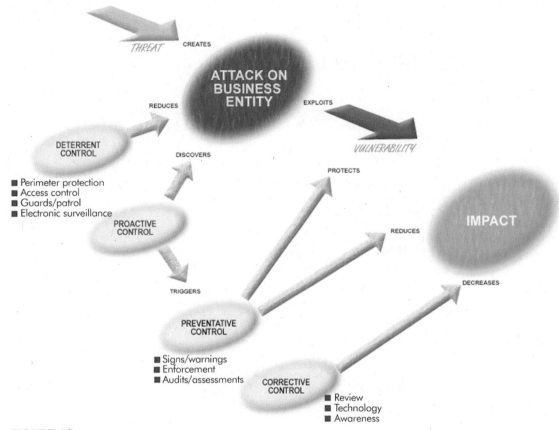

FIGURE 4.7
Attack on business entity

❖ Consider Project Constraints

Some project constraints could interfere with enhancing protective measures at a site. For example, improving access control could negatively affect plant or building operations. Insufficient funds would make it impossible to implement security improvements without affecting other company operations. Each constraint, as well as available alternatives such as asset relocation or alternative physical measures, must be carefully considered. Legitimate constraints may sometimes force an owner to accept existing physical or electronic protective measures despite the vulnerabilities they cause. In this case, the owner has to rely more on procedural security and awareness measures.

Sample List of Vulnerabilities

The following statements of vulnerability are quoted from a security assessment prepared for a pharmaceutical manufacturing plant:

+ Insufficient control and accountability of materials and finished products
+ Insufficient control of company visitors and vendors
+ Lack of protection for company's proprietary production edge
+ Insufficient control of access to critical areas
+ Insufficient screening of employees for critical positions
+ Lack of segregation of public and private space
+ Insufficient procedures for guard force response to security/safety events
+ Inadequate delineation and control of parking perimeter
+ Insufficient access control to site and buildings
+ Limited application of guard force and technology
+ Insufficient access control/intrusion detection at main entry
+ Lack of integration of systems technologies, personnel, and procedures
+ Insufficient security operations and response procedures
+ Insufficient personnel background screening
+ Insufficient screening of material/packages entering the research building
+ Insufficient segregation of interior operations
+ Insufficient control over facility perimeter
+ Insufficient control and surveillance of parking lots
+ Insufficient lighting of facility perimeter and parking lots
+ Lack of control over vehicles approaching the research building

RISK ANALYSIS

Risk analysis concentrates on how to address the extent and cost of potential losses. After potential losses have been identified, an organization can mitigate the risk to its assets by setting and managing asset protection levels (e.g., through enhanced security measures) or adopting other ways to offset or transfer risk (e.g., insurance). Thus, risk analysis is not an end in itself, but a key step leading to a security design. During the risk analysis the need for various design and risk management strategies is established. The risk analysis also serves as the basis for formulating functional security design requirements.

Concepts of risk control and risk management are central to the planning and evaluation process. Risk control strives to minimize or eliminate—to the extent possible—each identified risk through the application of appropriate security strategies and measures. Risk management, in contrast, evaluates and quantifies identified risks, then prioritizes the requirements for security measures based on asset criticality and vulnerability. The security analyst identifies risks that can be controlled. The client determines which ones to accept, transfer, or avoid, taking into account that security measures required to reduce or eliminate some risks might not be cost-effective or appropriate.

❖ Probability Assessment of Loss

The risk analysis phase of security assessment (diagrammed in Figure 4.8) is based on the asset vulnerabilities or exposure identified during the vulnerability analysis. A loss event probability and impact assessment is carried out to determine the existing asset exposure or loss potential and its potential effects on the organization. Considerations include whether

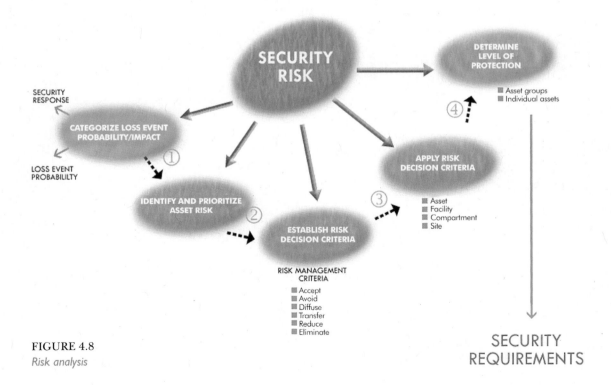

FIGURE 4.8
Risk analysis

there could be direct human loss, direct and indirect financial loss, and information compromise or image loss as a result of the postulated asset exposure. Potential loss events are then assigned a probability rating and a score ranging from certain (5) to not probable (1). Asset risks are prioritized, and risk decision boundaries are established (e.g., accept, diffuse, or transfer). This information is then applied to each identified asset to determine the level of protection for individual and groups of assets.

❖ Risk Management Strategies

Risk assessment is directed toward loss prevention and mitigation. However, the actual elements most often considered in this analysis are the probability that a loss event will occur, the expected frequency of such an occurrence, and the relative impact or consequence of the event if it were to occur as predicted. When client organizations insure assets against theft, they consider the actual cost of asset loss or damage. If the insurance company will replace or repair the item, the consequences of the loss will be substantially reduced. But if the client must repair or replace the item, the inability to use it and the related costs of replacement must be taken into account. Similarly, risk analysis weighs existing or proposed strategies to reduce both the likelihood and consequences of a risk-causing event.

Risk event probability is measured by the number of ways in which a particular event can result from a certain activity, divided by the total number of all events that could occur. Typically, a risk matrix is used to display this information because it provides an orderly and logical presentation of risk information from which decisions can be made. Probability ratings usually include terms such as "certain," "highly probable," "moderately probable," and "improbable." Severity of impact ratings normally includes terms such as "catastrophic" loss, "very serious" loss, "moderately serious" loss, or "not serious."

❖ Determining Levels of Protection

As part of the risk analysis, the appropriate level of protection is defined for each asset based on criticality and potential for loss or harm. At this phase, the security analyst categorizes assets and groups of assets according to the level of protection required (e.g., very high, high, moderate, low, and very low). These criteria become the basis for determining asset protection requirements and the eventual selection of security measures.

Sample Risk Summary Table

This risk analysis summary from an actual security assessment report lists expected major physical risks ranked as low, moderate, or high. Some security analysts may use a different rating scheme, scoring the level of risk from very high (5) to very low (1).

Interruption of business as a result of damage/destruction to facilities/systems and supporting resources	High
Loss of Company X's competitive edge in attracting quality staff because of significant incidents at ABC and XYZ facilities	High
Business operations severely impaired by actions of a disgruntled employee	High
Injury or harm to employees/visitors	Moderate
Loss of Company X's goodwill as a result of a significant injury/catastrophe/theft of highly confidential information/material	Moderate
Insufficient response to natural disaster results in damage to/destruction of Company X facilities and documents	Moderate
Loss or destruction of property and equipment	Moderate
Theft of and vandalism to Company X property and equipment	Moderate
Loss and/or compromise of sensitive and critical data and information	Moderate
Liability exposure created by lack of proper response to a security incident	Low
Increased operational and capital costs due to theft and vandalism	Low

Security Design Strategies

When a risk assessment determines that a client faces significantly higher and more consequential risks than the average organization, it is essential to design and implement security measures commensurate with those risks. Security measures are selected on the basis of their individual and collective ability to prevent, detect, control, and mitigate risks to assets from any or all of the design basis threat scenarios identified in the risk analysis.

Since 9/11, virtually any scenario has become plausible for some high-profile, high-value targets—especially infrastructure and highly visible, symbolic targets. To ensure the measures they take are commensurate with the perceived risks, building owners should be cautioned to conduct a security analysis of their facilities at least annually. Certainly, any collection of recommended measures may not prevent or deter all attack modes. Nevertheless, a well-planned, well-implemented, and well-maintained building security program can substantially increase the level of protection for an organization's assets, enhance the safety of high-risk working environments, and reduce employees' fears for their personal safety.

DETERMINING FUNCTIONAL SECURITY DESIGN REQUIREMENTS

The findings of a security assessment are used to develop a general set of security objectives such as the following

+ Prevent crime and other security incidents.

+ Integrate Company X's facility security requirements into the company's overall security program.

+ Reduce employees' fear of crime and potential feelings of vulnerability.

+ Maintain the company's creative, innovative work environment by ensuring safe and secure work and research facilities in an open-campus setting.

+ Based on anticipated risks to a new facility, seamlessly integrate physical and information security countermeasures into day-to-day facility activities and company operations to create a layered security effect.

While these objectives clearly establish overall, top-level design guidance, more specific objectives are needed for the security systems designer. Basic security objectives are usually expressed in terms such as "to prevent," "to control," or "to detect." Objectives for security design, however, are stated with more specificity; for example, "The security system has been designed to protect company assets by *deterring, detecting,* and *preventing* selected adversaries from perpetrating loss-causing events." Such basic security concepts are applicable regardless of the environment of the security system being designed.

Figure 4.9 lists functional security design terms and concepts. Virtually every recommended measure in a security assessment should have a direct relationship to one or more of these concepts. For example, natural features such as berms and bodies of water *delay* intruders; intrusion detection systems both *detect* and *assess* intrusions with respect to type and location; CCTV systems detect and *assess;* and access systems *control* and *respond* electronically to intrusion attempts. Finally, security personnel *detect, con-*

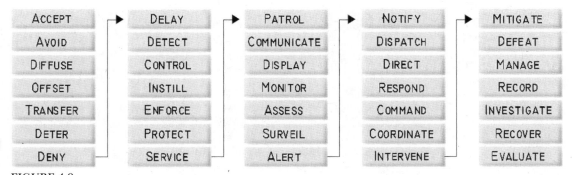

FIGURE 4.9

Security terms and concepts

trol, enforce, patrol, communicate, assess, surveil, respond, defeat, record, and *investigate*. Using these concepts, the security designer identifies functional requirements from which functional statements are prepared describing the functional level of protection for given assets. Using these statements and identified DBT scenarios, the security consultant develops a number of design strategies for individual and collective asset protection.

The consultant then presents the design strategies to the client, who selects appropriate ones for integration into the company security program. If the client feels that cameras for perimeter surveillance are too obtrusive or expensive, other strategies and measures providing comparable protection can be identified, or the original functional requirement can be changed or modified after reevaluating the risk. Sample functional design requirements from an actual security assessment of a university research reactor building are shown in the box on the next page.

SECURITY DESIGN OPTIONS

An integrated program of building security measures recommended to the client may include the following security program design options:

- ✦ Architectural barriers and spatial definition to deter, delay, and deny entry
- ✦ Building control systems and interior layouts to channel vehicular and pedestrian traffic
- ✦ Surveillance and assessment systems linked to electronic sensors and control elements
- ✦ Aesthetically placed electronic access control and detection technologies

Sample Functional Security Design Requirements

A security assessment for a university research building that houses a nuclear reactor resulted in the following functional security design requirements:

+ Provide for secure storage of special nuclear material.
+ Provide a high level of protection for organization's assets.
+ Provide a high level of protection for staff/employees/students/visitors that is consistent with perceived threats and risks.
+ Provide design solutions to detect unauthorized entry.
+ Control access to critical areas of organization's facilities.
+ Provide facilities for monitoring facility security systems.
+ Integrate systems for intrusion detection, access control, and electronic video surveillance/assessment.
+ Provide electronic means of assessing facility alarm function.
+ Maintain control of facility access through automated means.
+ Provide for adequate surveillance and lighting of parking lots.
+ Provide for continuous surveillance and monitoring of site entrances and facility lobbies.
+ Provide for effective incident management.
+ Provide for continuous surveillance/monitoring of facility perimeter.
+ Provide for effective central and remote monitoring of organization's facilities.
+ Enable detection of forced entry through exterior facility doors and windows.
+ Conduct sufficient background checks on personnel granted access to the containment area.
+ Provide assessment and surveillance capability.
+ Establish physical and procedural control over sensitive/restricted areas.
+ Provide a high level of protection for stored nuclear material.
+ Establish control over radioactive waste.
+ Provide a secure means to escort visitors.
+ Ensure rapid response to security/safety events.
+ Maintain security awareness through employee/staff involvement in security.
+ Communicate organization security standards to staff/employees/students/visitors.
+ Establish physical and electronic control over access to sensitive/proprietary/research information and data.
+ Restrict visitor access by establishing visitor badging and/or escort procedures.
+ Provide for internal and external control of organization-owned property.
+ Provide for electronic assessment and facility surveillance capability.
+ Establish strict controls over access to and use of proprietary information.
+ Ensure physical separation of public and private spaces.
+ Establish procedures to respond to identified threats and risks.
+ Provide for security training of organization's personnel.

◆ Environmental design concepts and strategies to prevent the incidence and fear of victimization on client property

◆ Communication and monitoring systems that allow for direction and notification of responders

◆ Comprehensive security policies and procedures to guide client security operations and provide security program control over all critical assets

◆ A computerized security management system that records security incident statistics, which can be used to enable proactive security responses

◆ Protection strategies for intellectual property and other proprietary information

◆ From a systems standpoint, all electronic design options are integrated through the security management system (SMS). The SMS is combined with personnel and procedures to create a total building security program.

▌DEFENSE IN DEPTH OR THE LAYERED EFFECT

As discussed in Chapter 3 and depicted in Figure 4.10, the *defense-in-depth* (layered) concept of physical security starts at the site perimeter, moves to the building exterior and then to the building interior, leading to the people and core assets. Each concentric ring can be protected through a combination of personnel and procedures, coupled with physical security components and technologies. Integrated lines of protective measures are generally configured in concentric rings around a protected asset to make it progressively more difficult for an intruder to reach it and to escape undetected. These protection schemes place time delays in an intruder's path.

The selection of security strategies is critical to forming effective layered asset protection schemes. For example, a well-conceived security system should detect penetration attempts as far away from the asset to be protected as practical as well as at several points along the likely path of an intruder. The point or area where an intrusion can be detected is defined as a *zone* or *line of detection*. A comprehensive system protecting highly critical assets, either on the exterior or interior of a building, may require multiple lines or zones of detection and/or delay. A security consultant determines the number of zones to be used and their configuration according to the perceived degree of asset protection required to ensure a timely response to a specified risk-causing event.

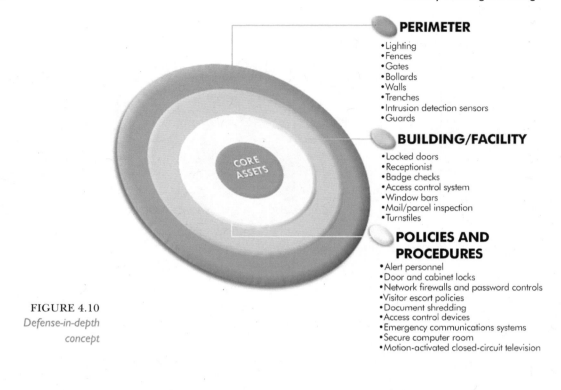

PERIMETER
- Lighting
- Fences
- Gates
- Bollards
- Walls
- Trenches
- Intrusion detection sensors
- Guards

BUILDING/FACILITY
- Locked doors
- Receptionist
- Badge checks
- Access control system
- Window bars
- Mail/parcel inspection
- Turnstiles

POLICIES AND PROCEDURES
- Alert personnel
- Door and cabinet locks
- Network firewalls and password controls
- Visitor escort policies
- Document shredding
- Access control devices
- Emergency communications systems
- Secure computer room
- Motion-activated closed-circuit television

CORE ASSETS

FIGURE 4.10
*Defense-in-depth
concept*

Security Strategy Selection and Integration

Which security measures a client chooses from the options presented depends largely on their cost-effectiveness. Factors that affect the cost of proposed security measures may include operational restrictions, nuisance alarm susceptibility, installation cost, maintenance costs, probability of detection, mean-time-between-failure contribution to personnel reduction, contribution to asset vulnerability, and reduced risk, normally expressed as the monetary consequence of loss or destruction. Following are cost issues to consider, whether measures are considered individually or collectively:

✦ Operational impact

—Time required for site or building access identification alternatives (hours/dollars)

—Estimated cost of physical reconfiguration of space or facility layouts to accommodate security concerns

—Effect of security measures on safety and operational efficiency

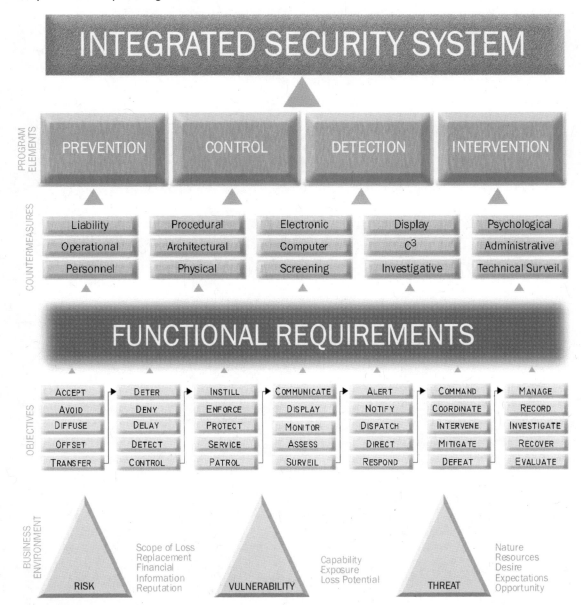

FIGURE 4.11
Integrated security system

◆ Vulnerability reduction potential

—Estimated savings due to reduction in known loss experience
—Reliability and coverage of physical security measures versus personnel efforts
—Reduced risk of loss

◆ Cost of operation

—Estimated installation and operations cost
—Estimated life-cycle maintenance cost

◆ Contribution to overall organizational efficiency

◆ Savings in security personnel costs over the life cycle of the system

◆ User confidence in the security measures put in place

◆ Deterrence value versus perceived personal intrusiveness (e.g., of biometric access control technologies such as retina scanning) and inconvenience of countermeasures

While any one of the preceding considerations may result in selection or rejection of a security measure, the acceptable measures are eventually linked as a system to establish *overall* cost and effectiveness. This can be a difficult task, mainly because most organizations do not regularly collect and report security incident data. The lack of data, coupled with the fact that quantifying security's contribution to an organization's goals is difficult if not impossible, makes it challenging to compare the cost of applying security measures to the resulting reduction in exposure or risk. Security expenditures must be shown on an individual asset and a system basis to justify the projected costs of a total security system in relation to the cost of projected losses.

The assessment of threats, vulnerabilities, and risks for a given business or enterprise is used to develop a series of functional security design requirements stated as security design objectives. These objectives, in turn, are used to develop security strategies, which can include liability, personnel, physical, electronic, and architectural countermeasures. Figure 4.11 shows countermeasures that could be included in a security system. By aligning these measures with specific summary program elements, such as prevention, control, detection, and intervention, appropriate security design strategies can be selected and grouped to form an integrated security program to protect buildings, property, information, and other client assets and resources—including, above all, people.

5 Building Hardening

Peter DiMaggio, PE

The frequency and magnitude of recent terrorist bomb attacks against civilian structures, both in the United States and abroad, has alerted the building design community to the need for comprehensive design solutions to mitigate the effects of such attacks. Thwarting a terrorist attack through intelligence-gathering or law enforcement techniques is always preferable, but building hardening is increasingly seen as a last line of defense in any antiterrorist program.

The current state of the art in building hardening reflects the ways in which terrorist attacks on U.S. facilities have shaped the design philosophies of U.S. architects. This chapter presents basic concepts and techniques, both structural and nonstructural, for hardening buildings against forced entry, ballistic attack, and bomb blasts.

Forced-Entry and Ballistic Hardening

The field of building hardening in the civilian sector commonly addresses techniques for protecting buildings and their occupants from forced-entry or ballistic (bullet) attacks. Forced-entry (FE) protection techniques can prevent an attacker from entering a facility, either covertly or during a mass riot. Ballistic-resistant (BR) design can protect occupants or other critical elements of a facility from a wide variety of weapons, including handguns, shotguns, rifles, and machine guns. As with any building hardening principles, the first line of defense against both types of attacks is early detection. However, due to the relative ease of obtaining the tools and weapons needed for these assaults, it is not possible to completely protect a facility through detection alone. As a result, FE and BR hardening measures can be incorporated into a building design to minimize the danger from these attacks.

FORCED-ENTRY PROTECTION

A wide variety of tactics and techniques can be used to defend against an FE attack. These techniques range from high level to relatively low-level protection, but the main purpose is to detect and delay aggressors attempting to penetrate a facility.

The level of protection (i.e., the specified time to penetration) chosen for a property is often coordinated with the time required for an appropriate response. For example, it is typically not practical to harden a commercial facility to prevent penetration; therefore, it is imperative to coordinate the level of protection for these properties with the time of law enforcement response. For example, in an urban environment with fast police response times, a low-level FE protection (5 to 15 minutes) may be acceptable. However, in a rural setting, with long distances to law enforcement offices, a higher level of protection (60 minutes) may be advisable.

 The U.S. Army Corps of Engineers' technical manual "Security Engineering Concept Design" (TM 5-853-2) defines the time required to defeat an element as "the time it takes to make a 96-square-inch (man-sized) opening with the least dimension greater than 6 inches in a construction assembly using a given set of tools." This time to penetration, or level of protection, is directly proportional to the construction of the individual building components being attacked.

Once a level of protection, or required delay time, has been determined, the overall design concept for hardening a building can be developed. Regardless of the level of protection desired, the design should provide the required delay time through use of a layered or tiered defense system consisting of the site perimeter, building envelope, and internal building areas. Each layer is protected by a combination of surveillance and detection devices and some form of physical barrier to delay the aggressor. Surveillance equipment alerts building security personnel and local law enforcement authorities, minimizing their response time. Physical barriers maximize the time required to penetrate each layer of protection. These two security tools should be designed concurrently and detailed to provide a coordinated level of protection.

The first line of defense in hardening a property is a contiguous, uninterrupted fence line around the entire perimeter of the site. Guardhouses are located at necessary fence penetrations, such as entrances and exits to the facility, to screen all visitors. The fence should be of sufficient height (7 to 9 feet high) to provide a psychological deterrent to aggressors and a platform for mounting surveillance cameras and other electronic detection devices. Use of a fence designed to be as difficult to climb as possible, incorporating primarily vertical bars without horizontal hand- and footholds, is recommended, although a determined aggressor can breach almost any fence relatively easily.

The second layer of defense is the exterior envelope of a building. A recommended approach is to harden the first floor, and any accessible higher floors (such as those with balconies accessible from the ground floor), to make them the primary means of delaying aggressors. This can be accomplished by modifying lightweight, typical building construction to force a longer penetration time. For example, brick and block façades provide more protection than exterior-grade plywood or exterior insulated finish systems (EIFS). For even more protection, thick reinforced concrete walls can be incorporated into a structure. In addition, any glazing accessible from the ground should be hardened to eliminate weak points that aggressors may target. Sensors, surveillance equipment, and alarm systems should be used in conjunction with hardening techniques to alert law enforcement personnel and to deter an aggressor.

The third layer of defense is the interior room or rooms containing critical assets. Techniques similar to those in the second layer of defense are typically used for interior room walls, doors, and, if necessary, windows.

BALLISTIC-RESISTANT DESIGN

As with forced-entry defense techniques, there are many options for providing ballistic- or bullet-resistant protection. In addition, the level of protection can be varied from a very low level of protection (e.g., primarily obscuring potential targets) to a very high level of protection (e.g., bullet-resistant construction able to stop jacketed assault rifle rounds). Comprehensive protection must protect the walls and all building apertures, including doors, windows, and mechanical openings, where assets are to be protected against a ballistic attack. While the detailed design of each component may vary, similar techniques are used for each element.

The first line of defense, possibly the only requirement for a low level of protection, is to minimize the number of openings, locate the openings out of direct line-of-fire sight lines, and obscure the view to any potential targets. This general approach is appropriate for all types of openings, although specific techniques vary slightly for every building component. For example, doors are designed to minimize the glazed openings, where possible. Windows, where necessary, should include at least a reflective film to obscure targets during the day as well as shades or blinds to conceal targets at night.

The second line of defense, typically used to provide a high level of protection, is to protect assets with bullet-resistant construction. This typically means thick brick or block walls, steel doors, and bullet-resistant glazing assemblies at windows and skylights. This high-protection category can be further subdivided into levels representing possible ammunition types and the velocity and energy delivered by specific weapons. A number of testing agencies have developed ratings based on this information; arguably the most universal is the Underwriters Laboratories (UL) rating system. UL defines eight levels of protection, plus a supplementary shotgun category. Level 1 is the lowest rating, requiring building elements to stop 9mm ballistic rounds, and Level 8 is the highest rating, requiring construction to stop 7.62-mm fully jacketed rounds. The table in Figure 5.1 lists the bullet resistance of various materials.

IMPLEMENTING FORCED-ENTRY AND BALLISTIC-RESISTANT FEATURES

Building elements designed to provide both FE and BR protection are typically based on empirical data gathered through well-documented testing programs. The designer is not expected to perform calculations to specify the element composition to resist these types of attacks. Rather, standard design procedure entails using test data available either in government references or from manufacturers' specifications.

In general, the design procedure can be broken into several basic steps. Initially, the design team must determine the level of FE or BR protection required. Then, when possible, the design incorporates general planning concepts such as providing perimeter fences, orienting the building to avoid direct lines of fire into apertures, minimizing fenestration, providing rugged wall construction at grade-accessible locations, and using concealment tactics such as reflective window film and shades at vulnerable window locations. If a building requires only a low level of protec-

Representative Ballistics Round	Thickness (inches)					
	Concrete	Concrete Blocks*	Brick*	Mild Steel Plate	Hardened Steel Plate	Bullet-Resistant Fiberglass
9 mm and .38 special	2	4	4	$\frac{1}{4}$	$\frac{3}{16}$	$\frac{5}{16}$
.44 magnum	2½	4	4	$\frac{5}{16}$	$\frac{1}{4}$	$\frac{7}{16}$
7.62 mm and .30-caliber rifle	4	6	6	$\frac{9}{16}$	$\frac{7}{16}$	$1\frac{1}{8}$
7.62 mm armor-piercing round	6½	8	8	$\frac{13}{16}$	$\frac{11}{16}$	N/A

FIGURE 5.1
Bullet resistance of materials

*Nominal thickness
Source: Security Engineering, TM 5-853

tion, sound-planning principles such as these may be sufficient. If higher levels of protection are required, the final step is to design and specify building components to provide the desired level of FE and BR protection.

As with all building hardening requirements, the key to successful implementation is to include a security professional early in the planning stages of a project. This involvement makes it possible to integrate security principles seamlessly into the project design.

Blast-Resistant Hardening

Several well-known terrorist incidents awakened the U.S. building community to the need for blast-resistant hardening features in the design of vulnerable buildings. These and other less widely publicized events—and the lessons learned from them—have played a critical role in shaping the design philosophy of building hardening in the United States.

In April 1983 a suicide bomber drove an explosive-laden truck into the U.S. embassy in Beirut, Lebanon, killing 63. In October of the same year, another terrorist drove a truck loaded with explosives through perimeter fences and crashed into the U.S. Marine barracks in Beirut, killing 241 Marines and sailors. The single most important lesson learned from these two events was the critical need for antiram architecture sufficient to protect the perimeter of vulnerable facilities from suicide bombers. In response, blast-resistant design techniques from military design manuals were modified to satisfy embassy design guidelines.

In 1993 Islamic fundamentalists attacked the World Trade Center in New York City for the first time, detonating a bomb in a van in the parking basement. Six people were killed, and about 1,000 injured. Although this attack did not cause the type of destruction intended, it clearly highlighted the vulnerabilities of buildings with uncontrolled underground parking.

In April 1995 Timothy McVeigh destroyed the Alfred P. Murrah Federal Building in Oklahoma City using a massive truck bomb parked at the curb in front of the facility. An explosive shock wave tore through the building, collapsing the entire front half of the nine-story structure and killing 168 people, including 19 children. This event highlighted the vulnerability of conventionally designed structures to high explosive loads.

Techniques developed to address threats such as these typically are intended to minimize human casualties if an incident occurs. A building and all its critical components are designed to resist the shock wave associated with a highly explosive blast. The objective is to prevent collapse, minimize hazards associated with flying debris, and facilitate evacuation of a facility—all with the primary goal of minimizing human injury and loss of life. Protection of property and the final condition of the building are normally secondary concerns. For this reason, design techniques are often used that adhere to minimum life safety requirements but could result in significant building damage, such as deformed steel, cracked concrete, and broken or fractured glass. This life safety concept allows designers to incorporate building hardening techniques but minimize their cost, aesthetic, and programmatic impact on a facility. For a project that includes building hardening, close coordination among all design team members is needed to achieve lightweight, cost-effective, and aesthetically pleasing structures that also provide significant protection to building occupants.

▉ BLAST LOADING

Understanding the concepts employed to defend a structure from a high-explosive terrorist attack requires a rudimentary comprehension of the mechanics of shock wave propagation. Three key variables govern the magnitude of blast pressure forces that reach a target structure: the size of the explosion, the distance from the explosion to the target (standoff distance), and the angle formed where the target meets the shock front (angle of incidence).

At the instant a conventional explosive device is detonated, a shock wave is propagated. As the wave moves away from the source of the explosion, the magnitude of the shock front dissipates exponentially as a function of distance. In addition, as the wave moves farther from the epicenter, the shock front moves significantly faster than the rear of the shock wave, increasing the overall duration of the wave. In short, the farther the target is from an explosion, the less the peak pressure on the target will be and the greater the load duration. Figure 5.2 diagrams a typical high-explosive shock wave.

As a shock wave generated by an explosion moves through the air and hits a surface, the magnitude of the load is reflected and magnified like a wave in water is reflected and magnified when it hits a rigid wall. The angle between the reflecting surface and the shock front will determine the amount of reflection and, subsequently, magnification. Assuming a blast load of 500 pounds of TNT at a distance of 10 feet from the target, the magnification factor can range from approximately 8 when the surface is 90 degrees (perpendicular) to the shock front to a factor of 1 when the surface is 180 degrees (parallel) to the shock front.

The first step in any building hardening exercise is to use the above information to reduce blast loading on the building. Typically, little can be done to minimize the size of the explosive a terrorist uses to attack a facility, but the design can control the distance between an explosive device and the target and can advantageously affect the angle of incidence. For example, locating a secured perimeter as far as possible from the target structure and effectively using the building geometry can significantly reduce blast loading on vulnerable building components.

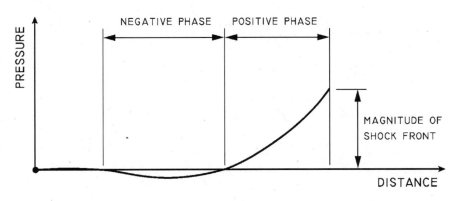

FIGURE 5.2
Typical high-explosive shock wave

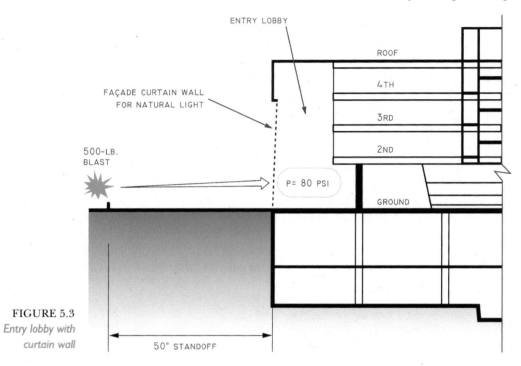

FIGURE 5.3
Entry lobby with curtain wall

    To illustrate this point, consider two options for providing natural light in the entrance lobby of a building. One provides a hardened perimeter, guaranteeing a standoff of 50 feet from the building, and seeks to infuse light into the lobby through a glass façade curtain wall (see Figure 5.3). The other increases the hardened perimeter and standoff distance to 75 feet and attempts to draw light into the building through skylights in the lobby roof (see Figure 5.4). A simplified calculation of blast loading can be used to compare the effects of the two design decisions. Increasing the standoff by 25 feet and modifying the angle of the reflecting surface of the glass from 90 degrees to 180 degrees reduces the peak blast pressure from 80 psi to 8 psi.

    This example is meant neither to advise against façade curtain walls nor to promote skylight systems. It simply highlights the need to consider blast-resistant design concepts at the earliest stages of project development and to use the site layout and building geometry to the greatest advantage possible. Minimizing the blast load of a building will reduce the need for costly strengthening techniques later in the design process.

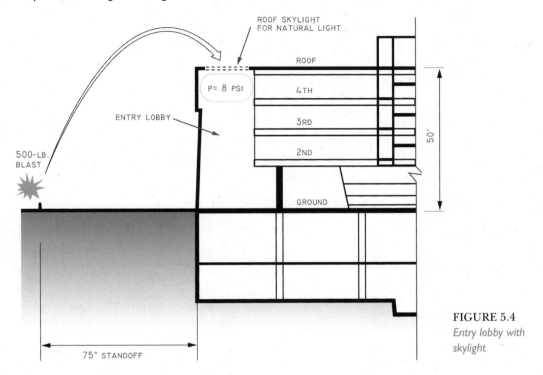

ROOF SKYLIGHT
FOR NATURAL LIGHT

ROOF

P= 8 PSI

4TH

ENTRY LOBBY

3RD

2ND

500-LB.
BLAST

50'

GROUND

75" STANDOFF

FIGURE 5.4
*Entry lobby with
skylight*

DETERMINATION OF BOMB THREATS

Despite the difficulty of quantifying the type and amount of explosives a terrorist may use, it is imperative that a realistic charge weight be used when planning hardening of a particular building. Although a comprehensive discussion of the methods for approximating a design-level threat is beyond the scope of this chapter, the basic principles are worth summarizing.

The wide variety of high-explosive devices that could be incorporated in any vehicle bomb—including fertilizer bombs (ammonium nitrate and fuel oil [ANFO]), dynamite (TNT), and military-grade plastic explosives (composition 4 [C4])—can be compared to TNT in terms of their relative explosive capacity. Therefore, this chapter will refer to all charge weights in terms of equivalent pounds of TNT.

The process of determining or assuming a design-level charge weight for a specific facility may consider some or all of the following variables:

✦ Type, size, and location of the facility
✦ Historical data from terrorist attacks

+ Building occupancy
+ Neighboring buildings and their occupants
+ Vehicle delivery sizes

The process of incorporating all of these variables into a charge weight determination can range from relatively simple to very complex, with detailed probabilistic models. Figure 5.5 summarizes the possible charge weights associated with certain vehicle types. It is imperative to remember that any method used to determine a design charge weight is only an assumption of what an attacker might actually use against a facility.

FIGURE 5.5

Approximate bomb sizes by vehicle type

+ Package Bomb: 50 pounds
+ Car Bomb: 500 pounds
+ Passenger Van: 2,000 pounds
+ Small Truck: 4,000 pounds
+ Large Truck: 10,000 pounds
+ Tractor Trailer: 40,000 pounds

PERIMETER SECURITY AND PROTECTION FROM VEHICULAR BOMBS

The first step in any building security project is to maximize and guarantee a secured perimeter around the facility. As indicated previously, one of the most important variables in determining the magnitude of a shock wave that might impact a target is the distance from the detonation to that target, or the *standoff distance*. Therefore, one of the most effective tools a designer has against a high-explosive terrorist attack is to force the terrorist to detonate the explosives as far from the building as possible. This is accomplished by surrounding the facility with a secure antiram perimeter, devoid of weak points, and by locating this perimeter as far from the target structure as the design allows. The look and design of an antiram perimeter are governed by two factors—the need to completely resist an explosive-laden vehicle traveling at maximum possible speed, and the designer's imagination in terms of the look and feel of the perimeter's elements.

Perimeter antiram architecture consists of two main types, active and passive. Passive devices are always in defensive position, while active devices can be raised and lowered to allow access by screened vehicles. Active devices, which may be activated either manually or hydraulically, are typically used at perimeter gates, sally ports, and garage and loading dock entrances. Passive devices typically constitute the remainder of the perimeter antiram system.

Whether a device is active or passive, its primary function is to prevent a terrorist from crashing through the controlled perimeter and from detonating an explosive device close to the target. A facility's overall blast resistance is based on a standoff distance that this perimeter security should guarantee. A terrorist who can advance closer to the target than the perimeter can defeat the entire building-hardening scheme. Therefore, any antiram architecture must be designed to properly resist the design-level moving vehicle threat.

The design-level threat for these elements depends on vehicle mass and corresponding approach speed. The larger the vehicle and the faster it is traveling, the larger the force imparted to the barrier. The designer can limit an approaching vehicle's maximum speed by locating and arranging access roads in a specific manner—for example, by eliminating direct,

See Appendix B for resources on building and structural hardening to resist bomb blasts.

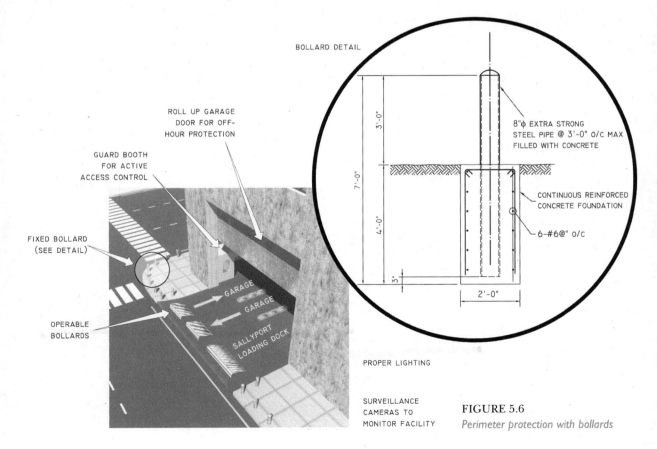

FIGURE 5.6
Perimeter protection with bollards

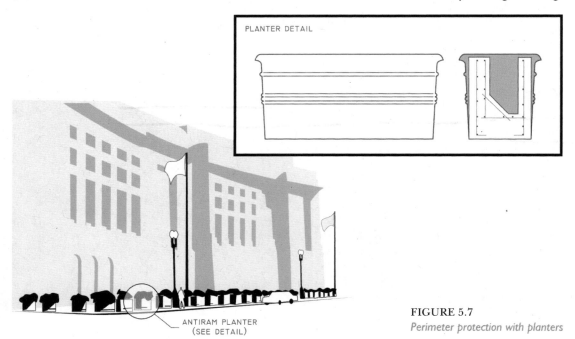

PLANTER DETAIL

ANTIRAM PLANTER
(SEE DETAIL)

FIGURE 5.7
Perimeter protection with planters

straight drive lanes to the perimeter access gates. Just as the building layout affects blast loading, limiting the vehicle approach speed will reduce the required hardening of the perimeter elements, saving costs and allowing for more aesthetically pleasing designs.

When considering whether to employ passive and active antiram barriers, as Figures 5.6 and 5.7 illustrate, it is important to understand that a controlled perimeter will powerfully affect a facility's overall aesthetic appeal. Any successful project will incorporate and coordinate the design of this critical element with the remaining landscape architecture early in the design process. Certain situations may require barriers that blend well with the terrain, such as rocks and boulders, while bollards or planters may be more suitable for other situations. Whether the building site is in a suburban environment, with a maximum standoff of 100 feet, or in an urban environment, with a curbside distance of only 10 feet, it is equally important to guarantee the standoff distance because it is the first line of defense in any building-hardening project.

PEDESTRIAN PACKAGE BOMB PROTECTION

Equally important to vehicular protection is protection from a package bomb delivered by a person, in a suitcase, backpack, or even strapped to an assailant. The first line of defense is to prevent that bomb from entering the facility, thus maximizing the distance from the targeted building element to the high-explosive charge.

The most secure facilities locate a screening station or guardhouse at the secured perimeter. There, everyone trying to enter the facility is screened for explosives, ensuring that any detonation would occur no closer than at the controlled perimeter. Because a package bomb certainly will be smaller than any design-level vehicular charge, it should not threaten the facility.

Where perimeter screening is not possible, as in the case of an urban building without a perimeter fence, it is critical that the location of any possible package bomb be contained to the extent possible. For example, screening devices in the lobby of a building can effectively confine an explosion to that area. Columns, beams, walls, and other important building components within the lobby could be designed to resist the effects of such a blast. However, locally hardening building elements is expensive and often aesthetically and programmatically undesirable. Therefore, it is best to limit the possible location of satchel charges to an area of the building designed for screening, thereby limiting the amount of internal building hardening required.

Building Hardening Techniques

Once a design team has determined a likely size for potential vehicular and personnel charges, and determined the requisite controlled perimeter or standoff distances, the nature and magnitude of blast loading for the building can be determined. Given these design loads, the team can begin to harden the vulnerable aspects of the facility to resist the specified loading conditions.

FAÇADE HARDENING

In any conventionally designed building, the component most vulnerable to blast loads is the building envelope. Conventionally designed glazing—or glazing designed to resist typical environmental loads such as wind and water infiltration—has been the largest contributor to human casualties in almost every terrorist bombing. To understand the many concepts that can be used to harden conventional wall systems, it is first necessary to understand what makes these systems so vulnerable.

❖ Glass and Glazing

Glass is aesthetically pleasing and an important element in most building designs; however, it is extremely susceptible to damage from a shock wave. Strong enough to resist even the highest loads associated with hurricane-force winds, glass is relatively weak and typically not nearly strong enough to resist the forces generated by even a small blast relatively far from the building. Coupled with this, the brittle nature of monolithic glass results in sudden, catastrophic failure when the glass is overstressed. Due to these material properties, glass fragments generated during a failure are extremely hazardous to building occupants and, if not properly designed, can cause mass casualties when propelled at high speeds into occupied spaces. As with each building component this chapter covers, design solutions can mitigate the hazards associated with glass by addressing each of its weaknesses, for example, by making the glass less brittle and modifying its failure mode.

Glass can be fabricated in a variety of strengths, the weakest being annealed glass and the strongest thermally tempered glass (TTG). Heat-strengthened glazing falls between these two types. Heat-treating conventional annealed glass prestresses it, significantly strengthening it. The heating process also changes the breaking pattern, or failure mode, of the glass. Annealed glass tends to fracture into large, daggerlike shards, while TTG tends to break into small, rock-saltlike particles. Most residential and typical office construction includes monolithic annealed glass, and a typical broken window illustrates the dangerous fragmentation produced by failure of this type of glazing. By comparison, an automobile's side windows typically are made from TTG and tend to fracture in a much more forgiving manner.

Although tempering glass increases its strength, it does not adequately address the problem of glass brittleness, nor does it sufficiently modify the overall failure mode of the glazing. Laminated glazing addresses these issues. Laminated glazing consists of two or more panes of glass that are glued together with a polyvinyl butyl (PVB) layer between them. This inner layer completely alters the failure mode of the original monolithic glass. When laminated glass fails—for example, in an automobile's windshield—the inner layer tends to hold the broken shards of glass together and prevents them from splintering. With each of the glass types (annealed, heat-strengthened, or TTG), this laminated glass concept can provide a tailored windowpane that is both stronger and less brittle than conventionally designed monolithic glazing. Almost all new, properly designed blast-resistant facilities incorporate some form of laminated glazing.

For existing buildings undergoing blast-resistant upgrades, it is often more convenient and cost-effective to apply window film to modify the behavior of the glazing than to replace all of the conventionally designed monolithic glass with properly designed laminated glazing. Window film is a thin polyester sheet, .04 mm to .15 mm thick, that is applied to the back of the existing glass with a bonding agent. This film serves the same purpose for monolithic glass that the PVB laminate serves for laminated glass. Although it does not strengthen the glass, the film is effective at capturing and gluing together fragments of the glass once it has failed.

Window film can be installed either in a *daylight application*—installed just to the edge of the glass but not captured by the window frame—or in a *captured application* connected to the frame. If a window filmed in a daylight application is loaded with a shock wave, the effect will be to propel the entire sheet of glass into the occupied space. Although this is still a hazardous failure mode, it is significantly safer than, and preferable to, the large number of glazing shards from failure of the original monolithic glass. A captured system can significantly improve the behavior of the filmed glass if the existing window frame and mullions can resist the loads it transfers to them. If the existing frame is weak, however, as is typically the case, attaching the film to the frame provides little or no additional protection, and the frame may actually add to the hazardous debris.

As with every hardened building component, the final design of building glazing must be tied to the design-level bomb threat, the perimeter standoff distance, the actual blast loading on the facility, and the desired level of building performance. Computer programs are available to help designers specify the proper glazing for any design situation. Several of the most common, based on national standards and criteria for blast resistance, are the Window Fragment Hazard Level analysis (HAZL) from the Army Corps of Engineers, Window Lite Analysis Code (WINLAC) from the U.S. Department of State, and Window Glazing Analysis Response and Design (WINGARD) from the General Services Administration. These codes are available to designers meeting certain security requirements by contacting the agencies indicated.

❖ Mullions, Framing, and Anchorage

Once the required glass type, thickness, and lamination requirements have been determined, the next consideration in designing the building skin is the window framing and anchorage. Properly designed, blast-resistant

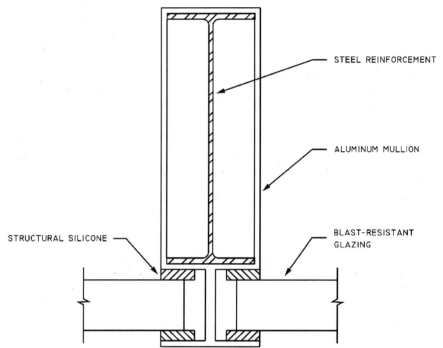

STEEL REINFORCEMENT

ALUMINUM MULLION

BLAST-RESISTANT
GLAZING

STRUCTURAL SILICONE

FIGURE 5.8
*Steel-reinforced
aluminum mullion*

windows will transfer significant reactions to a blast to the window framing, and it is imperative that this framing—including the mullions, framing connections, and anchorage to the structure and building skin—be sufficient to transfer these reactions. The larger the design blast loading, and the heavier the window design, the larger the reactions the framing and anchorage must be able to accommodate. (Figure 5.8 illustrates a steel-reinforced aluminum mullion.)

It is always preferable to design glazing to resist blast loads and remain securely anchored in the window frame. If glass cracks but is retained by the laminate, the force of a bomb blast is likely to cause large window deformations. Therefore, it is desirable to increase the glazing bite to keep the glass from slipping out of the frame. When the calculated bite becomes too large to be aesthetically acceptable, it is often necessary to bond the glass into the frame using a structural silicone adhesive. However, it is not possible to design reasonable glazing that can fully resist very large blast loads, such as those associated with a large truck bomb at close range. If such a threat is anticipated, it may be necessary to design the glazing to fail in a controlled manner to increase the level of protection without building a bunker. The following list describes possible designed window performance, in order of most to least desirable:

1. The glass cracks, and the laminate holds it together without failure. The glass and the laminate transfer the entire load to a properly designed framing system. This performance prevents any of the blast load or debris from entering occupied spaces.

2. The glass cracks, and the laminate fails in the middle, although the edges of the laminated glass are still held within the window frame. Some of the blast pressure is allowed to enter the occupied space.

3. The glass cracks, and the laminate fails at the frame bite, allowing the entire laminated pane to enter the occupied space. The framing remains in place.

Window framing and its connections to the structure do not fail before complete glazing failure in any of these scenarios. The window systems described are balanced and desirable regardless of the magnitude for which the blast load is being designed. In other words, an overdesigned glazing makeup is neither desirable nor cost-effective. It is extremely important to use the weakest glass that can provide the desired performance, thereby limiting the forces transferred to the mullions, the façade, and, ultimately, the building structure.

❖ Façade Wall Systems

A glazing and mullion system designed to resist a specified blast load must be anchored to an adequately designed building wall system. While a blast-resistant curtain wall system may be anchored directly to the building structure, most punched or banded window systems are connected to some form of exterior building wall. This building skin must be capable of resisting not only a reflected shock wave but also reactions transferred from the blast-resistant glazing system. It is imperative that the wall system be designed and detailed to resist these loads without failing in a catastrophic fashion.

A wide variety of wall systems can provide a blast-resistant building envelope if they are properly designed. Very light systems, such as heavy-gauge steel studs fronted with a thin steel plate, can resist low-level blasts, while reinforced masonry and precast concrete systems can resist larger-level threats (see Figures 5.9 and 5.10). Finally, heavily reinforced, cast-in-place concrete walls are often used to resist the highest-level

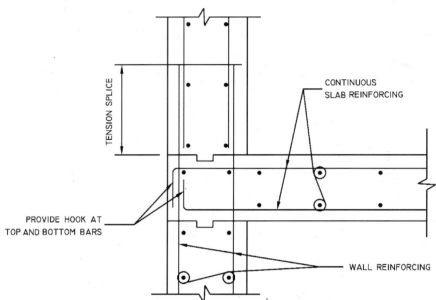

TENSION SPLICE

CONTINUOUS
SLAB REINFORCING

PROVIDE HOOK AT
TOP AND BOTTOM BARS

WALL REINFORCING

FIGURE 5.9
*Typical reinforced
concrete blast wall detail*

threats. As with any building component, a variety of methods can satisfy
the required design needs and architectural requirements, and they
should all be evaluated to determine the most cost-effective solution.

Regardless of the wall system chosen, pay close attention to the
design of the connection details that attach the wall to the structure. Reinforced concrete wall-to-slab connections can be made resistant to
high-reaction forces in a fairly straightforward way by providing ductile
reinforcement detailing and tension lap splices. However, it is often much
more complicated to provide adequate connections to the structure from
precast panels or reinforced masonry walls. Although properly designed
walls are specified early in the design process, all too often the detailing is
left until the last minute, leading to rush design decisions, surprise aesthetic implications for the architect, and unnecessary cost implications for
the building owner. A balanced wall design requires connection details that
are able to resist the ultimate capacity of the wall system. This ensures that,
if the blast loading is large enough to overwhelm the system, the wall will
absorb a significant amount of energy before it fails.

STRUCTURAL DESIGN

Once a conceptual design of the building skin has been developed, the
design team can turn its attention to hardening the building's structural

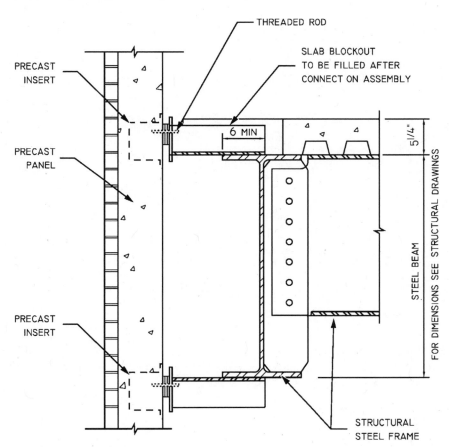

THREADED ROD

SLAB BLOCKOUT
TO BE FILLED AFTER
CONNECT ON ASSEMBLY

PRECAST
INSERT

6 MIN

5-1/4"

PRECAST
PANEL

PRECAST
INSERT

STEEL BEAM

FOR DIMENSIONS SEE STRUCTURAL DRAWINGS

STRUCTURAL
STEEL FRAME

FIGURE 5.10
Precast concrete tieback connection

system. When considering structural framing system concepts, it is critical to coordinate all of the design assumptions regarding charge weights, charge locations, and façade design requirements. If a building design includes a blast-resistant building envelope and no blast loads are expected to enter the building, interior elements designed to resist direct blast loads are unnecessary. If a façade is designed to completely resist the design-level blast load without allowing any blast pressures to enter the building interior, and adequate security measures have been provided to prevent delivery of a satchel charge against building columns, the structural design need only prevent the building from overturning. If a building façade is designed to sustain local damage or failure in the vicinity of the blast, or if several areas of the building (e.g., lobby, loading dock, or mailroom) are vulnerable to a suitcase or package bomb, individual structural elements such as columns, beams, and slabs are hardened along with

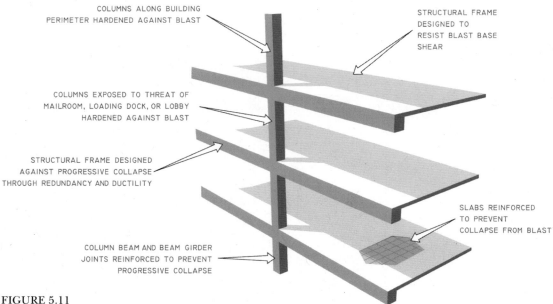

COLUMNS ALONG BUILDING
PERIMETER HARDENED AGAINST BLAST

STRUCTURAL FRAME
DESIGNED TO
RESIST BLAST BASE
SHEAR

COLUMNS EXPOSED TO THREAT OF
MAILROOM, LOADING DOCK, OR LOBBY
HARDENED AGAINST BLAST

STRUCTURAL FRAME DESIGNED
AGAINST PROGRESSIVE COLLAPSE
THROUGH REDUNDANCY AND DUCTILITY

SLABS REINFORCED
TO PREVENT
COLLAPSE FROM BLAST

COLUMN BEAM AND BEAM GIRDER
JOINTS REINFORCED TO PREVENT
PROGRESSIVE COLLAPSE

FIGURE 5.11
*Typical reinforced
concrete blast-resistant
construction*

designing to prevent progressive collapse. In this situation, these design requirements must always be coupled with the need to prevent global structural overturning (see Figure 5.11).

❖ Element Hardening

When individual building elements, such as exterior columns, are subjected to high-explosive shock waves, one design option is to design the elements to resist these loads. Nonlinear, inelastic, dynamic design methods will be most cost-effective. In simplified terminology, this means the analysis will take advantage of the time-dependent properties of the blast loading, namely its short load duration. The design will also take into account the ability of properly detailed structural elements to bend and deform without failing. In short, building members that sustain significant damage, without complete collapse, are typically considered to satisfy blast-resistant design criteria. This concept is known as *life safety design*, and contributes to the utilization of far smaller and more economical members than if conventional static, elastic design principles were used. These techniques may be used for all structural components regardless of their material properties, geometric orientation, or location on a building. In this way, each element of the building can be designed to resist a specified threat.

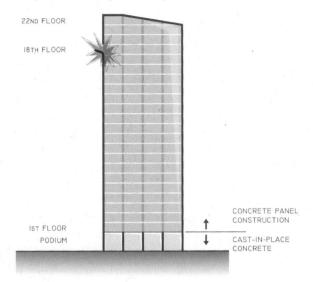

22ND FLOOR

18TH FLOOR

1ST FLOOR
PODIUM

CONCRETE PANEL
CONSTRUCTION

CAST-IN-PLACE
CONCRETE

1. FAILURE OF PRIMARY STRUCTURAL ELEMENT

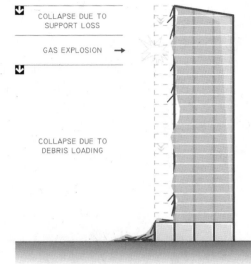

COLLAPSE DUE TO
SUPPORT LOSS

GAS EXPLOSION →

COLLAPSE DUE TO
DEBRIS LOADING

2. CHAIN REACTION OF FAILURES

FIGURE 5.12
Progressive collapse

❖ Progressive Collapse Prevention

In certain instances, it may be impractical to attempt to design all building components to resist a specific charge weight, as with a slender element located very close to a very large threat. In other circumstances, an element may be capable of resisting a specified charge weight, such as a 500-pound car bomb, but may be incapable of surviving the shock wave from a 2,000-pound truck bomb. In either case, it is critical that the failure of one local element not cause a chain-reaction failure of a large portion of the structure (see Figure 5.12). This type of progressive collapse is among the most hazardous failures associated with a terrorist car bomb and is typically responsible for tremendous fatalities when it occurs.

To understand the options for preventing progressive collapse, it is important to gain insight into the phenomenon itself. Probably the best example of this sort of collapse is the failure of the Ronan Point apartment complex in Canning Town, England, in 1968. A gas boiler explosion on the seventeenth floor blew out the exterior bearing wall supporting the floor and walls above. As a result of the loss of this support, the structure above the eighteenth floor collapsed onto the seventeenth floor slab. In turn, the seventeenth floor slab, which had not been designed for this additional weight, also collapsed, followed by the sixteenth floor, fifteenth floor, and so on until the entire bay of the building had collapsed to the ground. While this incident did not result from a terrorist attack, it high-lights what might happen to a high-rise building if a critical column were removed at the ground floor. Occupants 30 or 40 floors up, who may not have been affected by the original blast, could perish in the ensuing building collapse.

Prevention of progressive collapse lies in a structure's ability to sur-vive, even with the loss or removal of a key element. An alternate load path or mechanism, by which the structure can redistribute loads to adjacent members, can prevent collapse. In theory, this is relatively straightforward. The structural engineer simply designs the building to remain standing in the absence of various elements critical to the original design. The diffi-culty lies in accomplishing this with the least effect on the cost, aesthetics, and programmatic functions of the building. As with specific element hardening, this is accomplished by reducing the factors of safety normally associated with conventional design, allowing large deformations in the structural members, and taking advantage of the inelastic behavior of properly detailed elements.

A simple example of these concepts is a typical concrete flat slab building with 30-foot spans, a 10-inch-thick slab, a 50-psf live load, and a typical spandrel beam with dimensions of 24 inches by 30 inches. Assum-ing the loss of one perimeter column, and the need for each floor to sup-port its own weight, each spandrel beam would be required to span 60 feet. The following design parameters could be used for this design:

1. The live load could be reduced to 25 percent of its theoretical value, or 12.5 psf, which represents typical, actual office live loading.

2. The load factors of 1.4 on the dead load and 1.7 on the live load could be reduced to 1.2 to account for the extreme nature and dynamic effects of the loading, as well as the inelastic response of the member.

3. The span would be increased from 30 feet to 60 feet to account for the loss of one column support.

To meet these new design parameters, the exterior spandrel beam would have to be increased to a 30-inch by 36-inch beam, and the rein-forcement would have to be increased from the original design. These effects would have to be accounted for, both in the architectural design and in the budget for the project. As with all protective design solutions, the benefits of this increased level of protection must be compared with the negative effects of increasing building cost and possibly affecting building aesthetics.

Other options to address the simplified design problem just outlined include providing a large truss at the roof level and hanging the remaining floors from above, or providing closely spaced columns that allow for Vierendeel truss behavior of the perimeter frames in the event of a perimeter column failure.

In summary, there are many ways to approach this problem, from the simplified to the extremely complex, and the method used for a particular project will be a function of many factors. These will include, but not be limited to, building materials, geometry and loading, the design and construction budget, the architectural flexibility of the façade, and the site constraints. It is important to evaluate as many alternatives as possible, early in the design phase, to achieve the simplest, most cost-effective solution.

❖ Building Overturning

The third element of structural design is protecting the structure from overturning when an entire façade receives the impact of a shock wave. This is done by providing an adequate lateral resisting system, incorporating shear walls, braced frames, or moment frames for global stability. The overall force associated with the blast load is compared to the forces associated with any wind and seismic load, and the building is designed for the most stringent of the three. This analysis completes the building hardening aspect of the design.

NONSTRUCTURAL COMPONENTS

At this point in the design process, the blast load has been determined, the building shell has been hardened, and the structural frame has been reinforced to resist the design loading and prevent progressive collapse and overturning. The remaining vulnerabilities are associated with nonstructural building components, which can be dislodged from their mountings and hurled as projectiles in the occupied space. This often occurs when blast pressures penetrate the façade or as a result of extreme building vibrations when the structure resists a shock wave. While the dangers associated with this type of failure are not as critical as window or glazing failure or progressive collapse, they nevertheless have been tied to fatalities during recent terrorist attacks. To provide complete, coordinated protection, it is recommended that consideration be given, when feasible, to properly tying and anchoring all nonstructural elements to the building structure to prevent them from becoming dangerous missiles.

Applying New Knowledge

While the threat of terrorist attacks against buildings and other important structures has increased over the last several years, so has the ability of architects and engineers to mitigate the damage associated with these events in more cost-effective ways. By learning from past experiences, taking advantage of advancing engineering capabilities, and using state-of-the-art materials and construction techniques, the design community has been able to respond to the increased need for security and safety.

Nevertheless, new and more effective ways to deal with this problem are needed, as well as more adept methods for dealing with today's highly trained and extremely creative terrorist element. The events of September 11, 2001, clearly highlighted the fact that future attacks may take a variety of forms, and the protective design community must become more flexible and capable of defending against all types of attacks.

In the wake of September 11, prominent engineers have repeatedly stated that the airplane attack and subsequent fuel oil fire were far too extreme to be addressed by the design community. Others have said the engineering community should be able to fully protect our buildings and the people who work in them. Neither of these statements is fully accurate, nor does either provide useful insight into the real problems or possible solutions. No commercial office building can be hardened sufficiently to avoid sustaining some level of damage from the vast array of possible attack modes. Even if all manner of possible loading conditions could be predicted quantitatively, designs that responded to them would be neither cost-effective nor aesthetically pleasing and certainly would not provide the functional workspace desired. On the other hand, methods can be employed to increase the performance of a structure under almost any loading conditions. What the design community must strive for is to provide realistic, cost-effective protection measures while continuing to promote the aesthetic ideals that characterize any great building structure.

Architects can incorporate protective design measures—such as increased fire protection capabilities; hardened egress routes; and ductile, redundant building structures—that will mitigate, to the extent possible, damage and loss of life associated with any malevolent attack. Such measures can be used without retreating into a shell of fear and protectionism that results in architecture that may be dull and responds poorly to its intended functions.

6 Building Security Technologies

Richard P. Grassie, CPP

Security systems technology is burgeoning in response to the events of September 11, 2001. The best way for architects and other design and construction professionals to keep up with the rapid advances in technology and the new developments in equipment may be to consult with specialists in security planning and design. Yet, to effectively apply security technologies in the buildings they design, architects must have a basic understanding of these technologies. This chapter addresses this need by presenting fundamental issues associated with selecting and applying security technologies, discussing a process-driven approach to security systems design, and providing profiles of available security technologies.

In deciding which technologies to invest in, each building owner must consider the range of threats and risks that potentially confront a building and its associated assets. In addition, owners must consider the consequences of information compromise, possible loss of life or equipment, and the degree of disruption to normal operations should an attack or a security breach be successful.

The owner's security concerns provide a planning baseline for determining how to combine architectural approaches to security with technological and organizational strategies. Well-integrated solutions can make it possible to effectively prevent, control, detect, assess, and respond to unauthorized intrusions and other related incidents in or outside a facility.

The security technology design process is part of the overall building design process carried out by the architect. It is therefore imperative that requirements for building security systems be incorporated at programming or conceptual design and flow progressively to the more detailed phases of systems engineering, plan documentation, and installation planning.

The response time needed for security personnel to locate and arrive at a secured building area after a verified alarm is a key factor in selecting security technologies.

Many building owners and security managers have been reluctant to integrate security systems with other building systems, believing security systems are expensive and sophisticated but offer little more protection than security personnel. However, a number of strategies are available for achieving state-of-the-art security system integration that is both affordable and effective.

A decade ago, security technology options were limited to relatively simple sensors; expensive closed-circuit television (CCTV) systems; archaic photo-identification systems; slow, one-dimensional access control systems that relied more on manpower than technology; and complex, expensive processing systems that had limited applications but required major capital expenditure approvals. Today, an assortment of capable and reliable security technologies are available at affordable prices. In addition, the continuing advancements made with desktop PCs provide robust platforms that can run access control, intrusion detection, and CCTV systems together with relative ease.

Architects today can use security technologies and systems to reduce the cost of providing essential security services for new buildings. For example, intrusion detection and access control systems—allowing remote monitoring of critical locations at lower initial cost—have become electronic extensions of organizational and operational security systems. These technologies enable a more economical and efficient use of manpower usually assigned to building patrols and fixed guardposts, and can be used in place of physical security measures that cannot be employed because of safety regulations, operational requirements, appearance, layout, or cost or for other reasons. Finally, security technologies can be used to provide increased depth of protection when an owner requires multiple protective measures for increased system reliability.

Design and Selection Issues

The selection and use of security technologies directly affect the architect's responsibilities in other areas of building design. Architects may find some of the following issues self-explanatory from a building design standpoint, but each has its own impact on the eventual performance and success of any security system.

■ MATCHING SOLUTIONS WITH PROJECT REQUIREMENTS

Security requirements are typically the outcome of the programming phase. Emanating from a complete and thorough security analysis performed by the owner, in most cases with outside assistance, they become the basis for the preliminary security design, which is then reviewed by the owner and modified as necessary. If a technological solution, such as lobby turnstiles, is identified later in the design process, and there is no requirement or traceability to a requirement for automated lobby control, the solution does not fit the design and should not be included. Only solutions associated with specifically stated requirements should be included in the security systems design.

■ OPEN VERSUS CLOSED PROPRIETARY TECHNOLOGIES

Security systems include some of the most proprietary systems offered on the open market. The reluctance to "open" these systems to integration with other systems stems from the early days of alarm panels and central stations when the panel was the heart and soul of a typical security system. Today these panels, or multiplexers as they are called, remain proprietary intentionally to garner market share, although the real heart of the security management system is now the software—also proprietary—embedded in the host PC.

Some manufacturers have elected to offer security software only as a basis for integrating various manufacturer panels contained in a building. Some security software dealers have become application service providers (ASPs), although with little success. For the time being, manufacturers of security system peripherals (e.g., card readers, CCTVs) are being driven to make their systems compatible with others, while security management systems (panels plus head-end software) are expected to remain proprietary for some time.

CODE COMPLIANCE

Security systems design sometimes conflicts with code requirements. For example, a device placed on a door may restrict its operation, or the use of physical means to control access may impede egress. Code issues may arise when the architect, usually with the aid of the security designer, selects door hardware. For instance, the electronic locking hardware selected often determines the suite of equipment required to meet building code. In the case of access control, use of electromagnetic locking devices tells the security designer that two means of egress must be provided, one electronic (request to exit) and another mechanical (push-button power interruption). Panic bars also have code restrictions and uses in security design, and access to selected floors via an exit stairway must be controlled without blocking exits.

The bottom line is that security designers must be intimately familiar with applicable building code provisions, and must be prepared to advise architects on door hardware selection or identify problem areas prior to final design.

TECHNOLOGY PERFORMANCE CRITERIA

Including performance criteria in security systems specifications is vital to achieving a successful system. Security specifications should comply with the format guidelines of the Construction Specification Institute (CSI) and provide clear, precise performance criteria for the individual technologies included in the system. Generally, the products section of a specification identifies at least two or three manufacturers that produce products that meet the stated performance specifications. The security specifications must also identify the performance criteria for operation once systems are installed and ready for testing. This is important because the success of some aspects of a security system installation depends entirely upon the ability of the security systems installer to combine various technologies into a working system.

FACTORS IN TECHNOLOGY SELECTION

Each security technology is intended to perform a specific function within a system design. Basic factors to consider in technology selection include, but are not limited to, the physical and operational environments in which the system will function and the level of protection needed. When these factors are not considered, the result is a nonresponsive or ineffective system, with an unacceptable level of false and nuisance alarms.

A *false alarm* is caused by a hardware or software malfunction anywhere between the outermost peripheral device and the control and display central annunciator. A *nuisance alarm* is caused by sensor system response to environmental conditions, vehicular traffic, disturbances in electrical power, electromagnetic interference, and vibration-causing machinery, to name a few. Controlling these sources of system degradation calls for careful consideration of the physical and operational environments in which the system will function.

Another factor affecting security technology selection is the decision to use concentric rings of protection to make it progressively more difficult for an intruder to reach critical targets and escape undetected. Such protection schemes use combinations of physical and technological measures to build time delays into the intruder's path to an asset.

CONCEALMENT AND AESTHETIC CONSIDERATIONS

Visible security systems are occasionally viewed as appendages to an otherwise clean, efficient building design. Some security technologies, especially CCTV cameras, are difficult to conceal and often disturb the feeling of openness and freedom of movement. Owners, however, generally view security technologies as deterrents to criminal behavior and an opportunity to have building controls without denying freedom of movement to authorized users.

The use of technologies that blend in with the building environment can answer many aesthetic concerns. One example is the slim-line access card reader. Made possible by recent advances in technology miniaturization, it is easily mounted on a doorjamb. Another example is dome housing for exterior and interior CCTV cameras. These are visually pleasing and small enough to present an acceptable profile.

Manufacturers and installers of security equipment are responding to their customers' interest in the appearance of security systems. Manufacturers are introducing more equipment that is aesthetically pleasing as well as functional, and systems installers have become more attuned to aesthetic considerations.

The continued miniaturization of microprocessor technology and an increasing awareness of aesthetics are improving security product design.

BASE BUILDING VERSUS TENANT SECURITY

Office and high-rise buildings of any sort typically distinguish between "base building" and "tenant" spaces. Security technologies designed for the building owner provide protection for base building spaces. Tenants, meanwhile, frequently have the option of either buying their own security systems or purchasing those compatible with the base building system. When tenants integrate their own systems with the overall building system, the cost is often included in the per-square-foot floor space cost. The tenant can elect to install its own local system, which could report to the base building security control center (SCC) or to an outside central station. When the owner occupies the entire building, the security design usually begins with a base building design followed by a tenant fit-out, which is often done by a different designer or architect.

■ INITIAL, OPERATING, AND MAINTENANCE COSTS

Architects and owners are occasionally shocked at the costs for security systems. Integrated systems employing access control, intrusion detection, and CCTV systems that offer digital recording and multiplexing/switching of video scenes in an ergonomic control console cannot be accomplished on a limited budget. An approximate cost for access control systems is $3,500 to $4,000 per door installed, and $1,500 per fixed camera and $4,500 per pan-tilt-zoom camera installed.

Another rule of thumb is that the initial capital expenditure for installation of a complete building security system, not including personnel and procedures development, can range between $1.00 to $1.50 per square foot, depending on the type and levels of protection desired.

After the first year, maintenance costs of security systems generally run in the vicinity of 11 to 12 percent of initial capital cost escalating over a five-year period.

Security management systems should be able to handle at least 16, and as many as 32 to 64, supervised alarm points from a single access control panel, as well as at least four to eight access-controlled doors. Thus, an installed security system with 30 access-controlled doors and 25 cameras might begin at a cost of around $250,000. This would not include other devices such as turnstiles, interior and exterior sensors, photo identification equipment, equipment for digital recording and multiplexing of camera scenes, and security control room costs for consoles and equipment racks.

Operating costs during the warranty period are typically personnel-oriented, as the system installation is warranted for technology and installation defects.

■ STAFFING IMPLICATIONS OF TECHNOLOGIES

The security staffing required for a project is affected by building control needs and by the degree to which security technologies can minimize the need for monitoring and maximize the ability of the operator to control and view multiple areas. Some building owners will choose to integrate a lobby screening desk with monitoring systems for security. The disadvantage of this arrangement is that lobby security personnel tend to become engaged with visitors/contractors when monitoring tasks need to be fulfilled. High-rise buildings typically provide lobby desks with remote or client stations and minimal CCTV monitors, while the main security monitoring and control center is located in a more secure area.

Some building owners elect to use security personnel for visitor screening functions, whether these activities are carried out at a screening station or at the lobby desk. In any case, security control centers should be designed to require minimal staffing. Most SCCs, even for high-rise buildings, require only one, or at most two, trained and qualified persons, particularly if the systems are integrated and the number of CCTV monitors has been minimized.

Adding more monitors than are needed for effective operator control is confusing, adds space requirements (console and floor area), and escalates costs unnecessarily.

A single operator can reasonably manage four to six monitors, even with video camera scene multiplexing on a single monitor. With the advent of digital recording, operators can easily archive recorded events generated by the video system (motion detection) or an event generated by the security management system (door contact alarm, area sensor, invalid card read, duress, etc.).

Insurance carriers require most building owners to conduct regular building safety tours, especially after hours. Technologies such as microprocessor-based wands that security officers use to record these tours can be easily integrated with security operation centers.

LIGHTING CONSIDERATIONS FOR MONITORING

Adequate lighting for monitoring activities is important. In addition, lighting serves as a crime deterrent, discourages unwanted visitors, and gives building occupants a sense of safety and security. Security lighting for CCTV monitoring generally requires at least one to two foot-candles (FC) of illumination, whereas the lighting needed for safety considerations in exterior areas such as parking lots or garages is substantially greater (at least 5 FC). Recent advances in CCTV imaging allow adequate image viewing down to 0.06 lux or less, depending on the camera type.

Color cameras require more light for viewing than black-and-white cameras.

Generally, while interior lighting levels for elevators, lobbies, and stairwells range from 5 to 10 FC, exterior lighting requirements vary for different locations. Common lighting levels include the following:

✦ Building entrances (5 FC)

✦ Walkways (1.5 FC)

◆ Parking garages (5 FC)
◆ Site landscape (0.5 FC)
◆ Area immediately surrounding the building (1 FC)
◆ Roadways (0.5 FC)

A related consideration for monitoring is the amount of light in the security control center. It must be dim enough for the operator to see the console, but the operator should be able to highlight specific work areas when needed.

Process-Driven Systems Design

The combination of electronic technology concerns, response force availability, and owner operational requirements places specific constraints on the security systems design. Therefore, a carefully considered process is important to the successful design and performance of a building security system. It is imperative that the requirements for the system design be incorporated into the project concept development (programming) phase and included in the more detailed phases of engineering, documentation, and construction (see Figure 6.1).

FIGURE 6.1
Integrated security design process

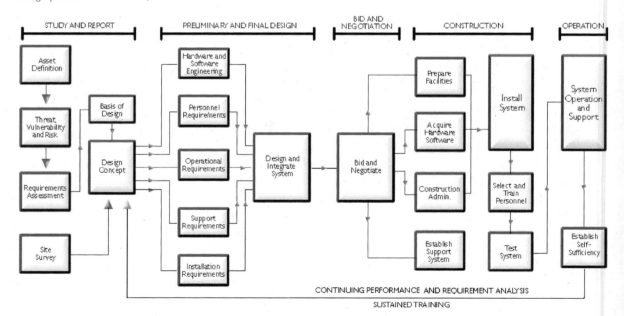

During programming, the owner and architect determine which security approaches are likely to be most cost-effective and appropriate for the building environment. Answering the following questions early in the programming phase will help the owner, architect, and security consultant make these determinations:

What is the purpose and objective of the system, and how will it be used?

Responses to the following preliminary queries will prove helpful in answering this question:

- Is the security system intended to protect critical assets, prevent escape of intruders, or detect unauthorized intrusions?
- What level of protection is required and acceptable for the owner?
- Will the protection objective and functional design requirements require the system to include interior or exterior intrusion detection, access control, and/or CCTV systems?
- Will the systems be integrated with one another and any other interior systems such as fire or building controls?
- What methods will be used to respond to alarms?
- How long a delay in criminal entry is desired?

To justify the use of an electronic access control system, the owner will need to know which critical assets are to be protected and what the potential loss or damages would be if no or minimal protection were applied. This is the risk management portion of the plan. Each security situation is unique; there are no packaged solutions.

Which operational aspects of the building will determine the required security technologies and systems, and what is their priority?

The types of security technologies, such as access control and intrusion detection systems, needed for a particular facility depend on the number of users and their key preferences, the number of doors in the system, and the operational characteristics of the software. Other concerns are addressed with answers to the following questions:

- What rate of movement is required at access control points?
- What false alarm rate is acceptable?
- How will the building systems function during normal operating hours and after hours (e.g., what are the proposed communications methods from sensors to alarms—hardwired or radio frequency)?
- Will sensors be addressable or linked in a chain?

◆ Will the systems be monitored from a central location?

◆ Will remote locations be linked over the network?

◆ Will local panels operate over the owner's local area network (LAN)?

◆ How will alarms be assessed for effectiveness (with CCTV, personnel, lights, horns, bells, or printed records)?

◆ Does the system have tamper alarms, capacity for self-tests, or lightning protection?

What environmental factors will affect the security system?

◆ Will there be multiple users and high traffic flows at certain points?

◆ Will exterior conditions such as weather, wildlife, vegetation, and corrosive conditions such as acid rain or salt affect the technologies? Information is needed on site topography to address this concern.

◆ What are the conditions of the site?

◆ Are there any existing structures, traffic patterns, industry controls, or other restrictions that would affect security for the site?

Security Equipment Profiles

At minimum, applications in an integrated building security system include electronic intrusion detection, perimeter protection, access control, and CCTV technologies. Some buildings, such as high-rises or government buildings, may require additional screening techniques. Each technology has distinct performance characteristics that offer various advantages to the owner and/or tenant. Each also has different requirements for installation and maintenance; for this reason, it is important for the installation company to have the specifications for each technology so the security management system will function properly. These and related considerations are discussed in the following profiles for major groups of security technologies.

■ INTRUSION DETECTION TECHNOLOGIES

Detection technologies provide electronic sensing and reporting of movement across, over, under, or through restricted areas of a building and its perimeters. They can be used to increase control over specific points or spaces outside or within a protected area, but their primary purpose is simply to alert security personnel of the possibility of an intrusion or other security incident.

❖ Exterior Sensor Technologies

Exterior sensors can be deployed either singularly or in an overlapping configuration to maximize the probability of detection around an area or along a facility or site perimeter. Various technologies are used to manufacture these sensors, including microwave, pulsed infrared beam, passive infrared, electrostatic e-field, ported coaxial cable, fiber-optic cable, and taut wire.

Exterior sensors capable of detecting all reasonable intrusion scenarios are applied in either an overt or covert mode, installed either aboveground on a fence or other supporting structure, or buried belowground (see Figure 6.2). Single, dual, or multiple lines of detection may be used to develop the required protection. For instance, at the site perimeter, fence

FIGURE 6.2
Exterior sensor

sensors can be used to protect against an intruder attempting to cut or climb the fence. Another line of detection can be formed in front of, between, or inside the perimeter to protect against an intruder attempting to walk, crawl, run through, tunnel under, or jump over the protected area. Together, these technologies form a complementary perimeter sensor configuration.

Exterior sensors are costly to install, particularly when a configuration has multiple lines of detection. Sites with highly critical assets typically require two lines of complementary detection, along with 100 percent CCTV assessment coverage. Exterior sensors require considerable site preparation, and they are extremely susceptible to the environment in which they are installed. However, if early detection and response to a potential intrusion is a sacrosanct requirement, exterior sensors may be the only alternative.

❖ Interior Sensor Technologies

Interior sensors can minimize the need for staffed security posts by providing an alarm when entry into a building or access to critical areas has been detected. Point sensors protect doors, windows, and other openings as well as critical and special stand-alone assets. Volumetric sensors placed strategically along building corridors send an alarm upon detection of the presence or movement of an intruder inside a confined space.

When several lines of interior detection are required, a line may be formed at the building envelope using interior glass-break sensors or wall-penetration detection sensors. In these applications, the sensors should be able to detect all likely intrusion scenarios (e.g., break-in through the roof, ceiling, or wall). If a building has windows strung along the ground floor, combined acoustic/shock glass-break sensors may be appropriate. When detection inside a facility is necessary, sensors can be used to detect presence, movement, disturbances, or the penetration of interior windows, doors, or walls. Close-in protection of an individual asset, if required, may entail the use of sensors capable of detecting touching, tampering, or removal of an object.

Infrared, ultrasonic, or microwave sensors are most commonly used to protect objects and avenues of approach because their energy can be focused. However, the effects of environmental conditions, the difficulty of restricting sensor energy to the object(s) involved, and cost are important trade-offs in deciding whether to apply a volumetric sensor to protect objects.

The active infrared sensor (or photoelectric beam) operates on the principle that a transmitted light beam forms a visible or invisible line of detection to be breached. If the beam is interrupted or broken, an alarm is produced. If the beam is continuous, the receiver may be "captured" by the substitution of another light source, permitting bypass. Therefore, infrared sensors that "pulse" the beam at a frequency making substitution difficult are generally preferable.

Door "switches" or "contacts" are the most commonly used point intrusion detection devices (see Figure 6.3). A switch-type sensor incorporates electrical contacts that make or break an electrical circuit as a result of the physical movement of a door or window. Surface-mounted door switches used in high-security applications are usually equipped with a tamper alarm. Recessed models are better protected from tampering because the actual doorframe must be attacked to gain access to the switch components.

Although not intrusion detection sensors, duress alarms are frequently used to signal distress or a life-threatening situation. The activation of a duress alarm is an automatic call for special reaction(s) by the responding security force, thus these sensors should never be designed to annunciate at the point of threat. The two technologies used to transmit duress signals are hardwired and radio frequency alarms. In specifying and designing duress alarm installations, high reliability, silent activation, and annunciation remote from the area of the duress situation are primary considerations.

Sensor technology advances have made possible sensors with complementary technologies, such as infrared and microwave or ultrasonic devices (see Figure 6.4). Combined in a single sensor housing, these sensors can provide increased protection in more difficult environments and from more sophisticated intruders. Other advances in sensor processing have resulted in the introduction of "smart sensors," which effectively filter

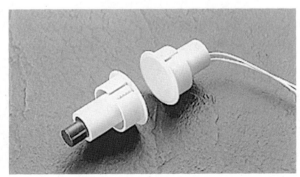

FIGURE 6.3
Door contact

FIGURE 6.4
Passive infrared sensor

out common sources of nuisance alarms and respond more accurately to valid intrusion stimuli. However, even smart sensors cannot eliminate nuisance alarms caused by the use of interior volumetric sensors in areas frequently used by inhabitants. Thus, if interior sensors are used, they should either be programmed to be inactive during normal building operating periods or to be controlled by authorized building occupants using an electronic keypad control device usually located at the entrance.

An alarm or access control panel collects signals from intrusion sensors and reports any change of state to the security control center. Burglar panels typically are stand-alone panels engineered exclusively for alarm input. They have light-emitting diode (LED) indications of alarm or trouble states. Access control panels, receiving both sensor and access device input, are usually linked in a network configuration, and transmit either an alarm or access authorization or a denial of transaction signal to a manned central response area.

SCREENING TECHNOLOGIES

Technologies for detecting contraband materials have been developed sufficiently that wide arrays of advanced detection systems are now available for screening applications in buildings. Metal detectors, X-ray screening systems, and explosive trace detectors are the most widely used systems for detecting items such as plastic weapons, plastic explosives, and radioactive materials.

Portal or hand-held metal detectors can be strategically deployed at entry points to screen individuals for hidden firearms and other potentially lethal objects. An audible alarm is generated when any metal object, contraband or otherwise, is detected. Portal detectors usually serve as the initial building screening point. If an alarm is generated, a secondary method of screening, perhaps with hand-held metal detectors, is used to locate the metallic object on the person.

X-ray systems are used to screen items such as handbags or luggage. These technologies depend either entirely on operator assessment of an image projected on a screen, or can be equipped with semiautomatic screening capabilities that prompt the operator. Either way, each contraband item generates a unique "signature." Mail screening is accomplished in much the same manner with various-sized screening devices, including recently introduced prototype chemical "sniffer" systems.

Building screening systems generally employ secondary screening methods for detecting concealed explosives. These more sensitive systems require a trained operator and must be programmed for the type of explosive to be detected. In addition, their accuracy depends entirely on the presence of residual traces of explosives on the objects being screened. Portal explosive detection systems and systems that detect large vehicles carrying bombs are commercially available, but the technology has not yet been perfected.

ACCESS CONTROL TECHNOLOGIES

Access control is a process used to permit or deny entry into a building or area and to regulate the flow of personnel, vehicles, and material. Criteria for approving access include verification of an individual's authorization to enter a facility and, in some cases, validation of a person's identity. A decision about what proportion of personnel, equipment, and procedures to use for authorizing access to a protected area involves analysis of the threat(s) specific to that area as well as its operational requirements. Automated access allows personnel to enter, and in some cases exit, a building or area without intervention unless the system initiates an alarm. If a remote video scene of an access point is available in the security control center, security staff can assess and respond to an invalid access transaction when an alarm does occur. Otherwise, the activation of an access transaction alarm requires security staff to initiate the proper personnel response action, which often arrives long after the event has transpired.

Electronic access control systems employ a card reader linked to an electronic locking device to grant or deny access to cardholders based on authorization criteria encoded in a badge or card (see Figure 6.5). The access authorization sequence must be communicated to the equipment in a form recognized by the electronics. In general, an electronic access control system comprises an enrollment station, a central controller containing database tables for access authorization, a transaction display (computerized and/or hard copy), and individual portals controlled by a coded credential. Keypads can also be used based on a programmed sequence of numbers, although these systems are less secure than coded credential systems.

Coded credential systems have several advantages. They decentralize access authorization, are centrally managed by a single systems administrator from a remote location, and are literally pickproof, as compared to conventional lock-and-key controls. If a badge is lost, it can easily be replaced or voided by deleting identification data from the system. The host processor constantly refreshes the access authorization information stored in remote access panels, monitors the condition of remote readers and associated portal devices, and logs all access activities in an archive record for later retrieval if necessary for investigative or other purposes.

The popularity of automated access control systems has increased primarily because of their affordability. The use of microprocessor technology and recent advances in coded credentials have lowered costs for

FIGURE 6.5
Proximity or contactless card reader

electronically controlling access and performing a host of ancillary functions from a single security control point. Rather than a manned security post, the employee credential or badge is now commonly accepted as the primary means of access authorization. Part of this system is a host processor continuously providing central operators with alarm display, control, and related system integration functions. With the robust memory and processing speeds of PCs, a single integrated access control system can control and monitor virtually thousands of entry points in multiple buildings in multiple locations. In addition, the simple introduction of the coded credential allows these systems to perform highly sophisticated authorization and reporting functions.

Access control elements may be integrated with barrier elements such as optical turnstiles (Figure 6.6) or gates in building lobbies to channel the flow of people and facilitate entry and egress during busy periods.

Entry authorization and verification processes are performed using a variety of technologies and mostly automated access criteria. These systems range from small applications providing control over a few portals in a building to large, distributed computer-based networks capable of performing multiple functions without significant geographic limitations. Elements that make up these systems may include the following:

✦ *Card-based entry control devices.* These electronic devices read programmed data unique to each card and authorize or deny access attempts at specific portals or record departure from an area. Cards can be imprinted with photo identification, which is stored

FIGURE 6.6
Optical turnstiles

on the host processor, and may serve as identification badges. Card readers may be employed on both entry and exit as stand-alone units or in conjunction with number keypads as a secondary means of access verification. Many different card technologies are available, but building owners generally prefer proximity cards and readers because they are easy to use and offer relatively good security. (See Figure 6.7 for some examples of access card equipment.)

✦ *Positive personnel identification/verification equipment.* Used increasingly in high-security applications where more than one access authorization level is required, this equipment may include coded keypads built into the card reader, CCTV for facial confirmation at the SCC, or biometric readers that key on unique features of each authorized individual.

✦ *Host and distributed processing for remote field control panels.* The host processor (file server) incorporates various automated access criteria based on area authorization, time zoning, access rules, antipassback prohibitions, or other features. Remote devices such as card readers and sensors are connected to remote area field panels, which report transactions and alarms either via hardwire topology to the host or via the local area network. Simultaneous display of transactions and alarms is accomplished at the host server display, usually located in the security room and at various remote client stations in the building or among multiple buildings.

FIGURE 6.7

Access readers and cards

Technologies commonly used for secondary verification include personal identification numbers (PINs), photographic image matchup, and biometric systems, such as the hand geometry reader shown in Figure 6.8. Such systems, with the exception of biometrics, are less secure than coded credentials because the identification media are easily read and the systems must accommodate variations due to environment, stress, and data entry errors. A PIN is the most commonly used secondary verification system because accurate data entry is relatively easy and this data is immune to environmental influences. Secondary means of access authorization are generally limited to high-security applications.

A relatively new development in the field of access control is the smart card. Smart cards contain a tiny microprocessor or individualized computer that identifies the owner/holder by recording unique details about that individual. A wealth of information can be stored, including personal identification data such as fingerprints or facial shape. A smart card can create encryption algorithms that generate unique PINs. Used mainly in Europe, Asia, and Japan, smart cards have proven prohibitively expensive for general application (approximately $25 per card), although this will change, as the technology becomes more affordable.

FIGURE 6.8
*Access control hand
geometry reader unit*

All card access badges are susceptible to alteration, decoding, duplication, and loss. The degree to which the technology and associated procedures resist these threats is important to the integrity of a security system. For more critical access verification requirements, use of secondary verification systems may be advisable to minimize the vulnerability associated with insider collusion and lost or stolen cards.

Locking hardware compatible with automated access control systems includes electric strikes, electric bolts, and electromagnetic locks (see Figure 6.9). Designers choose the type of hardware that best fits the type of door to be controlled. Electric strikes are easier to maintain, and provide a relatively simple mechanical egress from the exit side using door hardware supplied with the door. These devices are configurable with one of two features termed "fail-safe" (open) and "fail-secure" (locked). Generally, all means of egress with electronic access must be configured to operate in a fail-safe mode in the event of a fire alarm. An additional electronic device, called a request to exit (RQE), is used on the exit side to shunt the door contact during egress and, in some cases, to interrupt power to the electromagnetic lock (see Figure 6.10). Building codes usually require an additional mechanical means of interrupting power to the electromagnetic locking device, such as a push-button mounted on the wall adjacent to the egress portal. The design of an automated access control system must consider such variables, as well as local and national fire and electrical code requirements.

FIGURE 6.9

*Electric strikes and
magnetic locks*

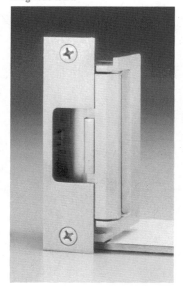
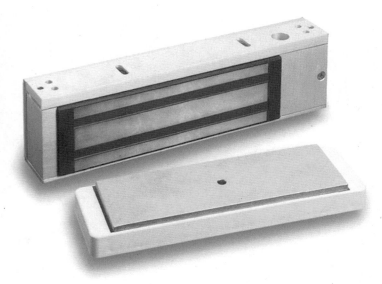

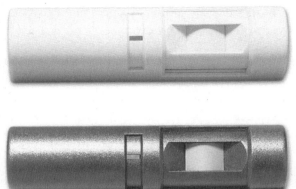

FIGURE 6.10
Request-to-exit sensors

Access control system selection involves many factors. Since systems will be chosen from commercially available, off-the-shelf systems, the two primary considerations are the capabilities of the proposed equipment and the experience and ability of the installation firm to support the equipment during its use. Incompetence in installation or service will negate the benefits of the most detailed design process.

ASSESSMENT/SURVEILLANCE TECHNOLOGIES

The security operator needs to be aware of the validity, severity, and nature of events that trigger alarms. Continuous surveillance of sensitive areas and assessment of alarmed areas can be accomplished with strategic placement of CCTV cameras or manned patrols and guardposts. Properly designed CCTV technologies can provide both control and response consistent with the threat source anticipated. Integrating equipment (e.g., lighting and CCTV) into the security system is often critical to achieving effective, confident, and safe responses by security personnel. Use of remote assessment devices directly affects the cost of overall integrated building systems because it can make it possible for a single operator to monitor and control buildingwide security, initiating a security response only when and where required.

CCTV technologies make possible three distinct yet complementary functions. The first is visual assessment of an alarm or other event. Video assessment may be employed to permit visual assessment of alarm zone activities, including activity at the site perimeter or areas inside a building such as a lobby or loading dock. When used with exterior or interior sensors and access-controlled portals, CCTV allows the operator to view and assess the nature of the alarm before initiating a response. CCTV is a cost-effective means of assessment that increases the efficiency and effectiveness of security personnel.

CCTV is also used for area surveillance and monitoring. It can perform automated video tours of a building exterior and interior, provided sufficient CCTV coverage has been designed into the system (see Figure 6.11). This feature permits the operator to become familiar with building operations, which increases the likelihood that suspicious events or activities will be identified during regular surveillance tours. CCTV can also be used to monitor activities in critical areas such as main entrances, loading docks, and product storage areas.

Another CCTV function is deterrence. The visibility of CCTV cameras may deter criminal or suspicious activity by increasing the likelihood of detection within the field of view of the camera, either during routine video tours or later review of the recorded data (see Figure 6.12). A feature of some camera systems is the ability to activate video motion sensory devices. In this mode, any movement detected within the camera's field of view automatically alerts the operator, displays the video scene on the alarm monitor, and begins constant recording.

Lighting is critical to CCTV performance and response force capability; therefore, the lighting system selected should support effective CCTV assessment and surveillance. To avoid costly retrofit, either of cameras or luminaries, lighting design should be coordinated with security system design. Each camera must be positioned to maximize available light. In exterior applications, particularly parking lots, CCTV cameras are most commonly mounted on light poles approximately 14 feet off the ground, placing them under the light source. Another common location for CCTV

FIGURE 6.11
Fixed CCTV camera

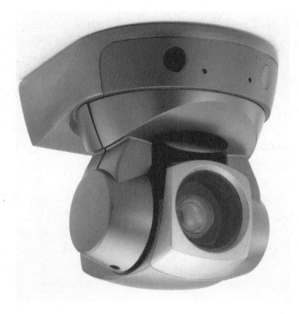

FIGURE 6.12
Pan-tilt zoom camera

cameras is on the building envelope, at least 14 feet above the ground and sometimes on a roof parapet.

The higher the location of the CCTV camera, the greater the field of view and distance of coverage. However, if the unit is mounted too far above the area being monitored, its usefulness may be diminished because the camera is looking down on the activities within its field of view. Nevertheless, cameras mounted in such positions can decrease the cost of CCTV systems and provide additional capabilities such as monitoring traffic.

The components of a basic CCTV system include the lens and camera, cable or other transmission media, and the monitor and associated components. Lightning surge protection for camera systems is an essential design component. Expanded CCTV systems use multiple cameras that may be identified by specific numbers and input into a video central processing unit (CPU) console. Basic and expanded CCTV systems can be used in either interior or exterior environments. In either application, use of modular CCTV equipment greatly aids routine maintenance and troubleshooting efforts.

Selecting the right CCTV cameras requires careful consideration of the setting in which the camera will operate and the performance that is expected. Color cameras display more detail for identification purposes, but they operate better during daylight hours than in the dark. Recent advances in technology have resulted in cameras that automatically switch from color to black and white as the light source decreases. Quality of resolution is another factor in camera choice. Generally, cameras with 480 or more lines of resolution are preferred. The monitor in an installation must have resolution of equivalent quality, however, or the resolution of the picture taken by the camera will not show in the display.

Monitor size is a design consideration based on the number of monitors, the size and configuration of the console, and the alarm assessment requirements. Operator fatigue and requirements for viewing the scene dictate monitor size. With recent advancements in the area of plasma monitors and wide-screen displays, monitors are generally available in the range of 6, 9, 15, and 20 inches. Monitors may be stacked in sets of two per alarm zone (up to five in a horizontal row). Pan, tilt, and zoom (PTZ) controls place an additional burden on the operator and may be detrimental during stressful situations such as simultaneous multiple alarms. However, the use of PTZ cameras increases an operator's ability to monitor a wide area, thereby decreasing the need for multiple cameras. PTZs can also be programmed to automatically pan and zoom to an alarm and automatically patrol an area as part of operator-assisted or archived video tours.

The aesthetic appearance of exterior CCTV cameras, their housings, and mounting brackets is a design concern. Recent-model cameras, especially of the unitized dome variety, have benefitted from miniaturization and are now available in many more pleasing styles. Cameras mounted inside buildings on walls or ceilings are small enough to be relatively inconspicuous, especially when housed in an aesthetically pleasing dome or when recessed. Architects wishing to improve the appearance of camera placement also have a variety of housings to choose from, including wedge and dome varieties (see Figure 6.13).

FIGURE 6.13
Vandalproof dome camera

■COMMUNICATIONS TECHNOLOGIES

The communications link that transmits information from sensors and video components to the security display and assessment equipment is a critical element in an integrated security system. The basic economic and technical requirements are factors to consider when selecting communications methods, but no one solution is best for all applications. The threat, cost, and other design parameters for each protected asset must accommodate them. In addition, however, several system-level considerations should be evaluated.

Security communications involves the transmission of sensor, CCTV, status, and control data. Hardwired, microwave, radio frequency, and fiber-optic communications methods may be used to carry the required electronic signals, voice, or video communications. Cabling and conduit requirements are the major elements of security communications system design. Cabling requirements should be defined early in a project and communicated to the electrical subcontractor.

Conduit is another issue. For most small- and medium-size security installations with up to intermediate protection requirements, it is acceptable to use conduit to carry the cabling for peripheral security devices into the ceiling, and then onto a cable tray from that point on. The cabling used should be plenum-rated cable.

Security systems that offer a higher level of protection typically require conduit end to end. Under no circumstances should security system data and signal cable be run in open trays with other power lines. Control signal, communications, and data transmission lines for security systems require line grounding as needed to preclude ground loops, noise, and surges. Applicable standards for cabling include those by Underwriters Laboratories (UL), Insulated Cable Engineers Association (ICEA), National Electrical Code (NEC), and Institute of Electrical and Electronic Engineers (IEEE) standards.

Hardwired communications typically involve a physical wire connection from point to point using twisted, shielded cabling. The use of more traditional telephone or landlines is considered too vulnerable for security uses unless as a last resort. The communications link between CCTV camera and monitor in a simple CCTV system is commonly achieved with coaxial cable or fiber-optic networks. The coaxial cable provides shielding and grounding characteristics that are critical for video signal quality. Long lengths of alarm communications wiring can be managed by existing or specially installed telephone company wiring; however, the transmission of video signals over landlines is still considered a secondary method versus network transmission. The principal consideration in sending video signals over a network is the capability of the host network to accommodate their size. For these reasons, the use of networks to convey video is usually limited to exception or alarm assessment transmissions only.

Radio frequency (RF) communications are occasionally used for security information transfer, especially in buildings where cabling penetrations are not feasible. RF communications, however, are subject to varying degrees of interference. Wireless RF systems work most effectively in conjunction with detection sensors. Microwave transmission can provide high-speed data transmission, television signals, multiplexed alarm signals, and multiplexed telephone signals. However, microwave technology is limited to line-of-sight transmission and behaves very much the same as light signals.

Fiber optics are perhaps the most reliable communications media for point-to-point security systems cabling, particularly for transmitting video signals. With virtually unlimited bandwidth, fiber-optic cables offer extremely high data transmission rates, plus simultaneous transmission of many data sources on a single fiber. In addition, fiber-optic systems provide adequate built-in line security, and they are often used where external electronic interference is a problem.

CENTRAL CONTROL TECHNOLOGIES

Central control and display technologies are the focal point for monitoring and communications, display of alarm information and system status, and system support and performance. Integrated systems containing alarm reporting, CCTV displays, access control PCs, and video assessment/surveillance modules provide operators with a display and control network that facilitates security functions in virtually any type of building or environment.

Regardless of the complexity of a building security system, its peripheral devices, intermediate controllers, and systems multiplexers eventually report back to a single location. This is usually designated as the security control center. In buildings or sites with multiple protected areas, the control network may comprise local control units that gather data from various subsystems and report back to the SCC.

When security protection for a building or complex is being upgraded, it is often believed that significant savings can be realized if existing equipment is retained. Although this is sometimes the case, the effectiveness of using existing components is determined by an analysis of how well the existing system counters identified vulnerabilities, the potential for seamlessly integrating the components, and the cost benefits that can be derived from new equipment. Another important issue is the extent to which the installer will include existing or retained systems in the warranty for the new building systems.

Existing intrusion detection devices are much simpler to maintain when incorporated in a new system than card readers. Existing cameras can be reused in a new system, but the cost of camera replacements is insignificant compared to the advantages offered by newer CCTV systems.

Two main considerations in system retrofits are the capabilities of existing equipment and the efficacy of existing cabling. If existing cabling is more than five years old or does not test properly for line continuity, it may not perform effectively in a new configuration. Also, cabling requirements between existing and new equipment may differ. Further, an older system may not perform as required under new or revised protection objectives, while the selection of more modern technologies may offer both cost and performance advantages.

Older control equipment is less likely to fulfill new integrated design requirements due to lack of expansion capabilities. Although caution is advised, compatible existing equipment from reputable manufacturers can be used in updating a control and display system. Care must be taken to design and engineer newer elements to be consistent with owner requirements.

Integration of security command and control services has not advanced as quickly as improvements in the security systems technologies themselves. Even with recent quantum improvements in the electronics field, control center designs all too often reflect a collection of manufacturers' equipment thoughtlessly stacked around a console. If properly designed, the control center environment—including lighting, colors, and atmosphere—can be a place where an operator can work comfortably and productively. Proper console design and integration of system functions can make it possible for operators to work more effectively, reduce unnecessary steps, and limit opportunities for mistakes.

RELATED SYSTEMS

A fully integrated security system incorporates other elements in addition to those discussed so far. These may include emergency communication and intercom systems, and procedural software that can help security staff respond to various incidents.

Involving security personnel and other users at early design review stages can help ensure that proposed security systems can be supported procedurally.

Emergency communication devices are commonly placed at strategic points around a property to enable employees and visitors to seek help in an emergency. These devices range from pole- or wall-mounted enclosures to stand-alone stations with integrated CCTV, and should operate in a duplex communications mode. Emergency communication devices, particularly useful in parking lots and parking garages, should be positioned in readily visible locations. When the devices are used in conjunction with nearby CCTV cameras, placing them under or near lighting sources helps the SCC operator assess a situation.

Intercom devices with push-to-talk simplex communications are typically used at employee entrances in conjunction with card access systems. These devices allow employees to request access if they forget their card-reader badges. Intercom devices can also be used at loading docks and visitor entrances to reach the dock master or security operator. In some cases, owners elect to provide a master intercom station in the security room and one or two submaster stations at other areas, such as in the dock master's office for control of incoming truckers.

Other building controls can also be linked to the security system; however, those controls typically provide only direct output that becomes input to the security system. For example, a facility control system that provides analog control of pharmaceutical storage refrigeration units can send a digital alarm signal to the security system when the storage temperature exceeds an acceptable range. This type of integration enables the security system to expand its emergency response capabilities, especially after normal business hours.

A variety of security control system manufacturers offer systems capable of integration with overall building control systems. Provided the security control systems remain operationally separate from the facility control systems while using common technologies, the advantages of such integration are significant.

Security Systems Integration

Considered individually, the technologies described in this chapter offer relatively little in the way of security protection. However, when carefully combined into an integrated system, they can provide unlimited opportunities for building owners and architects who want to establish many levels of building control to manage identified risks. At the very least, these sys-

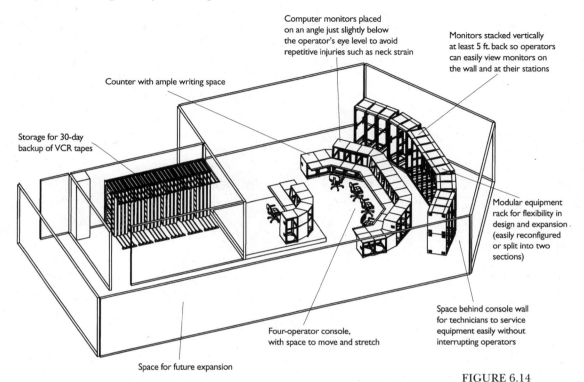

Computer monitors placed on an angle just slightly below the operator's eye level to avoid repetitive injuries such as neck strain

Monitors stacked vertically at least 5 ft. back so operators can easily view monitors on the wall and at their stations

Counter with ample writing space

Storage for 30-day backup of VCR tapes

Modular equipment rack for flexibility in design and expansion (easily reconfigured or split into two sections)

Space behind console wall for technicians to service equipment easily without interrupting operators

Four-operator console, with space to move and stretch

Space for future expansion

FIGURE 6.14
Ergonomic control console

tems give owners the opportunity to take advantage of capital investments and decrease recurring manpower expenditures.

Security technology is playing an increasingly important role in office, industry, and government building operations. Applications include contraband detection, walk-through metal detectors, explosive detectors, computerized antibomb-blast building designs, vehicle barriers, CCTV recording and motion detection systems, multiple credential readers, elevator floor and passenger control, security lighting, and security control and information display networks.

High-tech, integrated technologies not only offer greater protection opportunities but also help minimize costs by reducing reliance on multiple operators and roving patrols. Such savings can amount to as much as 30 percent of capital and recurring expenditures and can have an average payback period of less than one year. Nevertheless, even the best security technologies, regardless of how expertly integrated, can only communicate that there is a problem. The systems themselves do not stop determined intruders; if no one responds to an alarm, there is no protection, and the monies invested will be wasted.

Evolving security technologies such as biometrics, cargo-screening systems, more efficient airport-screening systems, and CBR sniffers may ultimately offer a greater likelihood of preventing, detecting, controlling, and intervening in everyday threats. Architects, design professionals, and security consultants will be challenged to find ways to apply such technologies cost-effectively. Architects seeking to integrate security systems more seamlessly into building design need to first understand the range of options, researching complementary subsystems and the corresponding advantages and disadvantages of a variety of possible solutions. Whatever the outcome, security risk control and management are always the end-game, while building control and management are the residual benefit.

7 Biochemical and Radiological Building Protection

Michael C. Janus and Robert Rudolph

The threats to commercial and government facilities throughout the world are constantly changing, and emerging threats now include chemical, biological, and radiological (CBR) terrorism. Terrorist attacks within the past 10 years include a Japanese cult's 1995 release of the nerve gas sarin in a Tokyo subway station, and the October 2001 release of anthrax bacteria through letters mailed to several U.S. locations.

The release of CBR agents inside or outside a building could seriously affect the health of building occupants as well as the use of the facility after the attack. Buildings are especially attractive and vulnerable targets for CBR attacks, for the following reasons:

+ CBR agents contained in a building can remain concentrated for long periods, in contrast to outdoors, where meteorological factors such as wind and sunlight may quickly dilute the concentration of an agent.

+ Mechanical and ventilation systems in buildings can effectively distribute CBR agents, increasing exposure and intensifying the contamination problem.

+ CBR agents can be delivered through a building covertly, for example, through mail or water systems.

✦ Facilities such as arenas, malls, theaters, or large office buildings accommodate thousands of people in high densities at predictable times.

✦ Terrorists may be attracted to buildings that house people and resources they want to target.

✦ Buildings can be difficult to restore to normal use after a CBR attack.

CBR Threats to Buildings

CBR threats pose special challenges to the design of a building protection system. These threats have extremely diverse and uncertain characteristics and, unlike conventional security threats, few historical analogs to help define them. This lack of predictability complicates development of design requirements for the components of a protection system. However, two key characteristics of a CBR threat that affect building protection systems can be studied—the *agent type* and the *delivery method*.

■ TYPES OF CBR AGENTS

Chemical and biological terrorism to date have delivered toxic industrial chemicals via food, water, and aerosol vapor, according to a study of non-military incidents presented in April 2001 at the Chemical and Biological Medical Treatment Symposia held in Dubrovnik, Croatia. The study also revealed that CBR agents used in terrorist incidents have included bacillus anthracis (anthrax), butyric acid, mercury, botulinum toxin, warfarin, thallium salts, ricin, arsenic, sarin, potassium chloride, sodium cyanide, lysergic acid diethylamide (LSD), paraquat, salmonella, strychnine, vibrio cholerae (cholera), and yersinia pestis (plague).

CBR agents possess a wide array of physical, chemical, and toxicological properties. Their variability can affect design requirements such as system response time, filter type and efficiency, and detector sensitivity and selectivity. This section summarizes the essential attributes of CBR agents.

❖ Chemical Agents

Chemical agents include both chemical warfare agents (CWAs) and toxic industrial chemicals (TICs). CWAs are relatively difficult to obtain and are produced to kill or seriously injure humans and to deny access to facilities or land. CWAs include GB (sarin), VX, HD (mustard gas), and phosgene.

TICs are used primarily for legitimate industrial purposes and are produced, transported, and stored throughout the world. TICs include ammonia, chlorine, and ethylene oxide.

The physical properties of an agent determine whether it can be transported throughout a building and how it will be removed from a building. Chemical agents may exist as solids, liquids, or gases at standard conditions. Their effective duration depends on their rate of evaporation, termed volatility. Highly volatile agents disperse quickly, while less volatile agents may remain in a building for an extended period unless it is decontaminated. Vapor density (whether a chemical agent is lighter or heavier than air) determines whether an agent will remain at ground level or be quickly dissipated by the wind. Most CWAs are heavier than air. Chemical agents that enter the body through inhalation, ingestion, or skin contact affect the human body quickly and vary widely in lethality. The table in Figure 7.1 lists the characteristics of various chemical agents.

FIGURE 7.1

Characteristics of chemical agents

Chemical Agent (CAS number)	Type	Physical State (at 20°C)	Volatility (mg/m^3)	Vapor Density (Air = 1)	Lethality[a] (mg/mm^3)
GB[b] (107-44-8)	CWA	Colorless liquid	22,000 @ 25°C	4.86	35 (LC50[c] inhal.)
VX[b] (50782-69-9)	CWA	Colorless to amber liquid	10 @ 25°C	9.2	0.086 mg/kg (LD[c])
HD[b] (505-60-2)	CWA	Colorless to pale yellow liquid	771 @ 30°C	5.4	1,500 (inhalation) (LD50) 10,000 (skin) (LD50)
Phosgene[d] (75-44-5)	TIC	Colorless gas	7×10^6 @ 20°C	3.4	8 (IDLH[c])
Ammonia[e] (7664-41-7)	TIC	Colorless gas	4×10^4 @ −45°C	0.6	348 (IDLH)
Chlorine[f] (7782-50-5)	TIC	Greenish yellow gas	3×10^7 @ 30°C	2.5	87 (IDLH)

[a] Lethality data from the U.S. Environmental Protection Agency, Chemical Emergency Preparedness and Prevention Office, List of Extremely Hazardous Substances (EHS) Chemical Profiles and Emergency First Aid Guides (www.epa.gov/swercepp/ehs/ehslist.html).

[b] Toxicity for GB, VX, and HD from the Centers for Disease Control and Prevention, National Institute for Occupational Safety and Health (NIOSH), Registry of Toxic Effects of Chemical Substances (RTECS) (1985).

[c] LC50 = lethal concentration, 50% fatalities; LD50 = lethal dose, 50% fatalities; IDLH = immediately dangerous to life and health.

[d] Toxicity for phosgene from NIOSH (1987), p. 192.

[e] Toxicity for ammonia from NIOSH and U.S. Department of Labor, Occupational Safety and Health Administration (OSHA) (1978), p. 44.

[f] Toxicity for chlorine from NIOSH (1987), p. 74.

❖ *Biological Agents*

Biological threats typically fall into the following categories:

✦ *Bacteria*, such as anthrax, are single-cell microorganisms that do not require a host and reproduce by cell division.

✦ *Viruses*, the simplest type of microorganism, consist of genetic material coated with a nucleocapsid protein, either RNA or DNA. Viruses lack a metabolic system and therefore require living hosts for replication.

✦ *Toxins* are poisonous substances created by living organisms that become toxic when introduced into human tissues.

Biological agents may be produced in a sophisticated laboratory or in a home with rudimentary equipment. Some key characteristics of biological agents include incubation period, lethality, stability, and transmissibility. The *incubation period* is the time between exposure and the appearance of symptoms. *Lethality* is the ease with which an agent causes death; the lethality of biological agents is many times higher than that of CWAs or TICs. *Stability* is the length of time the organism or toxin will remain effective in a particular environment. *Transmissibility* refers to the capability of an infectious agent to spread from a source to a host. The table in Figure 7.2 lists the characteristics of specific biological agents.

FIGURE 7.2

Characteristics of biological agents

Biological Agent	Type	Incubation Period	Lethality	Transmissibility
Anthrax	Bacteria	1–43 days	Inhalation anthrax after symptoms occur almost always fatal, regardless of treatment; 5–20% fatality if cutaneous	None (except cutaneous)
Smallpox	Virus	10–12 days	20–40% fatality	High
Plague	Bacteria	1–3 days	Pneumonic: 95% if untreated / 5–10% if treated / Bubonic: 30%–75% if untreated	High (Pneumonic)
Marburg	Virus	5–7 days	25%	Unknown
Ricin	Toxin	Hours–days	100% without treatment	None
Saxitoxin	Toxin	5 min. –1 hour	High	None

Source: Fatah, A.A., J.A. Barrett, R.D. Arcilesi, K.J. Ewing, C.H. Lattin, and M.S. Helinski. *An Introduction to Biological Agent Detection Equipment for Emergency First Responders*. NIJ Guide 101-00, Vols 1–2, 2001.

❖ Radiological Agents

Radiological threats typically are categorized by the type of energy emitted: alpha, beta, and gamma radiation and neutrons. Figure 7.3 lists the characteristics of radiological agents. Radiation is emitted by radioisotopes that may occur as aerosols or gases or be carried on particles. These radiological threats, and the means of protection against them, include:

♦ *Alpha particles* are able to travel only a few centimeters in the air and only a few microns in skin. They are an inhalation, ingestion, and absorption hazard, but individual or personal protection equipment (PPE), clothing, or even a piece of paper can effectively shield people from them.

♦ *Beta particles* are higher energy particles that can travel several meters in air and several millimeters in tissue. They are consid-

FIGURE 7.3

Characteristics of radiological agents

Locations and Materials	Radiation Sources	Source Strength	Comments
Cancer treatment areas	Cobalt-60 and cesium-137	~1 to several tens of grays (Gys)[a] over several hours at about 1 meter if the source is exposed	Found in therapy rooms.
Sources and applicators	Cesium-137, iridium-192, radium-226, phosphorous-32, strontium-90, iodine-125	Tens of millions of becquerels[b] (MBq)	Found in therapy and nuclear medicine areas.
Radiopharmaceuticals	Iodine-131, iodine-123, technetium-99m, thallium-201, xenon-133	Tens of MBq	Found in storage, nuclear medicine areas, and transportation.
X-ray machines and accelerators	X rays and electrons	~0.01 Gy min^{-1} at the source	Found in radiology or therapy rooms.
Various sources and devices	Tritium, carbon-14, sodium-22, sodium-24, sulfur-35, calcium-45, cobalt-60	Up to tens of TBq	Found in various areas and, if leaking, surface contamination.
Particle accelerators	X rays, alphas, protons, deuterons, electrons, gammas	~4 TBq to ~40 PBq	Found anywhere in an industrial area. Be aware of possible activation products.
Experimental reactors and critical assemblies	Fission products, neutrons, fissile and fissionable material, transuranics	Up to tens of TBq	Found in various areas, up to square kilometers in the case of widespread contamination.

[a] A Gray (Gy) is a unit of absorbed dose, equal to one joule per kilogram.

[b] A becquerel (Bq) is a unit given to nuclear decay, equal to one nuclear disintegration per second.

Source: Chemical and Biological Terrorism: Research and Development to Improve Civilian Medical Response to Chemical and Biological Terrorism Incidents. National Academy of Sciences, 1999. National Academy Press, 2101 Constitution Avenue, N.W., Box 285, Washington, DC 20055.

ered to be both an internal hazard (through inhalation, ingestion, and absorption) and an external hazard.

✦ *Gamma rays,* as the name implies, are not particles. They have a
high energy level, are very penetrating, and must be shielded
against. PPE is not effective against gamma rays. As a result,
gamma rays represent both internal and external hazards.

✦ *Neutrons* have the highest energy level of the four radiological
energy types. Emitted as the result of nuclear blasts or from a
nuclear reactor, they are highly penetrating and difficult to
shield against. However, they are not commonly regarded as a
threat when considering an incident involving, for example, a
dirty bomb made of conventional explosives with some radioactive material.

CBR DELIVERY METHODS

CBR delivery methods are significant to building design because they directly
affect the requirements of the building protection system. The means of delivery can affect the type, location, and quantity of protection equipment
required, in addition to influencing general protection strategies.

❖ Airborne Delivery

Different methods of delivering CBR agents have different effects on the
design of protective systems. *External standoff* threats, which release
agents at a significant distance from a building, can result in infiltration
of the agent into enclosed building spaces. Examples include the explosion of a tanker truck containing a TIC on a nearby rail line or a biological agent released by a crop duster. *External proximate releases* occur close
enough to a building for the agent to enter via the HVAC system rather
than by widespread infiltration; for example, a biological agent being
sprayed into an outside air intake. *Internal release* occurs inside a building; for example, if a chemical agent liquid is poured on a lobby floor or
a biological agent is released via small aerosol sprayer in a mechanical
room. Internal releases and external proximate releases require significantly smaller quantities of agent to reach lethal levels in a building than
do external standoff releases.

❖ Waterborne Delivery

A waterborne threat contaminates a building's water system at any point
prior to consumption or use for bathing or cleaning. Municipal water may

be contaminated at any point before it is treated, at the treatment plant, at storage sites, or during distribution. An agent also can be injected into water pretreatment devices inside a building. Bottled water may be contaminated en route to the facility or while in storage.

❖ Foodborne Delivery

A foodborne threat involves contamination of food at any point prior to consumption. Foodborne contamination can result from an airborne attack or from direct contamination of the food supply. Possible scenarios include food that is served in a facility cafeteria, delivered by an outside source, or purchased from a vending machine. Foodborne threats are not a major concern to building designers but may be a significant concern to building operators.

❖ Surface Delivery

A surface threat involves an agent that can harm building occupants when it is transferred from one surface to another. Examples include radiological particles spread on a lobby floor or anthrax-contaminated mail. Surface threats may become airborne threats if vaporized or reaerosolized from a surface.

THE VULNERABILITY OF BUILDINGS TO CBR THREATS

The vulnerability of a building to CBR threats is based on several factors. The design of standard building systems may affect this vulnerability as much as the integration of specialized CBR protection equipment, the development and use of response procedures, or the availability of trained personnel. Given the uncertainty associated with CBR threats and the many variables in building design, building environments, and building operations, a CBR vulnerability assessment is recommended as part of the security assessment process (see Figure 7.4).

It is important to keep all information on building vulnerability strictly confidential.

Designing for CBR Protection

Any or all of the following fundamental approaches can be used in the design of a CBR protection system:

Factor	Examples of Specific Issues to Address
Building layout	Segmentation of high-threat areas Standoff distances
Building structure and materials	Leakage characteristics Adsorption characteristics of materials
Mechanical system design	Location of external air intakes Filtration capability
Building operations	Occupancy patterns Critical operations
Building procedures	Mail-handling procedures Emergency response plans
Surrounding environment	Meteorology Proximity of CBR storage sites, rail lines, etc.
Specialized protection equipment	Usage of CBR detection equipment Usage of CBR filtration equipment
Personnel and training	Sheltering-in-place or evacuation training Availability of technical personnel
Security systems	Security of mechanical rooms Intrusion detection

FIGURE 7.4
Top-level considerations for CBR vulnerability assessment

◆ *Exclusion,* to ensure that CBR agents do not enter the building.

◆ *Containment*, to minimize the spread of contamination by confining the agent in a specific portion of the building.

◆ *Removal*, to minimize the spread of contamination by rapidly removing the agent from the building following release.

◆ *Evasion*, to remove the occupants from contaminated areas.

Although these approaches vary, they share the common objective of minimizing the number of building occupants exposed to CBR agents. Each approach may be implemented in either a *continuous* or a *standby* mode. In a continuous mode, a CBR protection system operates constantly, whereas a standby protection system is activated by a detection or warning system. Each approach may be designed with varying degrees of complexity, ranging from simple, low-cost solutions to complex, high-cost solutions. The following sections describe the basic components of a CBR protection system, the fundamental protection approaches, and examples of various system types.

CBR SYSTEM COMPONENTS

Regardless of the approach chosen, the components of each scheme must be selected and assembled in a logical and proper manner to ensure the system is effective. Complex systems may use all of the components, whereas less complex systems may use only some of them. Although some components may not be directly applicable to building design, all will affect it in some way. The components of a CBR protection system (diagrammed in Figure 7.5) may include the following:

- Detection equipment
- Collective protection (CP) equipment
- Personal protection equipment (PPE)
- Decontamination
- Physical security assets
- HVAC systems
- Control systems
- Communications equipment
- Building modifications
- Response plans and procedures
- Personnel
- Training.

❖ CBR Detection Equipment

Rapid detection and identification of CBR agents are vital capabilities of all CBR building protection systems. Detection is critical to protect building occupants, emergency first responders, and emergency medical personnel at local medical facilities. Identification of the CBR agent is important for effective treatment of casualties.

CBR detectors for building applications should have high sensitivity (below incapacitating levels), high selectivity (a low false-alarm rate), fast response time (in seconds), autonomous operation (no human intervention required during operation), and low maintenance requirements. However, CBR detection technologies are at different stages of development, making it difficult to use available technology consistently. In general, radiological detection technology is mature and reliable. Chemical detection technology is nearing maturity but still has limitations. Biological detection technology will require significant development before it can

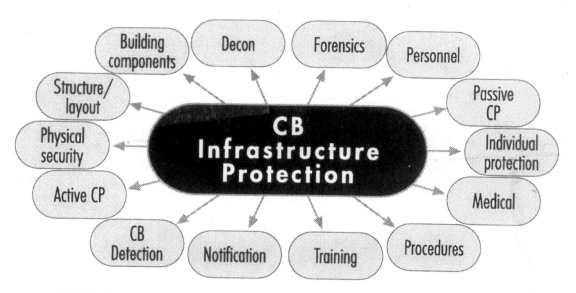

FIGURE 7.5

Chemical-biological

protection components become a useful part of a CBR building protection system. Currently, the cost of all of these technologies is relatively high.

A variety of chemical detection equipment is available commercially and through the government. Chemical detectors of varying sensitivity and specificity have been developed with different technologies. These include gas chromatograph-mass spectrometers (GC-MS), ion mobility spectrometers (IMS), surface acoustic wave (SAW) sensors, infrared detectors, flame photometry devices, and photoionization detectors. (Figure 7.6 shows a chemical detector located downstream of an external air intake.)

Biological agent detection systems must be highly sensitive (i.e., able to detect minute amounts of biological agents). Complex and rapidly changing environmental conditions also require these detection systems to be highly selective (i.e., able to distinguish biological agents from other harmless biological and nonbiological material in the environment). To enable them to make such distinctions, biological detection systems are often complex devices consisting of various subunits (trigger, collector, detector, and identifier). (Figure 7.7 shows a biological detector unit in a penthouse mixing plenum.)

Radiological detection is the most advanced of the detection technologies. Radiation and contamination detectors have been improved continuously over several decades. They are reliable and highly accurate, able to detect even the most minute quantities, and have extremely low false-

FIGURE 7.6
This chemical detector is located downstream of an outside air intake to provide early warning of an external chemical release. Detectors with rapid response times may be used to initiate active protection systems.

FIGURE 7.7
This biological contamination detector is located in a penthouse mixing plenum to warn of an internal or external release of biological agents. Currently, biological detectors are not typically used to initiate active protection systems due to slow their response times.

alarm rates. The most commonly used radiation detection technology includes ionization chambers, Geiger-Muller counters, proportional counters, and scintillation counters. Many thousands of continuous detection radiation detection monitors are in use throughout the world.

❖ Collective Protection Equipment

CP equipment is a critical component of any building protection system. CP is a generic term for equipment that provides safe breathing air for individuals. CP equipment includes particulate and gas filters, neutralization equipment (e.g., UV light systems), air movement devices, protective shelters and materials, airlocks, and associated components. (One such system is illustrated in Figure 7.8.)

The two primary types of CBR filters are gas and particulate. Gas filters capture chemical agents in gaseous and vapor form. Particulate filters (e.g., high-efficiency particulate air [HEPA] filters) capture the microscopic particles associated with biological agents, radiological agents, and chemical aerosols.

❖ Personal Protection Equipment

When warning of a CBR threat is not possible, or people must occupy CBR-contaminated areas within a building, they need PPE such as masks, respirators, coveralls, hoods, gloves, and boots. PPE has little effect on building design other than to require storage space. Numerous market surveys have identified and characterized available PPE.

❖ Decontamination

Decontamination is another critical function of CBR building protection. Removing or neutralizing CBR hazards prevents further damage and optimizes the chance for full restoration of a contaminated building. These processes sometimes include destruction of building materials. Because of the potential complexity of decontamination, adequate decontamination plans should be considered early in the design of a CBR building protection system. Market surveys have identified and characterized available decontamination equipment.

❖ Physical Security Assets

Standard physical security equipment also plays a key role in CBR building protection. Closed-circuit television (CCTV), intrusion detection equipment, perimeter fencing, and access cards can help thwart both internal and external threats. CCTV can be used to monitor highly vulnerable areas such as external air intakes or mail and package facilities. Intrusion detection devices may alert security personnel of unauthorized entry or signal when a mechanical access panel has been removed. Perimeter fencing can increase standoff distances to minimize the threat from an external release. Access cards may prevent unauthorized entry into highly vulnerable areas such as mechanical rooms.

❖ HVAC Systems

Given the vulnerability of building HVAC systems, every detail of mechanical system design—from damper closing speed to exhaust fan capacity to zonal segmentation to external access to water pipes—must be examined to determine the potential for transporting contamination throughout a building. Mechanical equipment design should enable precise and active control of all prominent airflow paths within a building. In addition, rapid activation is a key requirement for most mechanical components, including blowers, fans, and dampers.

❖ Control Systems

CBR protection typically creates additional demands on building controls, regardless of the complexity of the protection system. These requirements involve the ability to remotely control air handlers, dampers, exhaust fans, pumps, and other key mechanical components; the ability to program unique mechanical system response sequences; the ability to interface with CBR detectors, physical security devices, and communications equipment; and the need for enhanced cybersecurity. For example, a solution as simplistic as sheltering-in-place (SIP) may require configuration of the building controls so the entire mechanical system (e.g., all fans and air-handling units shut down, all dampers closed) can be shut down instantaneously with one button.

❖ Communications Equipment

Evasion approaches require personnel movement, which means communications equipment may be a key component of a CBR system design. Most protection solutions are extremely time-critical and will require quick responses from building occupants and equipment. In addition, different responses may be required depending on the location of the release. For example, the response to an internal release may be evacuation, while the response to an external release may be SIP. These two responses place opposing requirements on occupants, requiring a buildingwide communication system using intercoms, phones, pagers, or other devices. The current limitations of CBR detectors also dictate that awareness of a CBR incident may not come from a CBR detector but from a guard or occupant's observation (e.g., a suspicious device or injured people). This possibility underscores the need for buildingwide communication systems and a central command post or operations center.

❖ Building Modifications

The complexity of the protection system typically dictates the level of modification required for HVAC, plumbing, structural, electrical, and other building systems. The HVAC system will likely require the most significant modifications due to the critical role these components play in CBR protection. For example, some protection solutions may require mechanical dampers to be low-leakage and pneumatically controlled. Plumbing modifications typically are associated with decontamination equipment and protection from waterborne threats. Other modifications could include items such as larger mechanical rooms or tighter mechanical zones with minimal leakage. Structural modifications could include reinforcement of the roof structure to accommodate advanced filtration equipment or alteration of wall structures to provide radiological shielding.

❖ Response Plans and Procedures

Plans and procedures for responding to security incidents are vital to system effectiveness regardless of cost or complexity. Developing such plans and procedures is challenging because they must address many threat scenarios; moreover, they must be coordinated with local emergency responders and medical assets. Plans for maintenance and periodic testing of the protection system should also be developed, and procedures put in place to ensure the system is kept up-to-date and in good working condition.

❖ *Training*

The effectiveness of a CBR protection system depends on the skill level and training of the system operators and the occupants. In general, the more complex a protection system is, the more skilled the system operators must be and the less the system should depend on occupant action. Therefore, training for system operators is essential.

DESIGN APPROACHES FOR CBR PROTECTION SYSTEMS

The high level of uncertainty associated with the CBR threat does not currently allow for the effective use of standardized designs. Appropriate system solutions depend on factors such as the threat, vulnerability, level of protection required, user requirements, building design, building operations, budget, available technology, and other relevant issues. Numerous government research programs are working to develop and validate standardized approaches. The **Defense Advanced Research Projects Agency's (DARPA)** Immune Building Program and the **Defense Threat Reduction Agency's (DTRA)** Smart Building Program are two such efforts. Although a cookbook approach is not yet available, system solutions can be based on the fundamental approaches of exclusion, containment, removal, and evasion.

❖ *Exclusion Approach*

This approach strives to keep CBR from entering the building through the mechanical system, infiltration, surface contact (e.g., package), or other means. Exclusion, which the military has used effectively, may be accomplished crudely for airborne threats by SIP or in a complex manner using positive-pressure CP. The exclusion approach requires reliable CBR detection in a standby mode. To mitigate internal threats requires nonintrusive detection technology analogous to security screening devices (e.g., X ray or metal detectors) to ensure that CBR agents do not enter the building. Effective nonintrusive CBR detection equipment is not currently available.

❖ *Containment Approach*

This approach attempts to minimize the spread of contamination by confining the agent within a specific portion of a building. Containment of contamination may be accomplished by mechanical system zoning, variable pressurization schemes, knockdown sprays, and other techniques. The containment approach is most effective against internal threats and within buildings that have multiple mechanical zones. It requires identification of the release source location and depends on the availability of reliable detection equipment. Containment in a continuous mode is a useful strategy for high-threat areas such as mailrooms. This approach is similar to isolation wards in hospitals for patients with transmissible diseases such as tuberculosis.

❖ Removal Approach

This approach tries to minimize the spread of contamination by rapidly removing an agent from a building following release. Removal methods include dedicated exhaust, manipulation of outside air percentages, filtration, or neutralization. This approach is primarily intended for internal releases, and it requires reliable detection to be effective in a standby mode. Filtration and neutralization may also be used on return and supply airflows in a continuous mode for protection against internal threats. The removal approach is analogous to that used in smoke evacuation.

❖ Evasion Approach

This approach removes occupants from the contamination and thus requires minimal building modification. Evasion may involve the use of individual protection equipment such as masks and protective suits. The evasion approach may be effective against both external and internal threats. This approach depends greatly, however, on CBR detectors and advance warning because the approach is inherently standby and not continuous. Significant time may be required to train occupants before an incident and to don protective equipment during an incident. An evasion approach is sometimes used as an interim solution before more robust building protection solutions are implemented.

The system mode (continuous or standby) may affect a system's effectiveness, complexity, and cost. The primary distinction between the modes is the requirement for early warning or detection. The effectiveness of a standby mode system depends completely upon the availability of reliable and timely detection. Continuous mode systems are not as dependent upon detection but are typically more costly and operationally more obtrusive. It is important to note that an appropriate protection system may combine both continuous and standby modes. Each building and situation will likely pose a unique problem and therefore will require a tailored solution.

Sample CBR Protection Schemes

This section describes three hypothetical schemes to protect a building from airborne threats. The examples vary in complexity and cost. For each, a brief scenario describes a building where the proposed system scheme might be appropriate, followed by descriptions of the CP, detection, and mechanical equipment required because these components typically drive system cost.

EXAMPLE 1: SCHOOL

Objective: *To protect a school located close to a toxic industrial chemical plant that has received terrorist threats in the past. The external standoff threat is the prime concern, but the release of pepper spray by a student inside the building is also considered a possibility.*

A simplistic and low-cost system could combine exclusion and evasion approaches, using sheltering-in-place for external airborne threats and evacuation for internal airborne threats. SIP involves rapidly shutting down HVAC systems, closing doors and windows, and stopping other activities to minimize the infiltration rate. SIP involves minimal architectural modifications but will require a one-button control to shut down the entire mechanical system. Also, air handlers, fans, dampers, and other relevant components should be designed or configured to shut down as rapidly as possible.

Additional protection can be achieved with inexpensive equipment that can reduce infiltration and decrease CBR agent dosage within the building. Permanent architectural and mechanical modifications (e.g., caulking, foaming, and low-leakage dampers) are typically introduced to decrease leakage of the protective envelope. Temporary sealing measures (e.g., tape and polyethylene sheeting) may also be used for this purpose. Off-the-shelf recirculation filters with particulate and vapor filtration media may increase protection factors three- to fourfold, assuming low contaminant concentration levels. Evacuation is a well-understood technique and should not require any significant building modifications.

The primary weakness of this design is that it depends completely upon early warning. It needs at least two detectors, to identify internal and external threats. Detectors should be placed on the outside air intake and the primary air return. Exclusion and evasion approaches also require procedure development and training. The SIP approach may be challenging because staying in place during an emergency contradicts human nature.

For this scheme to be effective, protective actions should be taken before the contaminant reaches the building (for an external release) or before the contaminant has spread throughout the building (for an internal release). Because real-time biological detectors are not currently available, this solution is ineffective for biological threats (unless warning is received by another means). The cost of this approach is primarily driven by the cost of the detectors.

■ EXAMPLE 2: THEATER

Objective: *To protect occupants in a large theater from a small release of a CBR agent.*

A moderately complex system for protection from external and internal airborne threats can be achieved with a combination of the exclusion and removal approach. The design objective is to create a low level of continuous protection for the entire building and a high level of standby protection for a designated area within the building (i.e., a safe zone). The continuous low-level protection decreases the dependence on CBR detection by giving occupants more time to reach the safe zone. The system design uses low-efficiency filtration on the supply side of the air handlers and expedient CP equipment to provide protection for the safe zone. Expedient collective protection includes portable, easily installed and operated equipment.

Minimal building modifications are needed because low-efficiency (approximately 99 percent single-pass) CB filters can replace common dust panel filters on the supply side of the air handler. Because these filters typically have a pressure drop of between 0.5 to 1.0 inch of water gauge, air-handler capabilities may require enhancement. Low-efficiency CB filters on the supply side provide protection from both external and internal airborne threats and may be sufficient to independently provide protection from low-level threats.

The safe zone is protected in standby mode with the use of expedient collective protection equipment, for example, the Small Area Filtration Equipment (SAFE) Kit. This equipment can be installed in any standard door or window opening to provide positive pressure collective protection to a small zone (approximately 2,000 feet).

This system's primary weakness is its dependence upon early warning. It uses only one detector on the supply side of the air handler, and additional detectors to minimize response time and determine source location are always preferable.

Operation and maintenance training will be required to ensure that filters and expedient collective protection equipment are operating as designed. The protection afforded by this solution depends less on advanced warning since it operates continuously. The cost of this system depends primarily on the cost of the detectors and low-efficiency CB filters.

EXAMPLE 3: EMERGENCY OPERATIONS CENTER

Objective: *To protect the emergency operations center of a major city from an external CBR release. The emergency operations center does not expect to be a direct target but needs to ensure that it remains operational should an event occur in the city.*

A system may use the exclusion approach to address external standoff and external proximate airborne threats—the same approach used extensively by the military to protect key assets. The heart of this protection system is a continuous positive-pressure CP system that permanently integrates high-efficiency particulate and vapor filters into the outside air intake of the building mechanical system. Permanent integration means that air is filtered within the ductwork system rather than at a central location, as is done in many standby systems. The system is designed to create an overpressure in the building commensurate with local wind conditions.

Permanent architectural and mechanical modifications (e.g., caulking, foaming, and low-leakage dampers) typically are introduced to decrease leakage through the protective envelope. Airlocks ensure safe entry and exit during a CBR event. Although not required, a CBR detection system may be employed to ensure that occupants do not exit the building during an attack.

This system is costly and does not afford protection from internal threats. The cost is primarily driven by the type of filter media, the percentage of filtered air, and the required mechanical, electrical, structural, and architectural modifications. Assuming a 20,000 cfm system using military-grade filters, the initial cost of the filters alone could exceed $200,000. The system also requires significant periodic testing and maintenance. Its primary advantages are the high level of protection it offers and its lack of dependence on CBR detectors.

Application Considerations

The building owner and/or operator must conduct a detailed cost-benefit analysis to make decisions for the design of a CBR protection system. The analysis should include factors such as the specific threat to a building, the unique vulnerabilities of the building, the level of protection required, operational requirements, system operation and maintenance, building code requirements, budget, and the availability of technology.

Protecting against all potential CBR threat agents, means of delivery, and imaginable release quantities is exceedingly complex and costly. Consequently, focused and probabilistic threat and vulnerability assessments will enable the design of an effective system from both technical and cost perspectives.

The nature of a CBR protection system depends on the level of protection required. The CBR system designer must work closely with building owners and operators to fully understand their expectations and requirements. For example, does the building owner intend to provide CBR protection for the entire building or just the executive suite? Operational requirements also play an important role in system design. Complex CBR protection systems may be obtrusive and interfere with building operations. For example, detector false alarms could result in frequent and unnecessary building evacuations. New mail-handling equipment and procedures could result in significant delays in mail processing and delivery.

CBR protection systems may require a level of operation and maintenance that is unfamiliar to most building owners and operators. For example, high-grade filtration systems may require complex in-place testing several times a year. In addition, building code requirements may conflict with protection objectives. For example, does manipulation of outside air quantities conflict with requirements for acceptable indoor air quality? Do proposed automated responses of the mechanical system for CBR protection conflict with responses for the fire protection system?

Of course, the budget is usually the biggest design determinant. CBR detection and filtration equipment is extremely costly. CBR detectors may cost from a few thousand to a few hundred thousand dollars. High-grade CBR filters may cost anywhere from $10 per cfm to $50 dollars per cfm.

Finally, the availability of technology must be considered. For example, given the limitations of current CBR detectors, it may be prudent to focus on continuous approaches and minimize the use of standby approaches until detection technology has developed further.

An Evolving Threat

CBR terrorism is an evolving threat likely to require more attention by the building design community over the coming years. This threat poses significant challenges due to the uncertainty associated with it and the effectiveness of potential solutions. Systematic approaches are needed to address the problem, including threat, vulnerability, and protection assessments on a building-by-building basis. Standardized solutions have yet to be developed, but available options ranging from simplistic, low-cost to highly complex, high-cost solutions are currently available. Research continues in the effort to develop lower cost, more effective solutions that will be increasingly transparent to building occupants.

8 Security and Emergency Operations

Richard Grassie, CPP
Behrooz (Ben) Emam, AIA, PE, CFM

Knowledge of building operations is vital to the development of security programs and emergency plans that can help building owners and occupants recover from major disasters or disruptive events. A basic understanding of operating issues that facility users and managers are likely to face makes it possible for architects and other design professionals to gauge the effects of their design decisions on building vulnerabilities. This knowledge helps them reduce those vulnerabilities and ensures that design solutions support operational goals and objectives as fully as possible.

This chapter addresses the security and emergency preparedness aspects of building operations. Discussions of security operations describe surveillance, screening, access control, incident reporting, maintaining communications integrity, and associated activities. Discussions of emergency preparedness look at the development and use of emergency preparedness plans and response procedures. Although much of the material addresses specific facility types, the principles introduced could be applied to most building types.

Security Operations

Planning for building security operations should be developed during the early stages of building design. Such planning can help identify and isolate a host of security considerations, including locations and types of doors, cameras, and access control points as well as their impact on daily personnel and material traffic flows. Other important considerations in the plan are points of egress and potential choke points during emergencies, location of isolation or restricted areas, visitor traffic flow, security policies and procedures, standards for security personnel, and types and scheduling of building safety checks.

To ensure an operational plan addresses the people, procedures, and technology aspects of security, questions like the following should be answered: Will personnel and material movement patterns require a guard force? If so, how will they affect deployment of the guards? Will there be restricted access, and, if so, how much? Will all visitors and parcels be logged in and out? Will cleaning crews and contractors come and go at will, or will they be screened and issued credentials? A plan should also take

Elements of Security Operations

People, procedures, and technology are the foundation of effective building security operations. Key considerations for each of these elements generally include the following:

- *People.* The functions and movement patterns of a building's occupants, including workers, visitors, and contractors, are an important part of the programming information needed at the outset of a security design process. Preparation of a security plan includes determining the types of security personnel needed (e.g., contract or proprietary) and how and where to deploy them.

- *Procedures.* Specific plans and procedures—including evacuation, emergency response, and recovery plans—are developed in response to likely building safety and security threats such as fires, lightning damage, theft, explosions, and earthquakes. Once this has been accomplished, policies and procedures are developed to guide how security personnel respond to these threats and to assist in recovery from any incidents that may occur.

- *Technology.* State-of-the-art security technologies suitable for the operations or mission of a facility are determined. For example, how and where will screening of personnel and materials be accomplished, and what kinds of equipment and systems will be used?

into account how the building owner wants to handle security and emergency situations. Generally, security and emergency policies are accompanied by detailed procedures for specific risk scenarios to ensure that building operations suit expected situations. For example, both security staff and owner or tenant personnel may carry out visitor screening and processing.

SURVEILLANCE

Surveillance may be carried out with or without the use of security equipment (e.g., by guards in a lobby or secured area, by security officers walking beats, and by building occupants on an ongoing informal basis). The use of surveillance technologies such as closed-circuit television (CCTV), however, can supplement the actions of security personnel by providing four distinct yet complementary functions:

- ✦ *Assessment.* Surveillance technology can link intrusion/access systems to surveillance/assessment systems for automatic camera call-up to help personnel assess an incident or event. In most cases, a CCTV system is used to coordinate or guide a security guard's response to an incident rather than as part of an automated process.

- ✦ *Surveillance and monitoring.* CCTV technologies allow security staff to perform video tours of a facility. This enhances the overall security of a site, while helping to familiarize security staff with standard building operations during duty hours. This familiarity with typical activity helps the operator identify suspicious events or activities during regular surveillance tours.

- ✦ *Deterrence.* When visible or apparent, building surveillance technologies such as CCTV may deter criminal or suspicious activity by signaling that such activities are likely to be detected.

- ✦ *Archiving.* Archived images of technologically monitored events can support follow-up investigations of security incidents. State-of-the-art video systems can be programmed to record scenes of designated areas, capturing events or incidences that might otherwise go undetected.

SCREENING

In some facilities, the screening of people and property may become an important part of security operations.

Operational Security Factors

Following are some of the major factors that influence the development of security operation plans and procedures.

+ *Facility type.* Security operations are most difficult to manage in public facilities, which usually require free access because the occupant's mission is at least in part to serve the public. In semipublic facilities, such as hospitals, the task is somewhat easier because specific areas require heightened security and strict access control measures. In private facilities, the security operations depend much more on the type of business and on the organizational culture.

+ *Multiple buildings.* Typically, security operations for multiple buildings are handled by a small complement of security staff supported through security planning and technology applications. However, a single security officer can sometimes monitor the activities of multiple buildings from a single location, particularly after hours. For example, a single security officer can monitor multiple buildings when occupants adhere to set procedures such as using scanning devices or card readers for access control. In another situation, a building owner may place receptionists at the entry point of each building during business hours. After hours, a single security officer may be assigned to a control room along with one or more roving security personnel.

+ *Parking accommodations.* Parking facilities can offer adversaries opportunities to commit personal and property crimes without detection. Enhanced security operations in parking areas are typically supported by intercoms or emergency phones at strategic locations, and cameras, scream alert detectors, and motion detectors in stairways. CCTV cameras are used to conduct surveillance of parking facilities. Complementing these technological applications are security patrols and manned escorts upon request.

+ *Internal security resources.* Client or building user resources are an important factor when designing a building with security in mind. Hospitals, high-rise buildings, museums, transportation centers, corporations, public agencies, and so on all have vastly different capacities, capabilities, and available resources to deal with security issues. Some establish detection and reporting systems with local law enforcement backup and investigative support. Others assume responsibility for the entire security operation, occasionally relying on local law enforcement for offender profiles, arrest, and incarceration.

+ *Operating budgets.* The owner who has installed a building security management system typically has the entire system warranted for the first year. Thereafter, the owner must include sufficient monies for maintenance and support of such systems. A reasonable maintenance estimate for budgetary purposes is from 10 to 12 percent of the capital cost of the entire system to be maintained.

❖ Employees and Visitors

To control the movement of employees and visitors, the screening function is usually performed in the lobby according to procedures for categorizing and tracking movement of people in the facility. In some buildings, employees are issued color-coded badges, which can be further keyed to provide access to the base building, specific workspaces, and other restricted areas.

Personal visitors can usually be tracked most effectively with day passes issued on a day-to-day basis. These passes are requested by the person being visited and are logged in and out by the lobby guard or receptionist. Visitors with such a pass usually do not require an escort, although during periods of increased awareness or alert some buildings do require visitor escorts to heighten security. A supervisor usually approves general visitors. In a location with a high volume of informal or unexpected visitors, a generic daily visitor badge system can be used.

❖ Mail, Packages, and Deliveries

Mail and delivery surveillance and screening have become an extremely sensitive issue, and thus require a higher level of scrutiny than in the past. The facility manager generally oversees mailroom functions. Procedures should ensure the routine, safe, and expeditious processing of outgoing and incoming mail and packages. This includes specific drop-off and pick-up points and a procedure for after-hours deliveries.

All incoming deliveries should receive at least a cursory screening. A more thorough level of screening is determined, in part, by the type of business operating at the site. A detailed procedure should be in place to cover handling of suspicious items. In general, this includes reporting a suspicious item immediately, leaving it alone, and restricting access to it until appropriate staff arrives.

❖ Vendors, Workers, and Cleaning Crews

Regular visitors such as vendors, contractors, and cleaning crews are usually screened differently than other visitors. Vendors are typically salespeople, cleaners, contractors, or other personnel who will be on-site longer than the normal visitor. Generally, they are issued nonpicture day passes and logged in and out on a day-to-day basis. Workers to be onsite for long-term repair or construction work, temporary employees, and others as designated by a supervisor are usually issued picture badges for designated areas for a predetermined period of up to 90 days.

Cleaning crews generally receive a base building credential, which is issued directly to the crew supervisor(s). The supervisor on duty typically is issued a single card and is responsible for dispersing and controlling the cleaning crew throughout the building. Because access to a facility can be obtained easily simply by joining a cleaning crew, owners typically require that the cleaning contractor have background checks for all cleaning staff and that cleaning crews be supervised at all times while inside the building. In addition, some building owners require that building security staff regularly check cleaning crew activities and screen all contractor equipment and parcels before the cleaning crew leaves the facility.

ACCESS CONTROL

The term *access control* generally refers to physical or behavioral measures for managing the passage of personnel and vehicles into, out of, and within a facility. An access control plan strives to exert sufficient control to protect a facility while still allowing employees enough freedom of movement to work effectively.

Access control is typically an electronic or physical control process. A mix of technology and passive barriers can secure a site perimeter. Once this is accomplished, the next step is to control access to building interiors without disrupting facility functions and activities. Perimeter security keeps unwanted individuals out; but inside the building, access control can address concerns about internal theft and provide some limits on the movement of both employees and visitors. Each building presents a different set of challenges and requires unique security solutions.

The level of access control may vary significantly from building to building or be applied in a standardized fashion to all buildings on a given site. The appropriate level of access control depends on many factors: the degree of control the owner desires for a building; the number of employees who work there; hazards of materials present on the site; levels of pedestrian and vehicular traffic in and out of the building; the degree to which facility operations are controversial; the degree to which the assets, including the building, present an attractive target for various threats; and the proximity of the facility to populated, more criminally active areas, among others.

All areas of the building must be analyzed for potential unauthorized entry and exit, particularly for ways individuals could remove unauthorized or misappropriated property or contraband from the property. Dock or loading and delivery areas should receive special attention.

Access Control Measures

Building managers may use the following operational measures for controlling access into, within, and out of a given building or site:

- Post "No Trespassing" and "Authorized Access Only" signs, along with signs stating that vehicles and visitors are subject to search.
- Assign responsibility for security to someone on staff—the facility manager or security manager, if there is one—to allow for an orderly implementation of security access measures and procedures and subsequent daily monitoring.
- Train all organization and affiliate agency staff in basic security methods and procedures unique to the facility.
- Ensure that security awareness becomes a routine matter for all building occupants, in particular that the lobby security staff and the organization's tenants, employees, and visitors adhere to security procedures.
- Monitor performance of security duties such as the following: control of building entrances; regulation and monitoring of lobby pedestrian traffic; patrol and checks of the building and perimeter before closing and upon opening; inspection of incoming material and personnel; safety inspection of facilities and resources; and—in conjunction with the facility manager—responses to special situations and security activities.
- Distribute a simple, straightforward security policy statement, prepared by the organization's senior management, to all employees and tenants. The statement informs employees that security is a shared responsibility and serves as the foundation for issuance of security procedures.
- Develop and distribute a handbook of the organization's security policies and procedures, to be used primarily by guard and facility management personnel to respond to specific security events and emergencies in and around the building. The portion of the manual applicable to employees should be distributed to them with the general policy statement.
- Develop procedures to be followed in the event of a natural or man-made disaster, to include building evacuation, fire evacuation, civil disturbance, and power failure. Develop provisions concerning release of public information, availability of medical aid, emergency shutdown and restoration procedures, evacuation plans, and ways to regularly test and refine the disaster response and recovery plan.
- To the extent feasible, employ natural surveillance by arranging reception, production, and office space for easy observation of unescorted visitors.
- Restrict all visitors to building lobbies unless escorted by an authorized employee.
- Keep publicly accessible restroom doors locked, and establish a formal key control system using recognized quality hardware. If there is a combination lock, only office personnel should open the lock for visitors. Keep closets locked.
- Require visitor sign-in logs and escorts.
- Require material receipts or vouchers for any material leaving the building, especially for items such as laptops.
- Pay close attention to access control at loading and unloading areas.
- Institute a system of employee and contractor photo ID badges. Train employees to challenge persons who are not wearing badges as part of a security awareness program.
- Establish a system for determining which cars, trucks, and other vehicles may enter the site; through which gates, docks, or other entrances; and under what conditions. Such a system may be part of a pedestrian access control system, relying on card access carried by vehicle operators.
- Consider instituting parcel inspections (using magnetometers, X-ray screening, or devices to detect explosives). Require property passes to remove property from the site.

In addition, the right mix of alarm technology can indicate unsafe or emergency situations; unauthorized intrusion into a room or controlled area; and attempted intrusion through secured windows, doors, vents, and other openings.

Finally, credential systems are a vital component in any comprehensive system for controlling personnel and visitors. The most important qualities of a credential are that it be tamperproof and include a photo and some basic vital information. The best credentials provide universal access for multiple areas through multiple technologies (e.g., proximity, swipe, and bar code) on a single card.

INCIDENT REPORTING

Building owners must provide security operations with an information base that can collect accurate data about security incidents, losses and thefts, hazardous situations, security vulnerabilities, and general security operations. Knowing about, understanding, and keeping track of security incidents is critical to effective security planning and operations. The records management system should be simple in design but collect information detailed enough to be useful for archiving and investigative purposes and operations planning efforts. All data should be analyzed, evaluated, and reported to management and acted upon as required.

Once collected, incident data is subjected to asset protection analysis to determine security loss prevention and asset protection measures should be added or redirected. The asset protection analysis is the core of the loss control program planning process and provides much of the input for planning meetings. The gathered data will offer the security manager many options for addressing security concerns. The manager chooses which options to institute by weighing the effectiveness and cost of the countermeasure against the cost or potential loss caused by the problem.

MAINTAINING COMMUNICATIONS INTEGRITY

It is important to realize that the time a security force is least likely to get accurate, up-to-date information is in an emergency situation, when they most need it. Communications can be very difficult in an emergency for a variety of reasons, including varying frequencies, dead zones, cross talk, and overloaded circuits. The security manager's most important priority is to maintain connection between the security officers and the base station and dispatcher. Another priority is to stay connected to responding emergency (police, fire, and medical) personnel. Giving emergency personnel access to facility two-way radios or communicating by telephone usually handles this.

OPENING AND CLOSING BUILDINGS

The lack of clear operational procedures for periods when a building is open and when it is closed can lead to significant security vulnerabilities. Therefore, it is recommended that each facility develop operational procedures for both open and closed periods, taking the following into account:

- ✦ Which personnel are allowed access after hours and for what reasons?
- ✦ Are any doors to be left open, and why? Are they to be monitored electronically or by a guard?
- ✦ Are cleaning crews bonded? What, if any areas, are to be secured from access to the crew?
- ✦ Is there a process for receipt and shipment of mail and packages after hours? Where and under what conditions?
- ✦ Cargo and loading docks are extremely vulnerable. Are they to operate after hours? Will a guard be present?
- ✦ Is there a checklist for opening and closing the building and areas within the building?

BUILDING TOURS

Security personnel using a guard tour system conduct building safety and security tours on a regular basis. A predetermined series of stations throughout the facility require frequent checks. The guard uses a wand to record each visit at each security checkpoint, and this information is then electronically downloaded to a central file. Although a building access control system can be used for building tours, it is advisable to establish a separate system designed specifically for building tours because these offer more options for recording, processing, and archiving the tours and can be automatically integrated with other building control functions such as maintenance.

STAFFING REQUIREMENTS

Staffing requirements for a security operation vary, depending on the type of business or organization, the size of the facilities to be protected, the variety (and type) of assets to be protected, and other variables. A security staff can be retained through a professional security company or hired and trained as a proprietary entity. The present trend is toward in-house staffing for general security, with specific services provided by technology applications and contract guard operations.

As a general rule, the security budget is approximately 1.2 to 1.5 percent of total operating costs, depending not only on the factors cited but on the level of security protection that management is comfortable with. The process of security analysis seeks to achieve optimum security in a cost-effective manner. Therefore, it is generally recommended that a company or organization define a minimum number of security personnel to provide a level of protection commensurate with the company size, valued asset protection needs, combined production and retail activities (as applicable), and liability concerns.

Another staffing consideration that some organizations might consider is integrating security, safety, and possibly workers' compensation functions into a single department. These functions are similar in terms of employee contact, procedures, documentation, monitoring, and need for investigations.

Emergency Preparedness Planning

Research conducted following the January 1994 Northridge earthquake in California indicates that a company that is adequately prepared for emergencies experiences faster recovery and operational continuation after a disaster. For example, landmark medical facilities in California suffered major nonstructural damage to their equipment and systems in recent earthquakes. When this damage was coupled with lack of preparedness, the facilities were shut down from days to months.

Most business owners are not aware of either the potential for damage to their facilities or the accompanying business interruption. This lack of understanding, fear of the unknown, and lack of knowledge about how to proceed once the problem is recognized have left many companies unprepared for an emergency. This lack of preparation can cause business failure or the increased costs of an extended recovery period.

To begin planning for emergencies, companies must learn to identify the facility risks and hazards facing today's businesses, determine what types of training are useful, and categorize and deal with risks rationally. The goal is to be reasonably prepared and not to be swept up in a wave of hysteria.

Business owners can take advantage of one component of human behavior found in the aftermath of every disaster or stressful event.

Steps for Emergency Planning

The business environment today is constantly changing, and natural and man-made hazards appear to be increasing. For companies anticipating the future, emergency preparedness planning and training require a continuous cycle of activity, consisting of these steps:

1. Evaluate the risks a business faces.
2. Determine how these risks may affect business operations.
3. Develop steps to mitigate, respond to, work around, or reduce these risks.
4. Write an emergency plan.
5. Train employees to deal with emergencies.
6. Test the plan to make sure it meets objectives.
7. Revise the plan by reviewing these steps from the beginning.

Although some individuals respond to such events in an irrational and inappropriate manner, there are always others who rise above the chaos and respond with calm and clear thinking. When a company can find these persons and get them trained and involved in recovery activities, it can improve its chances for a successful recovery effort and reduce the recovery period.

Emergency preparedness plans should strive to achieve the following:

✦ Guide the goals and activities of the business in preparing, training, mitigating, responding to, and recovering from major emergencies.

✦ Establish an organizational structure and team to carry out an immediate response in the aftermath of an event.

✦ Frame a model for the creation of business contingency plans for operational units throughout the organization and its subsidiaries.

An emergency preparedness plan should be a living document, intended to be altered as requirements change. Because of this, at any given time, specific sections of the document may be missing, in transition, or under development.

DETERMINING POTENTIAL SECURITY INCIDENTS AND RESPONSES

Identifying security risks and determining their effect on an enterprise and its facilities are the most fundamental components of any security planning process. Recent events, both man-made and natural, have increased awareness of the need for businesses and other entities to prepare for emergencies. However, the same events have also increased the hype and fear that may cause business managers to have unrealistic views of such risks.

A list of potential events—such as fires, windstorms, earthquakes, bomb blasts, volcanic eruptions, electrical outages, weather-related emergencies, terrorist activities, major network or database failures, and localized flooding precipitated by broken water mains or malfunctioning systems—must be closely and objectively evaluated. Each potential event should be discussed in relation to the following factors:

◆ *Possibility of occurrence.* Is there a realistic possibility that such an event could occur at or near a facility?

◆ *Risk to or potential effect on the business.* Could such an event adversely affect the business and its continual operations, clients, customers, suppliers, vendors, employees, and the environment in which the business operates?

◆ *Options for mitigation.* Are there realistic options for mitigating such adverse effects?

◆ *Cost of mitigation versus cost of doing nothing.* What would be the cost of each mitigation option versus the cost of recovering from damage caused by not employing the option? Does it make economic sense to try to mitigate damage, or is doing nothing an option? What steps other than a complete mitigation strategy could reduce the risks?

For additional information on risk analysis, refer to the Federal Emergency Management Administration (FEMA) "Emergency Management Guide for Business & Industry," sections 1 and 3, available through the FEMA Web site at www.fema.gov/library/ bizindex.htm.

As an example, a business in a building more than 20 years old, in a downtown setting on the West Coast of the United States, has a high risk of damage due to fire, severe weather, or seismic event. However, depending on the type of business and its proximity to other high-risk businesses or organizations (e.g., a government facility or major tourist attraction), the risk of impact from a terrorist attack is comparatively minimal. In this example, concentrating all emergency preparedness and response activities on mitigating terrorist activities would be a waste of resources. However, investigating the facility's potential for damage from a fire, severe weather, or seismic event, and making appropriate plans might help prevent a business from failing or incurring major losses. Once a list of possible hazards is developed, it should be reviewed to determine whether existing organizational resources available on a day-to-day basis could deal with them. If not, it may be necessary to develop a separate response mechanism.

IDENTIFYING AN INCIDENT THRESHOLD

An incident threshold identifies the line between security incidents an organization handles as a matter of course and emergencies that require prescribed responses. Establishing an incident threshold for an organization helps security staff plan for and respond to emergencies that arise. Distinguishing between "Level I" and "Level II" incidents simplifies use of an incident threshold.

Level I encompasses common security incidents that occur as part of day-to-day business operations. Incidents that fall into this category include minor occurrences at a single business location; incidents that have no impact on employees, revenue, customers, or customer service; incidents that require only routine departmental and operational involvement; and events that local management staff and/or support personnel are able to handle. A Level I incident does not result in business loss, danger to employees, media interest, or danger to public life and safety. A bomb threat is considered a Level I event and should be handled using site-specific bomb threat response procedures.

A severe storm that affects the operation of a facility is another example of a Level I incident. The local business manager can mitigate this situation without business loss to the entire organization. In this case, business, facility, or security managers initiate a Level I response. During or immediately after the event, activities are documented, and corporate risk and facility management departments are notified.

Level II incidents have the potential to overwhelm local management and day-to-day business operations. Such incidents include those that may result in death or severe injury to an employee or visitor on company property; a major emergency that affects multiple buildings, business units, or operational systems; incidents that disrupt revenue or customer service; and incidents that cause a high probability of employee or public alarm and media interest. Examples include a major fire, a hazardous material (HAZMAT) spill, or an earthquake of 6.5 or greater on the Richter scale. In these cases, the company emergency director (ED) determines if a Level II response is warranted. If so, the ED starts up an emergency operations center (EOC).

The incident flowchart shown in Figure 8.1 highlights a sample process for event reporting and decision making.

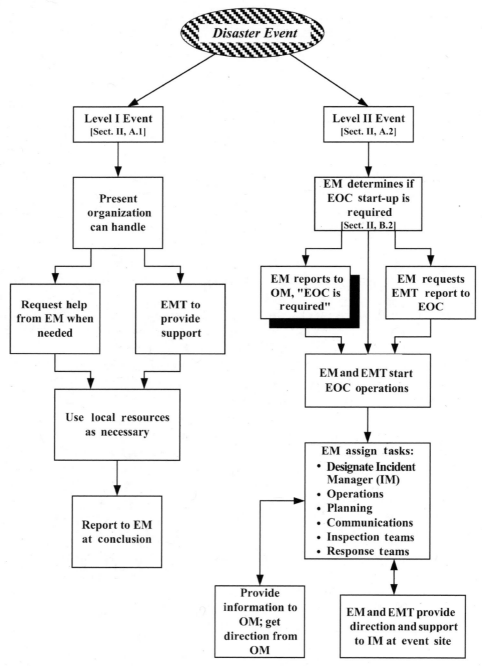

FIGURE 8.1

Incident flowchart

RESPONSE PARTICIPANTS AND TEAMS

A number of organizational and individual respondents should be trained and ready to respond to an emergency. These individuals may include an emergency director (ED), an emergency management organization (EMO), an incident manager (IM), and corporate executive management (CEM). The role and responsibilities of each is detailed below:

❖ Emergency Director (ED)

The ED is responsible for managing an organization's overall response and recovery efforts, for activating the EOC, and for assigning specific positions as needed. Several individuals may need to be identified to serve as ED, and a clear succession list for the team of emergency directors should be created. Major ED responsibilities include the following:

- ✦ Ensure emergency respondents' safety during an incident.
- ✦ Determine whether EOC start-up is warranted.
- ✦ Establish immediate priorities consistent with corporate policies.
- ✦ Determine incident objectives and strategies for response.
- ✦ Establish level of organization needed and continuously monitor the operation and effectiveness of the organization.
- ✦ Ensure that the IM mobilizes the response teams.
- ✦ Manage and plan meetings, as required.
- ✦ Approve and implement incident action plans (IAPs).
- ✦ Manage operations functions and coordinate activities of all assigned staff when no operations chief has been appointed.
- ✦ Approve requests from business operations for additional resources or for release of resources.

In response to Level II incidents, the ED quickly directs the EOC to coordinate and assign available resources and to manage the disaster effort. For large-scale incidents, the ED implements the overall policy and strategy, as set by the CEM.

❖ Emergency Management Organization (EMO).

An EMO consists of staff assigned from facility, risk management, and other business units of the company involved in some aspect of the emergency. The ED chairs the EMO and reports to the CEM for direction and priority on activities.

At the EOC, the ED assigns management of required missions to members of the EMO who are present. These assignments may include the IM and planning, logistics, and communications chiefs, among others.

❖ Incident Manager (IM)

The ED will assign an on-site IM at the onset of an event. The IM is selected from the site business manager, general manager, or other top manager designees. The IM is responsible for all activities at the incident site. The ED and EMO support the IM with resources and staff as necessary to respond to the incident.

For Level I incidents, the IM is responsible for establishing an incident command post at or near the incident, determining tactics and needed resources, and personally directing response teams.

❖ Corporate Executive Management (CEM)

Overall control and management of the corporation during an emergency rests with the CEM. The ED is responsible for managing activities related to emergency response; therefore, an order of succession must be established for senior management. A corporate succession list might begin with the chairman and chief executive officer (CEO), followed by the senior vice president or chief financial officer (CFO), general counsel, facilities vice president, human resources vice president, technology vice president, and finally the operations vice president.

❖ Coordination with Business Units

All incident response activities affecting or requiring involvement by individual departments or business units are coordinated through the business unit manager assigned to the EMO by the business unit vice president on the CEM team. The ED designates the on-site general manager, business unit manager, or a manager they assign as the IM to coordinate on-site response activities. The business unit manager updates the EMO on resources and manpower available during the operation of the EOC.

❖ Response and Recovery Teams

Hands-on, on-site response support is provided by a combination of facility staff and risk management and other business unit response teams. With support from the EMO, site response teams are created under the direction of the IM to handle requests and tasks assigned by the ED. The ED and the IM, with authorization from the CEM, retain resources required from outside the company. Figure 8.2 outlines response activities.

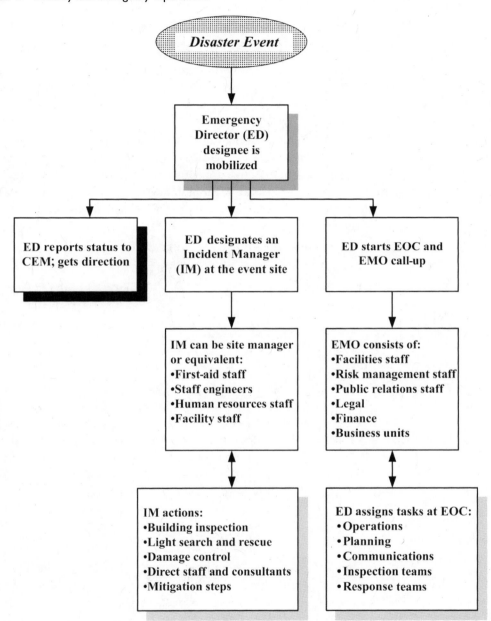

FIGURE 8.2

Response activities

DEFINING PREPAREDNESS, MITIGATION, RESPONSE, AND RECOVERY

An emergency—any unplanned event that causes damage or loss of life, production, resources, or assets—can be managed effectively only if the resources and staff required for a response have been identified, organized, and trained in advance.

Studies of past disasters indicate that the best way to ensure an organization's rapid recovery and continuing success in the aftermath of a disaster is to have an effective and practiced emergency response plan in place before the event occurs. Understanding and adhering to the following four principles of effective emergency preparedness is an important part of this planning:

- ✦ Preparedness through training, planning, and practice
- ✦ Hazard reduction through mitigation
- ✦ Prompt, skilled response
- ✦ Swift, efficient, and safe recovery

❖ Preparedness

Disaster preparedness requires evaluation of risks, determination of potential impact, and development of programs to train employees for effective, successful disaster response and recovery. Preparedness activities include conducting a vulnerability analysis, assessing potential damage from risks, developing emergency response plans, organizing response and recovery activities, conducting exercises to evaluate and improve plans, and continuous updating of emergency response plans.

❖ Mitigation

It is essential to identify and eliminate or reduce hazards to a facility. Areas of concern include organizational (human resources), economic, and physical (structural and nonstructural) aspects of facility operations. Physical aspects include structural systems, HVAC equipment, piping, transformers, lighting and ceiling systems, computer equipment, electrical connectivity, and evacuation routes. Evaluating whether nonstructural equipment and other elements are adequately attached and supported is also important. For all leased facilities, mitigation efforts must be coordinated with the building owner or management team.

❖ Response

After a disaster, short-term activities deal directly with the immediate effects of an event. These activities include assessing damage, creating response teams, mobilizing first-aid responders, evacuation management, employee/supplier/customer/PR communication, search-and-rescue operations, securing facilities, investigating structural integrity, and requesting shoring of structures to prevent additional damage or tagging to prevent loss of life. The responsibility for tagging (evaluation and identification) of damaged buildings lies with the building department of the jurisdiction in which the facility is located; it cannot be accomplished by building owners themselves.

❖ Recovery

Long-term steps are essential to bring facilities and operations back to normal. These may include relocating some or all building functions, organizing and managing damaged equipment and losses, replacing equipment lost during the disaster, documenting and managing a potential insurance claim, altering operations and work schedules, providing stress reduction programs for employees, and reviewing and updating emergency response plans. Prearranged contracting to allow short-term access to similar facilities outside the event area will help reduce the time needed for recovery.

Enterprises that rely solely on leased space to conduct business may want to discuss emergency arrangements with the owners of their buildings. Most building leases today allow the building owners from 60 to 180 days to decide whether to repair a badly damaged facility, a decision that often depends on the outcome of the insurance claim. Because most businesses cannot survive without access to their place of business for more than a few days, waiting two months or more for access to company property would be untenable. One proposal would be to change the lease language to allow the tenant to take whatever steps it deems necessary, at its own expense, to gain access to its place of business, records, or inventory. Once the insurance issues have been resolved, the business owners and building owners can determine how to address questions about cost.

RAPID INSPECTIONS AND DETAILED REVIEWS OF FACILITIES

Using trained on-site staff, an IM assembles damage assessment teams (DATs) and dispatches them to various areas in a facility to conduct postevent assessments. A rapid inspection form (RIF), illustrated in Figure 8.3, is used to indicate the essential information required within an hour of the onset of an event. DATs focus on life safety and the status of essential systems, looking for these types of problems:

+ Overall structural hazards

+ Specific structural hazards

+ Nonstructural hazards, interior

+ Operational hazards, equipment

+ Lifeline hazards (utility connections to the facility)

+ Key electrical systems

+ Life/safety hazards

For each property, the facility manager or facility coordinator develops a number of damage assessment survey routes. These routes are created to quickly lead trained personnel to important parts of the facility. The number of routes depends on the size of the facility and the availability of trained personnel to accomplish this task. For example, a large distribution center consisting of three separate building components (boxes) should have three inspection teams, each with its own inspection route. Each route should take a team (a minimum of two inspectors) by the essential structural (gravity and lateral systems) and nonstructural (equipment, utilities, and safety systems) building elements located in their portion of the property.

An overall assessment of a facility or some of its components is required, in addition to the quick review of major systems just described. A rapid assessment process, resulting in completion of a RIF, provides one or more of the following recommendations:

+ *No further action required.* Conditions encountered did not necessitate further review or action and can be remedied using normal company operations and procedures.

+ *Detailed evaluation required.* Conditions observed may be beyond the knowledge level of the reviewer. In such cases, further review is necessary to identify damage not apparent with rapid investigation techniques. Such damage could be severe enough to cause life safety or other hazards but require specific understanding of equipment, a component, or the type of hazard to determine the level of concern. Detailed evaluation must occur promptly (within 12 to 24 hours, if possible) and should involve a team of individuals with specific expertise as identified during the rapid

The Applied Technology Council has developed a damage assessment methodology for evaluating the structural integrity of buildings that survive an earthquake. The principles elaborated in ATC-20 can be applied to inspecting property after any emergency incident.

ABC Company Rapid Inspection Form

Inspector's Name:	Date & Time:
Cell Phone:	E-mail:
Facility Name:	Telephone No.:
Facility Type: Facility Size:	Facility Age:

Structural Systems, Gravity: Status:	Nonstructural Systems: Status:
Exterior Columns	Ceiling/M&E Fixtures
Interior Columns	Cladding/Glazing
Beams	Exterior Walls
Roof Diaphragm	Interior Walls
Floor Diaphragms	Parapets/Ornamentation
Other	Stairs/Exits
Structural Systems, Lateral: Status:	Other
Foundation Systems	**Lifeline Systems: Status:**
Braced Frames	Communication Systems
Moment Frames	Computer Systems
Roof Diaphragms	Electrical Systems
Floor Diaphragms	Fire Suppression Systems
Precast Concrete Elements	Gas Systems
Shear Walls	Mechanical Systems
Other	Plumbing Systems
	Other

Geotechnical Hazards:	
Slope Failure/Landslide	Ground Failure/Liquefaction
Ground Failure/Subsidence	Other

1. No Further Action Required:
Describe the situation:
2. Detailed Evaluation Required:
Describe the type of evaluation:
3. Barricades and Closures Required:
Describe the location and type:
4. Utility Disconnect Required:
Describe the location and type:
5. Immediate Facility Closure Required:
Describe the reason:
Additional Comments:

FIGURE 8.3

Sample rapid inspection form (RIF)

assessment. The expertise required may include any of the following:

—Structural engineering
—Automation and distribution system
—Mechanical and HVAC engineering
—Environmental remediation
—Electrical high-voltage engineering
—Low voltage, communications, telecommunications, and security systems
—Piping and utilities distribution
—Chemical hazard spills

The emergency director evaluates the availability of such expertise within the company and provides appropriate contacts and contracts to augment available resources when necessary.

✦ *Barricades and closures required.* The hazard area must be secured to protect employees and the public.

✦ *Utility disconnection required.* Further action is required to disconnect a utility that was damaged and is leaking due to an incident. This recommendation also indicates that the assessment team did not have the means or the knowledge to address the condition and that immediate action must be taken.

✦ *Immediate facility closure and evacuation required.* A major life safety hazard is present and requires the immediate evacuation of the facility and expert response to remedy the danger. Such required action should be immediate and accomplished in the shortest possible time using all means available.

MEANS OF COMMUNICATION

Recent events such as major earthquakes in California and severe storms in Washington State have demonstrated the problems associated with overuse and damage to a communications infrastructure. All modern means of communication have vulnerabilities that can be exploited or taxed during an emergency event. Local telephone infrastructures, often damaged during natural or man-made emergency events, can take from days to weeks to recover. Although cellular phone and pager systems fare better, the greater number of users in the immediate postevent environment can shut them down. Internet services have performed well in immediate and adjacent event areas. Several levels of advance planning are necessary to ensure some level of required communication during an emergency.

First, the organization must create a line of authority and a database of contact information. To accomplish this, each business unit should create its own line of authority and distribute contact information in both online and hard-copy form to EMO members. In addition, a telephone "tree" should be created to make it easier to contact essential employees.

Outside the region, contact telephone numbers should be set up to give employees information about what to do in the aftermath of an event and to disseminate general information on the status of activities and expected recovery times. This telephone system also gives managers who are unable to meet in person a way to set up conference calls immediately following an event.

The organization's public information department should be ready to provide updates to the media if the nature of an event creates interest from investors, customers, suppliers, and other parties. A prerecorded statement may be the first step, followed by regular news release packages prepared by the public information or legal departments, as necessary.

Several direct outside telephone lines not connected to the facility telephone switch system, and several mobile satellite telephone systems can provide an additional means of communication during postevent activities.

EDUCATION, TRAINING, AND EXERCISES

Creation of a plan is the first step toward emergency preparedness, but once created, such plans must be reviewed, tested, and continually updated. Training programs for employees and management are essential to keep staff engaged and ready to respond to events.

EMO members and other staff respondents should be trained in basic first aid, CPR, and light search-and-rescue operations. These training sessions are available from local American Red Cross chapters.

EMO members and other respondents should also be familiar with the principles of the Incident Command System (ICS). ICS is widely used by local, state, and federal emergency management organizations to respond to natural and man-made disasters. ICS training can be obtained through FEMA or local and state emergency management departments.

In addition, emergency respondents and facility and risk management staff should be trained using the Applied Technology Council (ATC) course methodologies for building evaluation and screening (www.atcouncil.org). The two courses described here were initially designed to provide a methodology for seismic evaluation of buildings; however, they are now widely used for all building damage evaluations:

✦ **Rapid Visual Screening of Buildings for Potential Seismic Hazards, ATC-21**, is based on FEMA document 154, published July 1988. The course includes a methodology for rapid evaluation of buildings using a scoring system for a building's lateral structural system and other important factors.

✦ **Procedures for Postearthquake Safety Evaluation of Buildings, ATC-20,** developed by ATC in 1989, provides a methodology for evaluating and tagging buildings following any event that causes structural damage and instability problems. Using this methodology, each building is evaluated and tagged to identify its damage state with a green (inspected), yellow (limited entry), or red (unsafe) tag.

Testing and exercising an emergency plan on an annual or biannual schedule ensures it will be reviewed and updated. The exercise should include a plausible event scenario developed by in-house staff or an outside consultant. This exercise should include minute-by-minute activities outlined to match potential event problems. It is helpful to have an exercise management team run the exercise.

The exercise management team plays the roles of outside resources, suppliers, emergency contacts, and other outside influences that would typically be involved in such an event. An evaluation team monitors and documents the exercise activities, and this information is reviewed against the expected and planned response steps in the emergency plan. Corrections are made to the plan, or additional training is provided to the emergency team in response to performance in the exercise.

Security operations and emergency preparedness will remain important concerns for many building owners in the future. By helping building owners anticipate security and emergency events and how to respond to them, architects are better able to choose design options that support the security operational and emergency preparedness needs of their clients.

9 Putting Security into Practice

Joseph Brancato, AIA

The previous chapters cover topics that include understanding threats, defining security needs and requirements, and developing security design concepts and strategies, among others. Practicing architects, at some point, also need to address the implications of threading security into the day-to-day business operations of their firms and in the delivery process of their services. This chapter provides practical advice on both of these aspects of incorporating security into architecture practice.

Security can only be achieved through constant change, through discarding old ideas that have outlived their usefulness and adapting others to current facts.
—*William O. Douglas*

Security Issues in Firm Operations

Regardless of firm size or focus, effective integration of security into architecture practice touches upon various business issues in a firm's operations. Such issues include acquiring needed skills and resources, identifying and selecting security professionals, contracting for security services, and determining professional liability and other insurance coverage.

ACQUIRING SKILLS AND RESOURCES

At this point, there are few formalized initiatives to help architects enhance their security education or training. However, much information about

Appendix A contains a list
of associations and other
entities that deal with
security issues. Appendix
B lists books and other
publications that archi-
tects may wish to refer to
for further information.

security is available, although there is no single clearinghouse for data. Architects generally work on their own to acquire skills, resources, and information through research and networking and by attending conferences, seminars, and workshops.

As with all specialized areas of knowledge, architects can gradually accumulate skills and knowledge as they work with independent consultants, security specialists, and security staff in client organizations. Such contacts afford prime opportunities for learning by providing an in-depth look at how security issues are analyzed and applied.

SECURITY CONSULTANTS

The Internet serves as a
useful gateway to security
resources and informa-
tion. Bear in mind, how-
ever, that information on
the Internet varies, and
the accuracy and com-
pleteness of the data may
need to be qualified.

Security consultants provide management consulting services specializing in security; loss prevention or security training; and security equipment system design, evaluation, and specification. Some security consultants provide architecture and design services to clients and architects. However, the focus of security consultants' efforts is to determine the security-related needs of their clients and to provide advice, information, and recommendations to clients. Security consultants offer their services by market or industry, by type of services, or by type of asset to be protected.

✦ *Certified Protection Professionals.* Architects are turning more often to a relatively small but qualified cadre of security professionals known as Certified Protection Professionals (CPPs), who are certified by ASIS International. These individuals generally have broad experience in the public and/or private sectors and, more often than not, bring a wealth of design project experiences to the architect. An increasing number of CPPs specialize in complex security design and integration projects, offering these services through practices similar in scope and depth to the architect's own practice.

✦ *Physical security professionals.* ASIS International is developing and introducing a certification program for an additional group of security professionals whose primary responsibility is to conduct threat assessments; design integrated security systems that include people and procedures; or install, operate, and maintain those systems.

✦ *Blast design consultants.* Few architecture firms have experience designing structures to resist the effects of bomb blasts. Blast design consultants offer analysis and design services to mitigate the direct and secondary effects of blast loads on structures. The blast consultant usually works with the architect and the structural

Categories and Types of Security Consulting Services

Services by Market or Industry
Aerospace
Commercial
Communications
Computer/data
Conventions
Criminal justice
Cultural
Education
Entertainment
Financial
Foreign embassy
Gambling
Government
Health care
High-rise offices
Hotels and resorts
Insurance
Manufacturing
Museums
Parking
Petroleum/oil/gas
Pharmaceutical
Residential
Retail
Sports
Transportation
Utilities
Warehousing

Types of Security Consulting Services
Antiterrorism
Classified programs
Counterespionage
Counterterrorism

Crime and risk statistics
Crisis management
Disaster planning and recovery
Executive protection
Expert witness testimony
Forensic science
Hostage negotiations
Investigation
Loss prevention
Manpower resource allocation and
  distribution
Personnel management
Policies and procedures
Program design
Project management
Site survey
Structural and blast mitigation
Systems design
Threat/risk/vulnerability analyses
Training

**Security Services by Assets
to Be Protected**
Artifacts
Buildings and construction sites
Data
Executives/VIPs/families
Intellectual property
Major sporting or other events
Negotiable assets
Nuclear materials
Pipelines
Power and communication grids
Priceless objects
Trade secrets

engineer during the design phase of a project, but the collaboration may also extend to other engineering consultants and landscape architects. While there are no certifying bodies for blast consultants, such consultants should have specific background and experience pertaining to the structural behavior of buildings under blast conditions

◆ *Engineering consultants.* An increasing number of engineering consultants are adding security design and engineering capabilities to their practices. While engineering consultants are typically members of a project team, their participation may be deeper on security-enhanced projects. Decisions regarding building systems, construction materials, air filtration systems, and other elements can affect the cost and effectiveness of implementing security-enhanced design.

◆ *Professional security systems integrators.* Because a building security management system is another form of building control, many clients and developers prefer to integrate the security function into one seamless building control system. Professional security systems integrators can help achieve such integration, which in turn allows for higher security, lower costs, and greater convenience. Because these individuals are well versed in all aspects of building security technologies and a variety of building systems, they can provide valuable input during security audits and during the design phase and can even install security systems after design has been completed.

Reputable integrators are authorized manufacturer installers trained in the systems they install, and they may warrant the entire system (as opposed to a manufacturer's warranty for pieces of the system). Most clients hire security designers with objective viewpoints to complete their systems design and then bid the design to at least three qualified integrators who can meet the specifications. Some clients, however, prefer to go directly to a single integrator, mainly because of a prior relationship or experience.

Although many security consultants have federal government, federal law enforcement, or military backgrounds, an increasing number of security experts emanate from the professional engineering, private security, or aerospace security sectors. As with any area of expertise, seeking recommendations from fellow practitioners is a good way to find a security specialist. In addition, several organizations (e.g., ASIS International and the International Association of Professional Security Consultants) can offer guidance and potential candidates. Security industry directories are another source. These include the *Security Industry Buyers Guide* (www.securitymanagement.com) and the *SDM/Security Buyers Guide* (www.securitymagazine.com). Security directors at larger client organizations can also be a source of recommendations.

❖ Qualifications of Security Consultants

As a rule, a security consultant should have demonstrable experience in performing threat, vulnerability, and risk analyses. Look for a consultant with a commanding knowledge of the security equipment types, systems integration methodologies, and engineering practice required to successfully translate a client's security needs into working security systems.

It is important to confirm the credentials of a security consultant (e.g., CPP, registered architect, or professional engineer). Some consultants may have professional memberships in organizations such as ASIS International or the International Association of Professional Security Consultants. However, there may be only a limited number of consultants among the membership of these associations with the qualifications for a specific project type.

Although truly experienced security consultants offer a breadth and depth of expertise that can be applied to virtually any type of project, it is best when a consultant has experience working in a client's project type. Personality is another consideration because the security consultant will work with sensitive information, collaborate with a variety of team members with different perspectives, and have to communicate accurately and comprehensively. A final consideration is whether a consultant carries professional liability insurance, and, if so, in what amount.

Other items to discuss with candidates include the following:

- ◆ Consultant's affiliation with security products and services, if any
- ◆ Type and extent of consultant's liability coverage
- ◆ Amount of time consultant dedicates to security consulting
- ◆ Types of work the consultant subcontracts to others
- ◆ Outstanding claims or lawsuits against the consultant
- ◆ Consultant's prior experience on a project of similar type and scope

❖ Cost of Consulting Services

The cost of security consulting services varies, depending on the nature and scope of a project. Typically, however, security design services range

When a security consultant contracts directly with the owner, the architect should allow adequate time in the owner-architect agreement to properly coordinate consultant services.

from 6 percent to 12 percent of the projected installed cost of the security systems. The fee may include security programming and a report, although a fee for these services may be charged separately. Likewise, bidding and negotiation services and construction administration services are either priced separately or wrapped into the cost for total security design and integration services. In either case, construction administration costs can vary significantly depending on the number and type of site visits required.

CONTRACTING FOR SECURITY SERVICES

Clients may contract for security evaluation and planning services through the architect, or obtain those services directly from a security consultant or specialist. Regardless of the contractual arrangement, these services should generally provide some or all of the following:

- ✦ A security assessment, consisting of asset, threat, vulnerability, and risk analyses
- ✦ An existing facility survey of the project site, building exterior and interior, mechanical and electrical systems, data and communications features, and an assets inventory
- ✦ A facility analysis of how the building is to be occupied and how its various functions will support owner and tenant operations
- ✦ A risk assessment, which determines the level of security required by the client for the project
- ✦ Development of security design requirements

As in any agreement, it is important to properly characterize the scope and nature of the services the architect will provide. As always, an architect should avoid providing any professional services that are beyond his or her expertise. Whether the security consultant is retained by the architect or directly by the client, the architect should determine the extent to which the consultant is insured for professional liability. When the architect retains the security consultant, the architect should also confirm whether such services are covered under its professional liability insurance policy. (Liability insurance is discussed in more detail below.)

One reason for a client to seek security enhancement is to reduce insurance costs, and tenants in a building with enhanced security levels may get reductions on their insurance rates to cover their losses. Many leading insurers have professionals on staff schooled in risk management who are more than willing to assist their clients with risk mitigation. Working with these individuals may help reduce insurance premiums.

Terrorism Insurance

The Building Owners and Managers Association (BOMA) International surveyed its members in September 2002 concerning the availability of terrorism insurance. An overwhelming majority of respondents cited difficulty in obtaining adequate coverage at affordable rates, and 27 percent of respondents were unable to obtain terrorism insurance at any cost. Of the 73 percent who were able to secure coverage, 80 percent incurred some or all of the following: higher premiums; caps on coverage; higher deductibles; cancellation clauses of 60 days or fewer; and exclusions for chemical, biological, or radiological acts. Increases in premiums ranged from an average low of about 20 percent to a high of 200 percent. For 69 percent of the survey respondents, a building's geographic location was among the factors that made it more difficult to buy insurance.

This BOMA survey provided clear evidence that insurance coverage for terrorist events has been unavailable at any price for one-fourth of office building customers and that the product that has been available does not meet the needs of building owners and managers. The outlook improved markedly, however, with the November 26, 2002, enactment of the Terrorism Risk Insurance Act. This act nullifies terrorism exclusions on professional liability policies as well as commercial property policies.

The new law, to remain in effect for three years (allowing the private insurance market for terrorism coverage to develop), makes available up to $100 billion in federal funds to cover losses from a terrorist attack. The federal government is to pay for 90 percent of losses above the deductible (set at 7 percent of premiums the first year, 10 percent the second year, and 15 percent the third year). Among the provisions of the law, insurers are to offer coverage for losses from terrorist acts that is basically the same as the terms, amounts, and limitations applicable to losses from other events.

When security services are part of the architect's services, the scope can be delineated in the architect's contract with the owner, for example, in AIA Document B141, Standard Form of Agreement between Owner and Architect. AIA Document B205, which is the scope document for Part 2 of the B141, offers a possible scope for security services.

When an architect engages a consultant to perform a security assessment or assist with security design and engineering services, documents from the C series of AIA documents can be used as a basis for defining the architect-consultant relationship. These agreements include C141, Standard Form of Agreement between Architect and Consultant; C142, Abbreviated Standard Form of Agreement between Architect and Consultant; and C727, Standard Form of Agreement between Architect and Consultant for Special Services.

Failure to properly identify and detail the scope of security services in a contract can undermine the overall budget and schedule, resulting in delivery of a project with less than the original planned content. When a change in scope is driven by enhanced security needs, the architect should provide a clear description of any modifications and suggested options, delineate the impact each would have on the project schedule and/or cost, and identify the risks associated with each. The architect should also suggest a clearly defined process for reviewing and approving the alternatives.

Architects who rely on the client or an unqualified security consultant to provide direction for security may find that major changes to the security scope are needed in later stages of design or construction. This may be due to an improper security assessment or an insufficient understanding of how security technologies and operations are to be integrated into the project.

PROFESSIONAL LIABILITY INSURANCE

Some security consultants carry insurance for security consulting services only and may not carry liability insurance for design and engineering services. It is advisable to confirm whether a consultant has such insurance before retaining him or her for design services.

In professional service agreements, it is important for architects to properly characterize the scope and nature of the services they will provide. They should also verify with their insurance carrier whether their liability coverage includes security services. Whether retained by the architect or directly by the client, the security consultant should be required to provide a reasonable level of professional liability insurance.

Historically, legislatures and courts have had little occasion to provide guidance on the legal aspects of designing for enhanced security, and this area of law is much in flux. Following are a few steps architects can take to protect themselves:

✦ Obtain knowledge of security adequate to meet your firm's professional responsibilities.

✦ Use care in qualifying consultants for security services.

✦ Address issues regarding provision of security services or inclusion of security features in architectural design that may concern scope, indemnities, and other factors that could affect the architect's liability to clients and others.

✦ Recognize that clients with high-risk facilities may not want to divulge the security measures and technologies used in their facilities. This could affect the types of information that can be released and the methods used to convey project data.

Ideally, the client will indemnify the architect from claims that might occur as a result of assessment or program evaluation by a security consultant, provided the architect follows a professional standard of care in implementing the consultant's recommendations during design and construction. However, because a third party is not a party to the owner-architect agreement, it can bring legal action if an event causes damages or loss of life or property. An indemnification from the client can provide necessary protection to the architect.

Prior to passage of the Terrorism Risk Insurance Act on November 26, 2002, some carriers that offer professional liability insurance to U.S. design professionals excluded damages caused by incidents of terrorism from their policies. The provisions of the act voided such exclusions with respect to foreign acts of terrorism within the United States (except in the case of air carriers, vessels, or occurrences on the premises of a U.S. mission). The insurers had 90 days from November 26, 2002, to advise their policyholders of the additional premium they would charge to provide coverage in conformance with the act. Upon receipt of the notice from the insurer, the policyholder had 30 days to accept the coverage and pay the required additional premium. If the policyholder declined the coverage, the exclusion would apply. Because of the complexity of professional liability issues, architects are strongly urged to consult both their attorneys and their professional liability insurance brokers and carriers for guidance.

Security Issues in Project Delivery

Security should be considered from the outset of each project and evaluated throughout delivery of project services. This means that attention is paid to security in all phases of a project, beginning with organizing and teaming efforts and continuing through programming, design, construction documentation, construction administration, and postconstruction services.

ORGANIZING AND TEAMING EFFORTS

On the cutting edge of the new frontier of security integration, architects increasingly rely on specialists—such as security consultants, code consultants, and engineering consultants—to help them understand what needs to be done to incorporate security in their designs. In that process, security looms as a truly significant element. Once the right team of experts and client representatives is assembled, dealing with security becomes a matter of organizing the knowledge, implementing the process, and identifying what needs to be protected.

When to Address Security Issues

It is never too early in the design process to raise the question of security. Rather than asking a client whether a project has security issues, ask what level of security is needed. If the level of security required exceeds the architect's expertise, the architect should promptly bring in outside experts. From the kickoff meeting, security issues should be on the table. The architect can come prepared with a list of initial recommendations related to security and the consultants with whom the team can work.

Architects must remember that raising the issue of security with a client may result in questions the architect is neither trained nor experienced enough with security issues to answer. Appropriate and balanced security responses can be achieved only through analysis and assessment of a complex set of personal and physical variables. Qualified, trained, and skilled security professionals can interpret the results of these studies and make recommendations for appropriate security measures.

❖ Role of Architect and Client

Every indication is that, in the future, security services will be a common part of both government and commercial projects that require higher levels of protection. In responding to this programmatic requirement, it will be important for architects to draw upon the expertise of all team members. Fortunately, collaboration is a natural part of the architectural process, so architects are skilled at facilitating and integrating the services of specialists. Close collaboration will become more critical as security, emergency, and basic building systems become more integrated. In leading the project team, the architect must be able to identify when the team has reached its collective knowledge limit and when it is necessary to pull in additional expertise (e.g., vertical transportation, kitchen design, structural/blast engineering).

Many large companies have a security staff, usually led by a security director. These individuals are closely involved in helping their organization deal with escalating incidents of terrorism, workplace violence, and cybercrime, and are responsible for providing the operational component of security programs. Their contribution can be invaluable to a design project, as they bring a knowledge of existing systems and procedures that is far broader than that of any consultant. The number and type of security personnel differ widely depending on location, property type, or industry. However, with the increasing complexity and importance of security, it is becoming more common for security directors to acquire MBAs and advanced study and certification.

❖ Coordination and Communication Procedures

Because projects with higher emphasis on security often involve multiple consultants and intensive client contact, it is critical for everyone to communicate openly, clearly, and consistently so that all parties understand all aspects of the project. To facilitate communication, the architect often becomes the organizing entity and clearinghouse for project information. Sometimes it makes sense to develop a project-specific template that gives all team members an easy-to-read snapshot of various elements of the project.

In a security-enhanced project, accurate documentation can help lessen the architect's potential exposure to liability. Throughout the project, the architect should maintain detailed records regarding the status of security-related recommendations and client decisions, as well as who was present when decisions were made. Having each participant sign off on these recommendations will minimize subsequent misunderstandings.

Ideally, it is the security consultant's responsibility to assess the threat, vulnerability, and risk levels of a project and to make a recommendation to the client based on those assessments. The client then either works with the architect to implement a design strategy to remove, alter, or reduce the risk, or accepts that level of risk. In reality, however, architects do not always work with a security consultant and, even when they do, the architect may still make recommendations about generic security issues (e.g., the different zones in an airport, a card reader in an office building, or controlling access to different floors). It is important, therefore, for an architecture firm to clearly define the scope of its services in its client-architect agreement and to require the client to make all security-related decisions.

Confidentiality Considerations

A fine balance must exist between the privacy surrounding a security strategy and the openness of information needed for project collaboration. The architect develops a coordination plan and communication procedures to accommodate the client's needs for confidentiality. Typically, once a coordination tactic has been chosen, appropriate procedures for communication logically follow.

PROGRAMMING

Perfect security is an unattainable goal. "There is no 100 percent, absolute protection," says David Morrison, executive director of AIA Pennsylvania. But it is possible to design additional degrees of security into a building, Morrison states. A security plan begins with a security assessment and a review of existing conditions. Security assessments comprise asset, vulnerability, and threat analyses, carried out using a combination of quantitative and qualitative techniques such as surveys and expert evaluations from intelligence and law enforcement bodies. The security assessment concentrates on determining real, likely, and historical risks, and the level of protection to be provided in light of these potential risks. After the security assessment has been completed, the next step is to prioritize concerns so the most critical functions can be stabilized first.

❖ How Much Security Is Enough?

Analyzing facilities comparable to the client's and benchmarking security against that of other companies in the client's industry can help establish the level of security appropriate for a project. A sufficient level of security may simply be a level higher than that of neighboring buildings. Most crimes are crimes of opportunity, and the same is likely to be true of terrorist acts. For a criminal or a terrorist, easy targets are preferable to more difficult targets. The goal is to give the impression that a client's facility is a hard target and therefore too risky for the adversary to target.

❖ Security Assessment as Part of Programming versus as a Separate Service

In the past, security assessment was exclusively the client's or building owner's ongoing assignment. Now, more integrated teams conduct the assessment as part of the programming effort. Nonetheless, the client (and especially government entities) often performs a security assessment separate from the programming process. In this situation, the assessment is typically performed by the security consultant as part of building evaluation. After the assessment, the client informs the architect of specific facility vulnerabilities and issues that must be addressed in the design.

❖ Defining Protection Levels, Strategies, and Potential Measures

The key to achieving successful security solutions for a project is establishment of an overriding security concept that is incorporated into the overall

The Client View of Security

Clients are primarily focused on the day-to-day protection of employees and facilities. Other client security matters relate to equipment to maintain business continuity, intellectual capital and data, corporate brand and image, security with a minimum of inconvenience, tailored yet flexible solutions, and cost considerations. A key concern for clients is the proper, or "sensitive," integration of security equipment and systems into the architectural environment.

Business Continuity

Loss of revenue is the obvious result when a business must suspend operations due to building damage, building systems failure, or unsafe working conditions. Beyond this direct impact on the company's bottom line, the consequences of suspending business operations include the emotional and financial effect on employees, the perception of the community, and potential disenfranchisement of clients.

Protection of Intellectual Capital and Data

Companies must protect intellectual capital, especially critical information needed to get a business up and running after a crisis. If a security breach disables data, a business can suffer huge losses. In recognition of this risk, many businesses are now focusing on plans for data redundancy on- or off-site. Driven by the growing dependence of the economy on information and communication systems, many companies are also merging IT departments and security departments. In "Give Your LAN a Hand," which appeared in the December 19, 2001, issue of *Security Management*, John Jackson describes what a company must do to ensure that computer systems will not remain out of commission too long after a disruption. The process begins with a business impact analysis to determine which functions are critical and what the company will lose when it is down. This information helps determine how quickly systems must be restarted, which is the framework for the disaster recovery program.

Design for Convenience

Security, at its core, is about education and knowledge, focusing on human behavior in a social situation. Therefore, the dynamics of anxiety and avoidance must be considered in security design. Hassles disguised as security won't improve anything. If security leads to inconvenience, people will resist it. People may tolerate inconvenience while images of terror are fresh in their minds, but standing in line on a rainy day is another matter. Indeed, congestion itself poses a security risk because intruders can use confusion to sneak through security systems. Appropriate levels of security and risk must be balanced. Holistic approaches to security can create a safer workplace at the same time they contribute to the user's sense of well-being.

Corporate Brand and Image

Placing a company's corporate identity on a building exterior can increase the risk level of the building. Each client needs to decide whether to make its corporate identity visible and accept that level of risk, or to follow a more subdued tactic. The approach the architect adopts is, in reality, a cultural issue for each client. The corporate identity chosen for the exterior of a building should enhance the corporate brand, not detract from the building, and be sensitive to the context.

Organizations that want to create an inviting atmosphere in a building may choose to put the access controls—in the form of card access or security personnel—at a point in the lobby that restricts admission to elevators and tenant spaces yet allows visitors to enter the building before facing security barriers. If a more visible security presence is desired, barriers may be located closer to entrances or even outside. Urban properties tend to opt for a more welcoming lobby atmosphere, while suburban properties often place tighter restrictions on interior access. Reduced access also allows security personnel to focus on the larger property surrounding company buildings.

Customized Yet Flexible Solutions

In the security world, one size does not fit all. Security needs vary from city to city, from building to building, and from business to business. Security elements must be customized to a specific site to create a safer workplace. Every facility needs to be examined from a variety of perspectives, specific to the user, so that design responses can be defined by its unique set of security challenges.

In one building, the owner or manager can implement only one level of security in public spaces. This level may be sufficient for other tenants but not for the client's business. In this case, the architect finds a way to upgrade security for the client's spaces or explores relocating the client to a more secure building.

Security design solutions by nature address changing programmatic needs and should be dynamic rather than static. As architectural changes occur and new technology appears, the program can be modified accordingly. Proactive security programs should be capable of ratcheting up and down without significant equipment modifications and with minimal inconvenience to users. It pays to periodically reassess the threat environment by analyzing vulnerabilities and the risk to company assets.

Cost Implications

The level of security for a building is limited by financial considerations. The cost depends on the security need and differentiation between localized damage and overall damage. New building design may focus more on preventing collapse, and some structural integrity measures can be implemented with minor cost implications. The surest way to obtain upper management's commitment to a security strategy is to raise awareness of the economic impact of a security problem and of the benefits to be gained from a safer environment.

building design. To accomplish this, security programming must be an integral part of the project process just as planning for other building systems is. In other words, security should not be "bolted on" later in a project; it should be built in.

DESIGN CONSIDERATIONS

Architects can do little to diminish the potential risk inherent in a facility. However, they can respond to a facility security survey and assessment by designing solutions that address security requirements and by ensuring that security strategies and measures are integrated into the overall building solution. The inclusion of security need not diminish the quality of a facility. Architects apply the same design skills in controlling risks inherent in client occupancy that they use in creating attractive buildings.

❖ Choices and Trade-offs

Businesses interested in taking security seriously do not necessarily have to buy the most sophisticated or expensive security systems, but they do need to take precautions to ensure that business operations remain intact and to minimize their employees' exposure to attack. The project team faces the challenge of balancing cost with security objectives and then prioritizing needs for a valid response.

Determining how many client resources to spend on security involves defining a client's proposed protection level. One way to better understand the choices and trade-offs involved in making such decisions is to develop a matrix that includes project goals, levels of required security protection, and projected cost. Identifying comprehensive project goals and priorities will make it easier to balance risk mitigation during the design process.

Building owners and occupants will no doubt pay more attention to building security issues in the future. However, security factors will have to be considered in a total project context, regardless of the level of security protection that clients deem desirable. For example, some building owners may want to maximize new physical space at the lowest possible cost, which could influence how much can be spent on security measures. Other clients may place a priority on having buildings that reflect a certain image or brand identity or that engender a quality of openness. Such goals would have to be weighed against security approaches that could conflict with them.

It is best if architects and their clients work closely together to define all project needs—including security—and to understand the interrelationships among those needs. With this information in hand, architects can apply the necessary knowledge and skills to achieve balanced design solutions.

❖ Codes

The nature of security is subjective; no standards, best practices, or codes currently exist to provide clear, universally recognized guidance on how to regulate building security. In the future, building codes may change to reflect security requirements. Building security concerns will, however, always be secondary to life safety. One of the most important issues for life safety is to minimize the amount of time it takes people to get out of the building in an emergency.

While security matters remain in the purview of the building owner, codes mandate minimum-level safety standards and therefore have some applicability to the subject of security. In most current prescriptive building codes, requirements are set forth in a manner that dictates precisely how a building will be built, adhering to a "one-size-fits-all" approach to construction. Thus, new technologies and analysis tools can be difficult to use until they have been recognized by and incorporated into building codes. Since building codes are usually developed in three-year cycles, a new technology, approach, or design may not be incorporated until several years later.

Performance-based design for structural safety is well-established in the construction industry and is based on concepts developed by the American Society of Civil Engineers, the Structural Engineers Association of California, and the Federal Emergency Management Agency. Performance-based design provides for safe building design because it is grounded in science, yet it offers flexibility not always afforded by its prescriptive counterpart.

The important point for architects to remember is that all security elements must be code-compliant. The challenge is to ensure that appropriate equipment and security devices satisfy both code and security requirements. For example, the security mandate may require stairwell doors to be locked in a certain way to deter access, while the code requires doors to be unlocked to ensure speedy egress.

❖ Leveraging CPTED Concepts

As stated in an earlier chapter in this book, architects can apply the principles of crime prevention through environmental design (CPTED).

Basic Design Opportunities for Security

Long-term solutions should be planned thoughtfully to balance security, the desire for openness, and financial priorities. The following are some opportunities to consider when integrating security into building design.

Layering and Zones of Security

As described in Chapter 4, it's important to think of a building as a series of concentric layers and zones within those layers (site, façade, interior, interior specialty spaces) and to consider the level of security required for each. The level of security increases relative to one's proximity to the building and its most critical functions. A "targeted protection" strategy, which locates certain assets in a specific protected area, can be more cost-effective than trying to protect those assets in multiple areas. Installation of perimeter security is common when standoff distances are required.

Blast Standoff

Security perimeters are set as far out from a building as the site permits to decrease the likelihood a bomb, particularly a vehicle bomb, could damage the structure. The greater the standoff distance, the less hardening a property needs. Effective standoff is easier to achieve when the tactic is considered before construction rather than as a retrofit. In government buildings, a 50-foot standoff distance is now the requested norm. In congested urban areas, however, such a standoff distance is nearly impossible to achieve.

Hardening the Building

When a standoff distance cannot be achieved, another option may be to harden the building. This can be accomplished by constructing more mass, perhaps by using more concrete, incorporating fewer windows, and enhancing the structural system. Windows may also be designed with a blast curtain that absorbs the force of an explosion instead of resisting it. These curtains diffuse the blast and catch shrapnel before it reaches the building's occupants.

Landscape Architecture

Landscape architecture can play an important role in providing natural security protection, not only for directing people through the grounds to appropriate entrances but also as barriers to protect buildings from vehicles. Planters and bollards in front of buildings may provide protection while enhancing the physical appearance of a facility.

The Parking Question

While garages serving government tenants require employee badges for parking or restrict truck access to patrolled areas, businesses often have fairly open access to parking. A parking garage may be, in fact, one of a building's most vulnerable areas. Potential solutions include requiring employee badges for garage entry, limiting self-parking to badge holders, and restricting large vehicles to controlled areas. The section titled "Security Design Examples" at the end of this chapter includes several hypothetical security design solutions, including considerations for parking facilities.

Access Control

Some businesses are implementing stiffer measures for controlling access both inside and outside their facilities. Security at suburban sites tends to focus on exterior access control, while downtown office security focuses on interior access control. Variables such as the size of the building, the amount of pedestrian traffic, vehicle access and proximity, existence of loading docks, and type of parking available are considered in making decisions about exterior access control. Interior access control involves limiting the number of building entrances and elevators and incorporating the type of access desired by tenants. Some facilities limit points of ingress and egress to one or two entrances, which makes it possible for the architecture itself to assist in the security program. Another approach is to enlarge lobbies to accommodate enhanced security functions.

Space Planning and Adjacencies

Space planning and adjacencies can be used to protect key company functions. For example, the least-critical facilities may be situated in the highest-risk areas of a property; or a long-term storage area may be placed next to a parking area to buffer critical functions such as mechanical and electrical facilities. Size requirements for security features are often overlooked. When monitoring and explosive detection devices are required, sufficient room must be provided for both equipment and queuing, as well as effective segregation of people entering and exiting an area. Space should also be carved out for security command and communications centers.

Segregating Mailrooms and Entrance Lobbies

Mailrooms, entrance lobbies, and other areas where packages are delivered and await screening may need to be environmentally and physically separated from the rest of a building to prevent introduction of a dangerous package into the building. Some companies open mail off-site. Others open questionable mail under a fume hood to protect against cross-contamination.

Refuge Spaces

As a result of the Americans with Disabilities Act, areas of refuge are being identified to assist in building evacuation. Persons with disabilities can await assistance in these areas, which are located in a fire-protected envelope. In a high-rise building, reinforced areas of refuge are often located every few floors so occupants do not have to go to the ground floor to reach safety. The importance of getting people out of a building quickly is obvious, so training and evacuation procedures are important. (Chapter 8 addressed security and emergency preparedness issues in building operation.)

High-Rise Buildings

High-rise buildings present special security concerns, especially related to evacuation. An effective high-rise security strategy is a defend-in-place program, which protects occupants sufficiently inside the building to allow them time to exit safely. In designing high-rises, U.S. developers may look to Asia, where building codes are often more stringent—even if it means using approaches that sacrifice rentable space. The 95-story Shanghai World Financial Center, designed by Kohn Pedersen Fox, provides a fireproofed refuge floor every 15 stories to buy time for evacuees in an emergency. Special elevators in the core allow firefighters to haul equipment up without interfering with the exodus of evacuees.

Speculative Office Buildings

In a depressed real estate market, developers often want to attract government tenants to their speculative office buildings. To compete, some developers have positioned their buildings as "medium-level" security properties, which are attractive to most government tenants. To accomplish this, security must be built in from the outset and upgrades for a potential government tenant anticipated in the building design. Appropriate measures may include the following:

- ✦ Make the structure more resistant to progressive collapse.
- ✦ Make the skin more blast-resistant and omit expensive windows in the base contract (with a provision for adding them later as a tenant cost).
- ✦ Design the lobby to accommodate surveillance and screening equipment, but install it after tenant occupancy.
- ✦ Harden the slabs where required but do not jacket the columns against blast.
- ✦ Create a secure entry room outside the typical building footprint.
- ✦ Provide an external mail facility and, if possible, an external parking facility (difficult in an urban area where below-grade parking is common).

These principles can be used in a variety of contexts, including security-specific risk management. In conjunction with other allied professionals, architects can apply CPTED methodology to create a safe climate in the building environment. By building on the four key CPTED strategies (territoriality, natural surveillance, activity support, and access control), architects can design a physical environment that positively influences human behavior. CPTED principles differ from traditional building hardening techniques by leveraging environmental factors that can affect user perceptions of a space. The way people react to an environment, more often than not, is determined by the cues they pick up from that environment.

❖ Developing and Refining Concepts

Hypothetical security design solutions are included at the end of this chapter to illustrate concepts for addressing security issues in selected building functions. A list of security measures to consider for each application is also included.

The design process embraces problem solving to meet the client's objectives. For security-enhanced projects, the architect's challenge is to determine how to create a design solution that integrates security concepts while projecting an inviting, friendly appearance. Rather than turning ground-floor streetscapes, public buildings, airports, and lobbies into walled fortresses, the architect can integrate modern design concepts and aesthetics with efficiency and security.

Quite often the basic design of a building can greatly enhance or greatly reduce the amount of security needed in that building. For example, design of new buildings should take into account the security of entrances, including lobbies, as well as the placement of parking lots and vehicle access points. In addition, technology exists to make buildings resistant to all sorts of attacks or natural disasters without requiring a design that exudes a "bunker feeling."

CONSTRUCTION DOCUMENTATION

The construction documentation phase of a security-enhanced project presents some challenges to the project team. One is specifying products and equipment that may be unfamiliar, such as surveillance cameras and antiram barriers. Another is the need to omit some details from the construction drawings for security reasons. For example, it may be acceptable to show a surveillance camera for purposes of quality and pricing, but it may not be permissible to indicate its exact location or range of vision. Instead, the architect will walk through the project with the client and contractor to confirm placement and range information.

❖ Selecting and Specifying Security Components

For projects that require a high level of security, use of materials and products that can contribute to security (e.g., glass, cladding, monitoring equipment, bollards) must be considered from the beginning. This awareness makes it easier to integrate such materials and products into the project design. Specifications for materials that affect security are based on function and performance; however, architects who write specs strive to balance functionality with aesthetics in every specification. Often, clients demand products with a strong technical response, although some select vendors based on peer recommendations or an established long-term relationship.

Security design changes requested during design and construction are likely to be functional or operational. On the functional side, security measures might separate traffic in public and private spaces. On the operational side, one public entry and exit could be used to maximize security control.

More and more client companies, particularly those with multiple offices, are developing design standards that incorporate security considerations. When the architect specifies security equipment for a building, it is important that the client's security policy and application standards drive technology selection and application.

Although the American Society for Testing and Materials (ASTM) has some security-related standards, there is no definition of a "secure" product, no industry consensus on basic terminology related to security design, and no recognized methods for testing product performance. The limited amount of information available from any single source and the lack of a recognized clearinghouse for product information means architects specifying security products have to do research. Specifications for "secure" products are generally based on successful experiences with particular products in applications and environments unrelated to the client's business or on proven security equipment offered by the client's security vendors. Architects can also rely on the advice of security consultants or fellow architects more experienced in security-related projects. Nonetheless, product research or testing provides valuable information, and much more attention is paid to performance research in projects that require integration of security systems into other building systems.

Specifications for high-security projects may require a different approach to some standard building products, such as glass and cladding. For example, functionality is an especially important factor in specifying glass performance and blast resistance. Flying glass shards cause the majority of bomb injuries. Techniques and materials such as strengthening the glass and the frame and using window film, blast curtains, or blast-resistant glazing materials are likely to play a larger role in building design. However, the reflective qualities of glass increase as its thickness increases, reducing light transmission and minimizing views. Thus, archi-

Specifying Products for Security-Enhanced Projects

The following issues may be applicable when architects specify products for projects with high-security requirements:

◆ *Appropriateness.* The greatest issue in specifying security products is determining whether a product is appropriate for the level of protection the client needs. Is it overkill? Is it inadequate? Is the protection provided worth the cost?

◆ *Appearance.* Since security-related products can be quite massive and heavy, accommodating their size can be an important factor in building design.

◆ *Cost.* Products and equipment to enhance security levels are by nature specialized and therefore expensive. For example, bullet-resistant glass can cost $300 per square foot, while a glass wall system typically costs $35 to $40 per square foot. Lamination for bullet-resistant glass comes in multiple layers, approximately 2 to 3 inches thick; this thickness significantly increases the weight of the glass, requiring a corresponding increase in load-bearing capacity throughout the building structure.

◆ *Testing.* Custom-designed assemblies are not tested for performance related to air (drafts) or water (leaks) or blast or bullet resistance. Such criteria may need to be defined for each project.

◆ *Sensitive material.* Often, specification criteria are classified and cannot be published. In these cases, specs may not include the name of the building and its location.

◆ *Long lead times.* Many security-related products have long lead times for delivery and should be ordered as early as possible, especially for fast-track projects.

◆ *Codes.* It is important to check a piece of equipment for compatibility with local codes. For example, in New York City, certain "optical portals" cannot be used in a path of egress because they don't "crash out" in a single motion, as required by New York City code.

tects must consider the visibility, reflection, and UV resistance of different materials in order to achieve a satisfactory level of performance for both security and aesthetics.

Another common building material that may affect security performance is cladding. Cladding materials (precast, metal, or stone) affect not only blast resistance and bullet resistance but also the amount of building debris that could result from a blast. Furthermore, exterior building ornamentation can loosen and become lethal flying objects. The more mass a cladding material has, the more resistance it gives and the greater damage it can cause if airborne.

❖ Specifications and Security Consultants

Architects writing specifications for projects with high-security requirements benefit from consultation with qualified, knowledgeable security
professionals. Conflicts between the aesthetics and durability of a product
and its security performance may arise during preparation of specifications. In such cases, architects and security consultants work together to
arrive at an appropriate compromise. The architect shares the design
intent and concept with the security consultant. In turn, the security consultant verifies that the required security criteria can be achieved using the
architect's design. Depending on the contractual scope of work, the security consultant can review the architect's specs or prepare a portion for
insertion in the project specifications.

❖ Document Checking

Security requirements increase the need for document checking and coordination among design team members. Generally, a security review of documents occurs during schematic design, design development, and
construction documentation. In checking the documents, the security consultant ensures that the specified equipment and systems will provide the
level of security required by the client. In some cases, the security consultant
prepares separate computer-aided design (CAD) schematic, design development, and construction document sets indicating security applications. In
either case, CAD documents produced by the architect or security consultant
are usually checked via hard copy because the architect, consultants, and
client often do not use the same software. When consultants or clients are
expected to mark up drawings for the architect, each is assigned a color for
their comments, so all markups can be done on the same document.

For projects with a high level of security, the way documents are handled is especially critical. All participants (including architect, contractor,
client, and consultants) must adhere to project-specific procedures to keep
the security aspects of the project confidential. Such procedures include
instituting a chain of custody for preparation and review of drawings, a safe
storage location, and control of printing (sometimes at a special location).
Someone on the team must know at all times who has custody of the drawings. It is also accepted practice for the security portion of the design to be
separated from other project documents and marked according to the
client's documentation classification scheme.

A requirement for a higher level of security raises a number of collat-
eral questions about security during document production and contract

administration. Typically, anyone can access project drawings during construction. Does that change for this type of project? Where do the drawings reside after construction is complete?

❖ Evaluating Security Performance and Costs

Evaluating the performance of any building function is challenging, but measuring the effectiveness of a security strategy in an architectural project, especially in an integrated strategy framework, is particularly problematic. The goal is to ensure that the client gets the most appropriate level of security for the most reasonable price. The cost for security measures should be commensurate with the threat level identified for a project. Too much security enhancement is wasted money, and too little may heighten threat exposure.

While the negative result of too little security—loss of life and property—is obvious, how is it determined whether a strategy is more or less than what is required? To help a client make decisions about a security program, create detailed cost and performance models. Begin at the outset of a project and focus on specific security measures, related costs, and anticipated performance or benefit of each measure. The initial outlay should be weighed against long-term cost considerations. For example, installing security-monitoring equipment may be expensive, but once such systems are in place, the resultant monitoring capability may make expensive security guards unnecessary. Capital improvements that enhance security operations may make it possible to eliminate costly recurring expenditures such as personnel. Furthermore, security equipment or systems can be an added value when a building goes up for sale. Generally, if a client is willing to spend money on equipment and technology, the level of security can be significantly elevated.

CONSTRUCTION ADMINISTRATION

The construction administration phase of a project with high-security needs is not significantly different from that of any other project. One critical aspect is to keep the entire consultant team (including all security and engineering experts) involved during construction administration. The goal is to ensure project conformance to the design intent and to make it possible to make adjustments quickly and cost-effectively. In the most effective strategy, the contractor makes frequent reports and remains a focused, responsive part of the team. On some government projects, security equipment is installed after construction is completed and the architect is no longer associated with the project. Communication is critical to ensure the best and most appropriate response.

BUILDING OPERATION AND USE

Quality assurance and quality control testing usually occur immediately before a space is occupied, rather than earlier in the construction process. In this way, modifications can be evaluated under actual conditions. For many clients, the ultimate test is whether a facility is perceived to be user-friendly; the client's operations group thus has a major voice in evaluating whether the security in a building design works.

Some architecture firms require the security consultant to regularly use commissioning activities, which usually include training client staff to operate the building systems properly. Through commissioning, it is possible to evaluate whether building systems were installed properly and are operating as designed. Typically, the commissioning process involves prefunctional performance testing (verifying the installation of equipment, materials, and/or systems as stated in the construction documents), functional performance testing (reviewing operation of installed systems, alone and with other systems), functional performance test notification (reporting performance results to all team members), and training the client's facility staff.

❖ Contingency Planning and Recovery

Respondents to a Building Owners and Managers Association (BOMA) International survey (see the sidebar "Terrorism Insurance") cited that more emphasis is generally given to emergency preparedness procedures, such as fire evacuation plans, than to terrorism prevention and response methods. Hot sites, cold sites, or contingency centers are the backbone of any operation in a disaster. A contingency center should be set up in advance exactly as the business itself, with identical software, hardware, other equipment, and enough space to accommodate the number of employees. An alternative strategy for large companies would be to provide reciprocal coverage from one location to another.

Another priority should be the review of existing building emergency plans, which typically include information on water supply, ventilation, communication, and elevators, in addition to general building data and construction information. Such plans allow emergency workers to respond quickly and effectively. By knowing certain facts about a building, emergency crews can make informed tactical decisions, which in turn save lives and property. Most emergency plans are fire-related and often useless in the event of security-related emergencies. Fire-related emergency plans operate under the assumption that elevators must be avoided and that floors closest to the fire must be evacuated first. In some situations, elevators can be employed during evacuation, and the entire building must be evacuated at once. In fact, new technology may soon permit the use of elevators in the case of fires.

❖ Building Information Management

Security enhancement doesn't end with project completion; it often carries over into facility management. Manufacturers are aggressively pursuing new systems and equipment that will allow building managers and owners to more effectively monitor access to buildings as well as specific floors and areas within buildings. We are moving toward increasingly linked data management and facility management systems, which most likely will become Web-based. Besides technical and design integration, enhanced building security will also involve information integration. The potential result will be a unified building management system.

Sharing Experience between Government and Private Sectors

The General Services Administration (GSA) has instituted the First Impressions program "to change the way people perceive government buildings—and the government itself." Through the program, the federal government has learned from the private sector that a building can convey a sense of professionalism and welcome, even with security measures in place. The private sector, on the other hand, wants to learn more about building security from the federal government, particularly regarding security analysis and building systems modifications.

Beginning in 1997, the GSA has developed security design criteria connected to the risk level of a facility as part of its *Facilities Standards for the Public Buildings Service* (for more information, see Appendix B, "Publications"). The intent was to learn from buildings that have "failed" in the past—for example, the Murrah Building in Oklahoma City. Any building can be made substantially more secure, but because U.S. government buildings belong to the people, they must also seem accessible to the public. It is the mission of architects who design for the federal government to ensure that public buildings are not only inviting and comfortable, but secure and—at best—inspiring.

New Practice Outlook

Faced with questions about balancing security with freedom of movement and market realities, architects are grappling with their role in this new practice environment. They are learning worthwhile lessons about making informed decisions that are appropriate for their clients, their firms, and their communities. Architects may find it helpful to follow several simple guidelines to ensure that any security response is appropriate:

- ✦ *Gauge the real threat.* Think about the range of threats that may apply to a project—and the fact that threats are dynamic and thus subject to changes in nature and operations over time. After the Oklahoma City bombing, the government spent $1.2 billion on protection from truck bombs, which at that time were the greatest perceived threat. The spectrum of potential threats has grown remarkably since September 11, 2001.

- ✦ *Be cost-effective.* Balance costs with perceived risks and alternative risk management options. There is not enough money in the world for 100 percent fail-safe security, even if it were possible. Make decisions that are both security-effective and cost-effective.

- ✦ *Use common sense.* At the end of the day, do not check your common sense at the door. Work with security consultants to assess real threats, help clients make cost-effective decisions, and create integrated security solutions that function well for the end user.

Security-enhanced projects challenge architects to seamlessly merge architecture, technology, and security elements to support facility use and operation and to balance security with other building functions. These projects also ask the architect to embrace the role of leader and integrator. Many security decisions involve areas of information and expertise new to most architects, but by assembling appropriate team members and focusing on particular aspects of contractual and design issues architects are succeeding in providing integrated design solutions.

Security Design Examples

There are no cookbook solutions for incorporating security into building design. Each design must be tailored to project functional requirements on a case-by-case basis. The hypothetical examples on the following pages are offered to stimulate "security thinking" by demonstrating how selected security concepts may be applied for representative building uses and functions. The examples include building grounds; a dock area; an office lobby; an apartment lobby; a school; and interior, surface, and stand-alone parking facilities.

Each example has a diagrammatic plan containing several security measures and features. The diagrams are accompanied by lists of potential measures that might be considered in addition to the measures shown in the diagrams. Several of the lists refer to more than one diagram (e.g., lobbies, parking). Each list organizes the security measures under the headings of natural, mechanical, and organizational to reflect the CPTED design concept groupings discussed in Chapter 3.

BUILDING GROUNDS

Security Objectives: *To provide a secured site perimeter and grounds, including a standoff zone commensurate with the security requirements of the facility (see Figure 9.1).*

❖ Natural Measures

- ✦ The access control/entry location is the focal point of the site perimeter.
- ✦ A staging area outside the site perimeter may be used to check vehicles before access to the site is permitted.
- ✦ Site elements such as landscaping (e.g., berms, shrubs), fencing, gates, and bollards provide positive control and form a secure perimeter around the site or campus.
- ✦ Consider standoff distances from the building to mitigate explosive effects within accepted client parameters.
- ✦ Consider establishing a 5- to 10-foot building perimeter zone with tangling underbrush or ground cover.
- ✦ Avoid nooks or recesses that can conceal intruders. Existing nooks and recesses should be observed closely.
- ✦ Use signage to direct visitors, staff, and tenants to security control points.
- ✦ When possible, consider designating entry and exit points as emergency exits, using a limited number of employee entrances (e.g., one at the front and one at the side), and operating only one visitor entrance at the main lobby.

❖ Mechanical Measures

- ✦ A CCTV system may be used to monitor key areas of the building grounds.

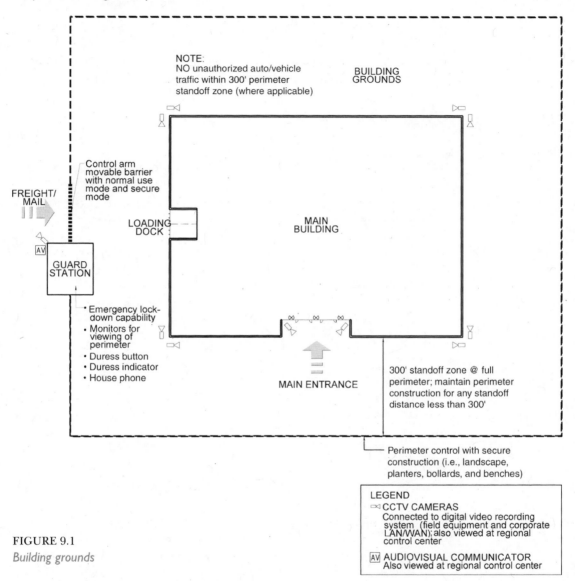

FIGURE 9.1
Building grounds

- ✦ Install secure windows with appropriate locks and consider installing window glass breakage detectors at all ground-floor locations. Consider using unbreakable plastics instead of glass and employing window bars where penetration is likely.

- ✦ Institute an electronic means of visitor control with badges.

- ✦ Consider electronic access control using proximity cards and readers at the main site and facility entrances, as appropriate.

- ✦ Consider instituting parcel inspection (using magnetometers, X-ray screening, or explosive detectors).
- ✦ Require property passes for removal of property from the site.
- ✦ Provide duress devices at reception and control points

❖ Organizational Measures

- ✦ A security guard may be posted in a kiosk or security station to control vehicular entry into the secured perimeter area. Visitors can be required to announce themselves to obtain authorization to proceed to the parking lot, loading dock, or building.
- ✦ Establish a system to determine which cars, trucks, and other vehicles may enter the site and under what conditions.
- ✦ Vehicles with deliveries that have been cleared for entry may be given access to the loading dock. Provide sufficient standoff so that an unauthorized vehicle may be quickly diverted to another area.
- ✦ Through awareness training, instruct employees in how to recognize the warning signs of a troubled or potentially violent person and how to respond.

LOADING DOCK AREA

Security Objectives: *To provide a level of protection for a dock area commensurate with perceived risks in delivery, shipping, and warehousing operations (see Figure 9.2).*

❖ Natural Measures

- ✦ The layout can separate exterior access, interior areas, warehouse spaces, and other storage areas from the main building.
- ✦ Some dock areas may provide a separate entrance leading into a dedicated room for drivers. Others may include a vestibule in which one door closes before the other opens to provide an effective means for monitoring, verifying, and controlling deliveries.
- ✦ Walls, ceilings, and floors may require blast-resistant, hardened construction, based on risk analysis. One exterior wall (i.e., wall with the garage door) may be designed to break away during an explosive event.
- ✦ Dock managers generally prefer an open-window office for controlling and monitoring dock operations. Open-window design is not appropriate for sensitive or critical dock areas such as the warehouse or shipment storage areas.

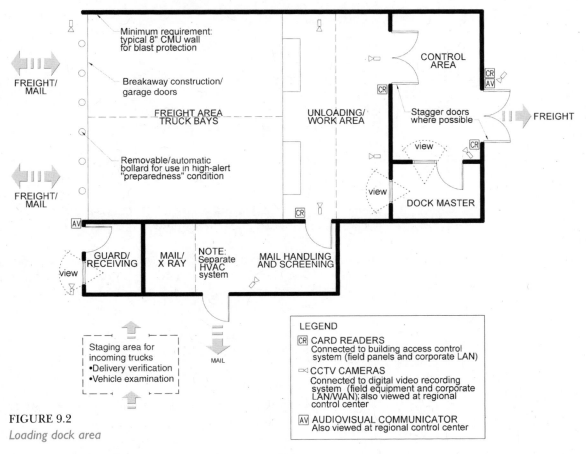

FIGURE 9.2
Loading dock area

✦ Waste management access doors are either manually or electronically controlled, or physical separation from the outside may be achieved by abutting the waste management vehicle or receptacle directly to the door.

✦ When mail is received through the dock area, personnel in a dedicated mailroom (usually behind the receiving area) can screen mail. Walls, ceilings, and floors of the mail screening area (if located in an area other than an at-grade dock area) may require blast-resistant and hardened construction depending on findings of the risk analysis.

✦ Underground dock areas as found in high-rise buildings typically require access restriction at the grade-level entrance along with an active delivery screening function. Loading docks below street level may have a road-blocker arm and riser-type barrier to prevent unauthorized entry during alert conditions.

❖ *Mechanical Measures*

✦ Security access controls are typically placed on personnel entrances in the dock area. Entrances not electronically controlled are generally monitored by a door contact. If a door is to be controlled at all times, a request-to-exit device is placed on the interior wall to avoid nuisance alarms.

✦ Door(s) leading from the dock area may be designated as emergency-only egress doors. These doors are typically monitored using an electronic door contact and are equipped with a local audible alarm device.

✦ An exterior fixed CCTV camera near the door for delivery personnel enables visual verification before access is granted. Some dock managers locate a CCTV camera and intercom submaster station inside the dock manager's office.

✦ Medium- to high-security warehouse facilities usually use CCTV coverage of warehouse activities and of entrance and egress points. CCTV cameras—either fixed, pan-tilt, or in combination—are used to monitor the dock area from a security station inside the building or in a remote location. Camera control is usually restricted to the central security operator, and the camera is typically activated when motion is detected in the field of view.

❖ *Organizational Measures*

✦ Dock managers generally exercise strict control over incoming and outgoing personnel and materials.

✦ Delivery personnel generally communicate with dock area personnel using an intercom.

✦ Roll-up dock doors are typically controlled manually or electronically from the interior and are not used for personnel access.

LOBBY AREAS

Security Objectives: *To provide a primary entrance and greeting area for employees, occupants, and visitors that reflects the intended safety and security principles of the building facility (see Figures 9.3 and 9.4).*

❖ *Natural Measures*

✦ Revolving or double access doors can lead directly to a waiting area with a separate seating breakout space for informal conferences or meetings with visitors. Consider panic hardware on the inside of lobby vestibule doors to ensure proper exiting in case of an emergency.

✦ Entrance doors may have full-height glass sidelights to allow natural surveillance of visitors and outside activities. Laminated
glass may be used on the exterior lobby face to mitigate the
effects of bomb blasts.

✦ Lobby areas may have a receptionist to greet, screen, and direct
visitors. Nonetheless, the design can restrict visitors from entering areas beyond the lobby without authorization.

✦ The focal point of the lobby may be a permanent reception desk
staffed by a concierge or other person. Visitors announce themselves at this point before obtaining permission to access elevators and unsecured stairs. In an apartment lobby, the station is
located close to the entry, with clear views of the corridor leading
to the elevator lobby.

✦ Design of the reception desk allows for a seated person to greet and
screen visitors. It may also accommodate equipment and a work
area for reception activities, including security monitoring and control. Access behind the lobby reception desk should be restricted.

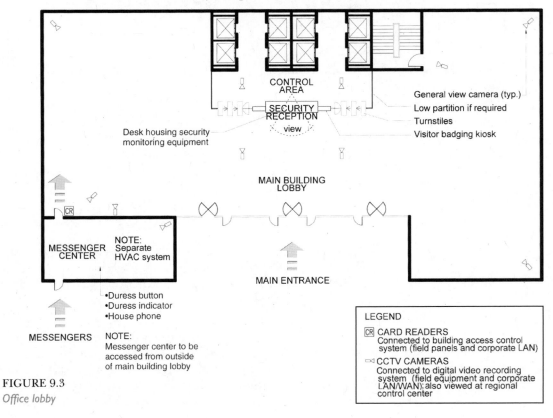

FIGURE 9.3
Office lobby

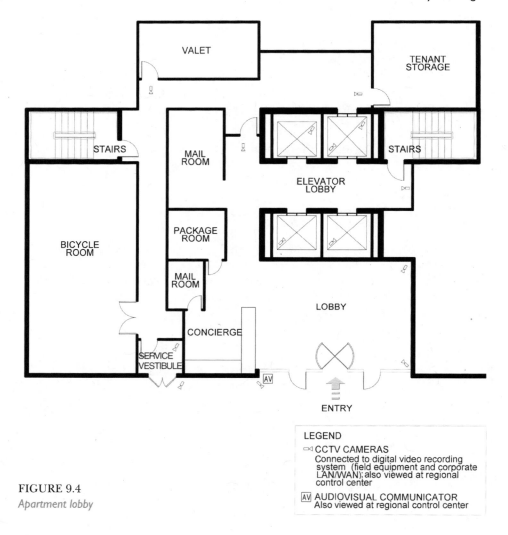

FIGURE 9.4
Apartment lobby

LEGEND
⊲ CCTV CAMERAS
Connected to digital video recording
system (field equipment and corporate
LAN/WAN); also viewed at regional
control center

[AV] AUDIOVISUAL COMMUNICATOR
Also viewed at regional control center

✦ When an access control device is used, the reception desk opening should be inside the screening point. The desk and turnstiles together should impede unauthorized access to the elevator banks or stairs and should give staff an unobstructed view of the lobby.

✦ The lobby design may encompass two distinct zones: one for public, nonscreened functions and another for private functions such as access to stairs and elevators leading to workspaces or living quarters. Employee entrances should be separated from main lobbies. If the interior control point for entry into secured areas cannot be located within the view of the receptionist, access doors to those areas may be monitored by CCTV.

✦ Stair and building doors located outside secure building areas such as lobbies are configured as "exit only" doors and are equipped with monitored door position sensors.

✦ A secure perimeter around the elevator(s) and unsecured stair(s) is another design option that can fill in gaps using architectural barriers (e.g., walls and screens).

✦ Access to interior building spaces should be behind the point of screening. Stairs, elevators, and common internal corridors should not pass through lobby areas.

✦ Visitor restrooms should be accessible from the lobby without entering workspaces or private quarters and should be within the receptionist's visual control.

✦ Consider a lockable storage area within the lobby area for visitor luggage, unclaimed packages, and so on.

❖ *Mechanical Measures*

✦ Optical or electromechanical turnstiles equipped with card readers to control lobby access create a "one-person, one-card" relationship for a higher level of control and accountability. The low profile of this equipment provides for an open atmosphere while creating a psychological barrier to inhibit unauthorized access.

✦ Screening equipment may be used to examine packages, handbags, and other items. Some building owners or users elect to keep the infrastructure in place for this function, allowing them to increase building security during periods of heightened alert and to revert to normal building operations when alerts are relaxed.

✦ Access points that accommodate the requirements of the Americans with Disabilities Act (ADA) need to be integrated with card access points. In more secure buildings, visitors use communication devices such as intercoms to request access. Security access devices would be situated at the main interior access points into the building from the lobby, again incorporating ADA considerations.

✦ Depending on the security systems used, the reception desk may be provided with a duress button, a door release button, a master intercom station, an alarm-monitoring workstation, CCTV monitors, and a video keyboard. The reception desk may have an elevator recall button in the event of an incident in the lobby.

✦ Some buildings facilitate a guest's ability to communicate with the host, either through the receptionist or a telephone for internal calls only.

❖ *Organizational Measures*

✦ Building security plans can provide detailed policies and procedures for the operation of lobby areas. Staff stationed in the lobby may oversee visitor access. Using a video keyboard and video monitors, this individual can provide surveillance of the facility perimeter and interior spaces.

✦ Main lobby doors may be kept unlocked when the reception workstation is staffed. Staff may electronically lock down the building so free egress is not impeded in an emergency but incoming traffic is restricted. Some facilities use access card readers after normal business or operating hours. Others may require card access all the time.

✦ Delivery of packages can be made to a mail or receiving area in or near the loading dock. In apartment lobbies, the mail or package room can be accessed without moving deeper into the elevator lobby.

▮SCHOOL FACILITY

Security Objectives: *To provide access control, surveillance, and response mechanisms consistent with perceived threats and risks. Specific objectives are to prevent crime, reduce fear of crime, and improve the quality of the learning environment by integrating security measures seamlessly into routine educational activities (see Figure 9.5).*

❖ *Natural Measures*

✦ Consider using separate entrances for freight and passenger vehicles.

✦ Use fencing with lockable gates around student parking areas at high schools when control of access and egress during designated hours is desired.

✦ Install lighting to adequately illuminate all parking and perimeter areas.

✦ Place new or relocated trees, shrubs, and other landscape elements to maximize sight lines for natural surveillance.

✦ Consider hardening the lower portion of enclosures around playgrounds in locations with high incidences of violence.

✦ Provide sufficient standoff distance between parking areas and the building to mitigate explosive effects within accepted client parameters.

✦ Double entrance doors may need to be in individual frames with separate latching and locking mechanisms.

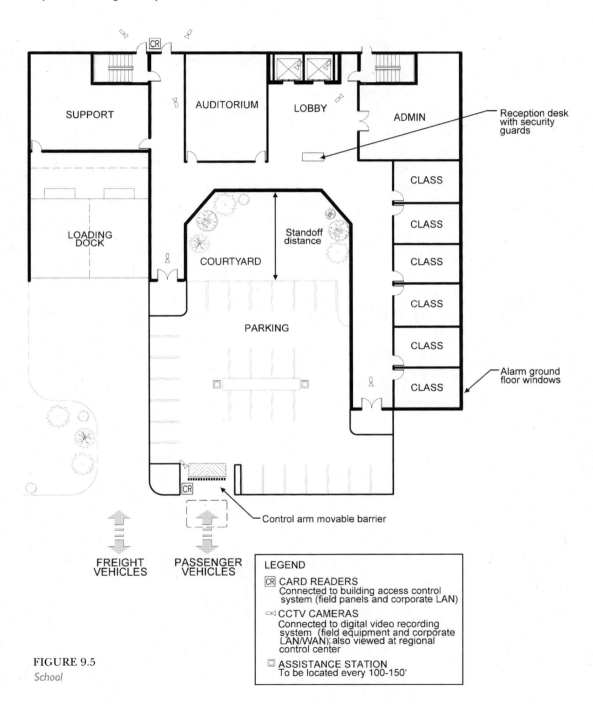

SUPPORT

AUDITORIUM

LOBBY

ADMIN

Reception desk
with security
guards

CLASS

CLASS

CLASS

Standoff
distance

LOADING
DOCK

COURTYARD

CLASS

CLASS

PARKING

CLASS

Alarm ground
floor windows

CLASS

CR

Control arm movable barrier

FREIGHT
VEHICLES

PASSENGER
VEHICLES

LEGEND

CR CARD READERS
Connected to building access control
system (field panels and corporate LAN)

CCTV CAMERAS
Connected to digital video recording
system (field equipment and corporate
LAN/WAN); also viewed at regional
control center

ASSISTANCE STATION
To be located every 100-150'

FIGURE 9.5
School

+ Use properly displayed signage at all entrances to communicate visitor and trespassing policies.

+ Maximize natural surveillance by locating entrances and exits to the parking area close to the building to prevent the need for electronic measures to control parking.

+ Channel students and visitors into the building through a single choke point to enhance screening opportunities and provide greater control over school property.

+ Locate a reception desk to provide clear sight lines to corridors.

+ At reception areas, consider using solid masonry for lower portion of walls or reception desks to shield personnel in an emergency. Consider eliminating glass in the lower portion of walls.

+ Avoid blind corners or alleys.

+ Consider hardened construction for exterior walls, and treat graffiti-prone areas with vandal-resistant surfaces, both interior and exterior.

+ Eliminate, monitor, or control hiding spaces throughout the school (e.g., recessed corridor doors and hidden alcoves).

+ Classroom doors can be locked from the exterior with free egress from the inside. Glass portions of the doors may be used for natural surveillance. Doors other than fire doors may also require safety glazing.

+ Consider providing entrances without doors to group toilets for better supervision of restroom use.

❖ *Mechanical Measures*

+ Electronic control of public access to the school and school grounds can be centrally monitored with visual and physical control from the administration area. Access to the administration area and others such as the kitchen can also be electronically controlled.

+ Two-way communications may be used from all classrooms, lounges, janitorial storage areas, and other areas.

+ Consider use of portable communications when teachers are outside the building (e.g., on playground or bus duty).

+ Panic or silent distress alarms can be installed at each teacher's desk and in the administration area.

+ Separate, dedicated outgoing phone lines for emergency purposes may be necessary in classrooms.

+ Panic hardware for exterior doors should be considered.

- Video monitoring, using CCTV cameras, of entrances and exits can be considered to provide a deterrent and an assessment mechanism.
- After-school protection of the school buildings from fire and intrusion is accomplished by means of installing separate or integrated systems.
- Consider alarms on ground-floor windows and doors.
- Card readers are optional for access control into the parking area.

❖ Organizational Measures

- Develop, document, and promulgate security policies and procedures, including identification of disciplinary situations (e.g., weapons violations) that require a security response.
- Monitor all exterior doors for access control both while school is in session and after school hours.
- Employ security personnel as required for control, screening, and monitoring functions.
- Encourage law enforcement personnel to make periodic site visits to indicate their presence and to increase safety and security awareness in students.
- Develop contingency plans for emergency and life-threatening situations.

■ PARKING FACILITIES

Security Objectives: *To provide safe and secure vehicular parking environments in configurations that may include surface parking adjacent to a building, surface parking remote from a building, a stand-alone parking structure, or an interior parking area in a building containing other uses (see Figures 9.6, 9.7, 9.8, and 9.9). The considerations and features described here apply to all of these configurations unless indicated.*

❖ Natural Measures

- Depending on a parking facility's proximity to other buildings and the results of a risk assessment, consider hardening the parking structure.
- For stand-alone parking structures, access and egress for vehicles and pedestrians is generally limited to a portal for each purpose. There are no points of entry leading to secure building areas.
- Parking areas in buildings are accessed through a control or entry point at street level. To the extent possible, interior parking is situated away from critical business units and other plant

facilities. Two lobbies (secured and unsecured) with open stairs providing full visual access are shown in Figure 9.6. Consideration may be made for blast mitigation of the area if the building superstructure is supported by the parking structure.

✦ Site and landscape elements may be used to enhance positive access control for remote surface parking areas.

✦ Adjacent surface parking can be controlled by a secure perimeter around the parking site. The perimeter can be protected through use of site elements such as berms, shrubs, fencing, gates, or bollards. Access and egress is limited to one portal.

✦ Both remote and adjacent surface parking facilities can maintain lines of sight from the building by having trees no higher than 8 feet and construction and landscaping no higher than 3 feet. The parking is situated with a sufficient amount of standoff distance

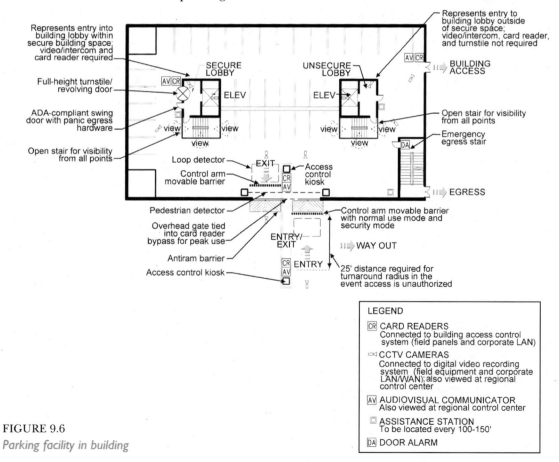

FIGURE 9.6

Parking facility in building

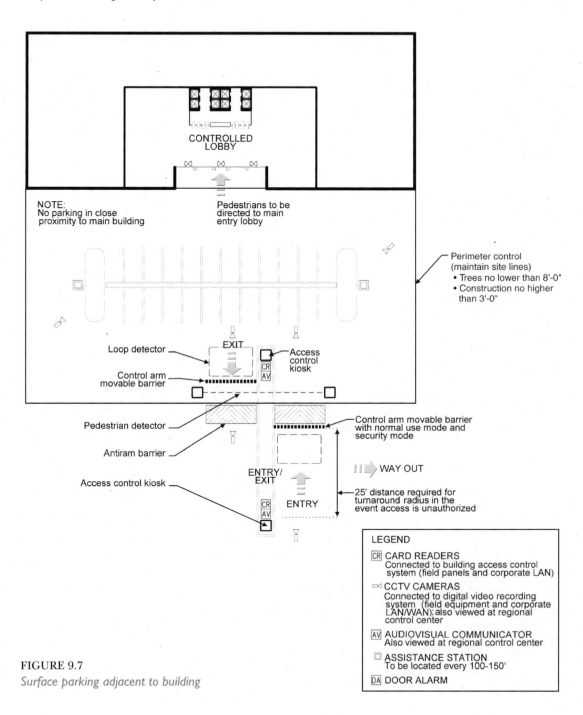

FIGURE 9.7

Surface parking adjacent to building

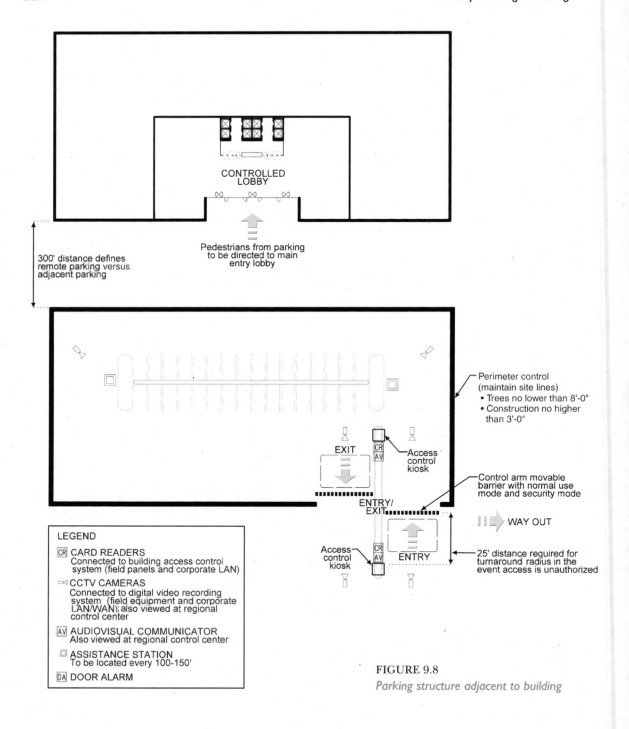

CONTROLLED LOBBY

Pedestrians from parking to be directed to main entry lobby

300' distance defines remote parking versus adjacent parking

Perimeter control (maintain site lines)
• Trees no lower than 8'-0"
• Construction no higher than 3'-0"

EXIT

Access control kiosk

Control arm movable barrier with normal use mode and security mode

ENTRY/EXIT

WAY OUT

Access control kiosk

ENTRY

25' distance required for turnaround radius in the event access is unauthorized

LEGEND

CR CARD READERS
Connected to building access control system (field panels and corporate LAN)

◁ CCTV CAMERAS
Connected to digital video recording system (field equipment and corporate LAN/WAN); also viewed at regional control center

AV AUDIOVISUAL COMMUNICATOR
Also viewed at regional control center

☐ ASSISTANCE STATION
To be located every 100-150'

DA DOOR ALARM

FIGURE 9.8
Parking structure adjacent to building

to mitigate explosive effects on adjacent buildings within accepted client parameters.

✦ Adequate lighting is critical to support surveillance and integral to personnel safety and security. Clear sight lines should afford surveillance of parking areas.

✦ Adequate standoff distance is provided between the access control mechanism (e.g., electronic gate or arm) and the entry portal so that unauthorized incoming vehicles can be moved so they do not interfere with authorized incoming traffic.

✦ Consider separating visitor parking from employee parking.

❖ *Mechanical Measures*

✦ Positive control may be accomplished through a road blocker and rising barrier configuration in both entry and exit lanes, card access or ticket dispenser for entry, and staffed egress controls at the exit barrier.

✦ Exit lanes can be equipped with a barrier (movable arm and tire shredder), to prevent entry, and a loop detector that allows egress from the secure side of the access control barrier.

✦ Staffed control points can provide continuous surveillance via fixed CCTV camera(s).

✦ Typically, card-based access control systems are used at all doors inside the parking facility with direct access to secured building areas or elevator lobbies. Elevator lobbies servicing parking areas provide free access at all points only when they are separated from main building elevators.

✦ Depending on the facility configuration, a mix of pan-tilt and fixed cameras or all fixed or all pan-tilt cameras can be used for surveillance of parking areas. The level of surveillance (100 percent coverage or other) depends on client preferences and risk assessment. With additional security devices inside the parking facility (e.g., intercoms, emergency telephones, area detection, and audio detection devices), automatic video scene call-up for operator assessment is desirable.

✦ Intercoms are typically used for access and egress control, along with elevator lobby communications. Intercoms used in combination with CCTV assessment provide for better security.

✦ Emergency call stations are strategically placed within parking facilities (central or multiple locations). Emergency call stations can be integrally linked with CCTV assessment.

✦ Audio detection devices may be used in stairs to detect screams or other signs of distress. These may be linked to fixed cameras in stairs.

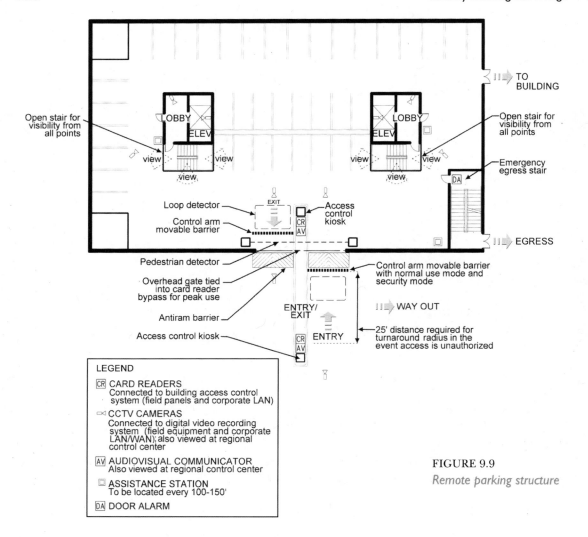

FIGURE 9.9
Remote parking structure

♦ Cameras can record constantly, or they may be event-driven. Video motion can detect oncoming vehicles or personnel entering a parking area.

❖ *Organizational Measures*

♦ Parking restrictions and procedures should be strictly followed.
♦ Security patrols of parking areas should be frequent.
♦ Contract parking operations personnel should have limited security functions.

Appendix A. Organizations

American Crime Prevention Institute
ACPI, a division of the AEGIS Protection Group, Inc., offers crime prevention education, publications, and on-site training for law enforcement agencies and the private sector, including basic and advanced CPTED seminars, Basic Crime Prevention and Counterterrorism Certification training, and on-site crime prevention training. (www.aegisprotect.com/acpi/Default.htm).

American Institute of Architects
The AIA Building Security Through Design Resource Center offers architects, their clients, and the public up-to-date, in-depth material about security information resources, publications, continuing education, and special industry events. (www.aia.org or call AIA Information Central at 800-242-3837).

American Society of Civil Engineers
ASCE formed teams to study the structure and collapse of the World Trade Center and the Pentagon due to the terrorist attacks. ASCE disaster response programs include its critical infrastructure response initiative (CIRI) and an online publication, *Vulnerability and Protection of Infrastructure Systems: The State of the Art,* which presents 24 journal articles concerning infrastructure vulnerability and strategies and guidelines for mitigating the effects of natural and man-made disasters. (www.asce.org).

American Society of Heating, Refrigerating and Air-Conditioning Engineers
ASHRAE conducts research to address safety in the design and operation of building systems, including prevention of hazardous material entry into ventilation systems. The ASHRAE Learning Institute offers education and training. (www.ashrae.org).

ASIS International

Formerly the American Society for Industrial Security (ASIS), this international organization serves professionals responsible for security. ASIS has been increasing its involvement with other professions, including architects, and includes a Security Architecture and Engineering Council as a resource for architecture, engineering, and technical integration design issues related to protection of assets within the built environment. ASIS offers educational programs and numerous publications, including a monthly magazine. (www.asisonline.org, www.securitymanagement.com).

Building Owners and Managers Association International

BOMA, representing the commercial real estate industry, provides research and resources, in audio and printed form, concerning security and emergency planning for the workplace. *The Property Professional's Guide to Emergency Preparedness* (a companion to *Are Your Tenants Safe? BOMA's Guide to Security and Emergency Planning*) presents a step-by-step guide to comprehensive emergency planning. (www.boma.org).

Federal Bureau of Investigation

The FBI's Awareness of National Security Issues and Response (ANSIR) Program provides unclassified information for espionage, counterintelligence, counterterrorism, economic espionage, cyber and physical infrastructure protection, and national security issues (www.fbi.gov/hq/nsd/ansir/ansir.htm). Its *Terrorism in the United States* report is updated annually. (www.fbi.gov/publications.htm).

International Facility Management Association

IFMA offers a Writing an Emergency Plan workshop. Emergency response material on IFMA's Web site includes information on disaster planning, recovery, business continuity, and a bulletin board. (www.ifma.org).

National Crime Prevention Institute

NCPI, part of the University of Louisville's Department of Justice Administration, offers training in all aspects of crime prevention for police, planners, and other government officials. Some courses are available online. (www.louisville.edu/a-s/ja/ncpi).

National Research Council

The NRC's books, published by the National Academy Press and available online or by purchase, cover topics such as blast-resistant construction, risk analysis, and other issues related to security and design and construction. (www.nap.edu).

Sandia National Laboratories

Sandia's Emerging Threats Program applies science and engineering expertise to nonmilitary national security threats. (www.sandia.gov/ENST.htm). Its Architectural Surety Program aims to make buildings more resistant to assault. (www.sandia.gov/archsur/C33.htm).

Appendix B. Publications

Security Planning and Design

American Society for Testing and Materials. ASTM E1946-98: *Standard Practice for Measuring Cost Risk of Buildings and Building Systems* and E1369-98: *Standard Guide for Selecting Techniques for Treating Uncertainty and Risk in the Economic Evaluation of Buildings and Building Systems*. Procedure for measuring cost risk for buildings using a simulation technique running on commercially available cost risk analysis software.

Broder, James F. *Risk Analysis and the Security Survey*, 2d ed. (Butterworth-Heinemann, 2000). Presents the principles of risk analysis, explains how to perform security surveys, and covers business impact analysis, business continuity planning, and response planning. Extensive appendixes contain survey worksheets, forms, checklists, and other useful information.

Crowe, Timothy D. *Crime Prevention Through Environmental Design: Applications of Architectural Design and Space Management Concepts*, 2d ed. (Butterworth-Heinemann, 2000). Updated version of CPTED methodology with practical guides for several environmental settings and facility types.

Garcia, Mary Lynn. *The Design and Evaluation of Physical Protection Systems* (Butterworth-Heinemann, 2001). Describes the design and integration process for security technologies within the context of determining objectives, designing the system, and evaluating the system.

McDowell, Bruce D., and Andrew C. Lemer, eds. *Uses of Risk Analysis to Achieve Balanced Safety in Building Design and Operations* (National Academy Press, 1991). Risk analysis for increasing building safety and security and protecting property values. Risk analysis procedures, references on risk analysis for existing buildings. Online at www.nap.edu/catalog/1907.html.

National Research Council. *Protection of Federal Office Buildings Against Terrorism* (National Academy Press, 1988). Guidelines for security management; threat, assessment, and vulnerability analysis; and security guidelines for sites and buildings (readily adapted for private sector facilities). Online at http://www.nap.edu/catalog/9808.html.

U.S. General Accounting Office. *Building Security: Security Responsibilities for Federally Owned and Leased Facilities* (GAO-03-8, October 2002). A broad review of 22 federal agencies' responsibilities for the protection of the federal buildings they own or occupy, including whether the agencies have completed security assessments for their facilities; the types of security forces and technologies used; funding for security operations; coordination of security efforts within and among agencies; and impediments to tightening security at federal buildings. An appendix lists sources of guidance for addressing building security vulnerabilities. Available online through http://www.gao.gov.

U.S. General Services Administration, Office of the Chief Architect. *Facilities Standards for the Public Buildings Service* (PBS-PQ100.1), Chapter 8: Security Design. (GSA, 2000). Guidelines for making security an integral part of a building; covering planning and cost; architecture and interior design; new construction; historic buildings; structural, mechanical, and electrical engineering; and electronic security.

U.S. General Services Administration, Public Buildings Service. *Balancing Security and Openness in Public Buildings* (GSA, November 30, 1999). A thematic summary of a symposium on security and the design of public buildings, jointly sponsored by the GSA Public Buildings Service, the U.S. Department of State, and the American Institute of Architects. Online at http://hydra.gsa.gov/pbs/pc/gd_files/SecurityOpenness.pdf.

Williams, Timothy, ed. *Protection of Assets Manual* (POA Publishing, 1999). Four volumes of information, updated monthly by subscription, covering hundreds of key management issues and all aspects of security training, including employee awareness, internal and external theft and fraud, security and civil law, investigations, ethics, and substance abuse. Now available in a searchable, online format at http://www.protectionofassets.com.

Building Hardening and Blast Mitigation

Hinman, Eve, and David J. Hammond. *Lessons from the Oklahoma City Bombing: Defensive Design Techniques* (ASCE Press, 1996). The structure of the Murrah building and damage witnessed by the authors, with identification of weak points in the design. Measures that structural engineers can take to limit damage from blast loads.

Leyendecker, Edgar V., and Ellingwood, Bruce R. *Design Methods for Reducing the Risk of Progressive Collapse in Buildings* (National Bureau of Standards, Washington D.C., NBS BSS 98, 1977). Provides general engineering guidelines and design methodologies that can reduce the risk of catastrophic progressive collapse in buildings. Provides qualitative recommendations and detailed examples.

National Research Council. *Blast Mitigation for Structures: 1999 Status Report on the DTRA/TSWG Program* (National Academy Press, 2000). Program of the Defense Threat Reduction Agency (DTRA) to reduce loss of life and injuries to occupants of buildings targeted by terrorists. Development of innovative techniques for new structures and for retrofitting existing facilities. Online at www.nap.edu/catalog/9861.html.

National Research Council. *Protecting Buildings from Bomb Damage: Transfer of Blast-Effects Mitigation Technologies from Military to Civilian Applications* (National Academy Press, 1995). Blast-resistant technologies and methods adapted to design of civilian structures, with commercial buildings as an example. Assessment of threats to civilian buildings, specifications for hardening existing buildings, and economic considerations. Online at http://www.nap.edu/catalog/5021.html.

Security Engineering, vols. 1–3, TM 5-853/AFMAN 32-1071 (Washington, D.C.: Departments of the Army and the Air Force, May 1994). Provides an excellent reference for a wide variety of building hardening techniques. Covers specific design recommendations to minimize the risk of forced entry, ballistic attacks, and high explosive bomb blasts. The manual is intended to guide designers in providing economical unobtrusive protective design solutions.

Structures to Resist the Effects of Accidental Explosions, TM 5-1300/NAVFAC P-397/AFM 88-22 (Washington, D.C.: Departments of the Army, Navy, and Air Force, December 1991). Technical manual originally intended to provide guidelines for the blast-resistant design of military installations. The concepts described in this manual have been successfully adapted to a vast array of building hardening projects, ranging from government office buildings, to corporate headquarters structures, to U.S. embassies overseas.

Biochemical and Radiological Protection for Buildings

U.S. Army Corps of Engineers. TI 853-01: *Protecting Buildings and Their Occupants from Airborne Hazards* (October 2001). Presents a variety of ways to prevent, protect against, and reduce the effects of outdoor and indoor releases of hazardous materials. Online at http://BuildingProtection.sbccom.army.mil.

U.S. Army Corps of Engineers. ETL 1110-3-498: *Design of Collective Protection Shelters to Resist Chemical, Biological, and Radiological (CBR) Agents* (February 1999). Explains and provides guidance on designing and installing positive-pressure and filtering protection systems. Online at www.usace.army.mil/inet/usace-docs/eng-tech-ltrs/etl1110-3-498/toc.htm.

Security Management and Operations

Building Owners and Managers Association International. *Are Your Tenants Safe? BOMA's Guide to Security and Emergency Planning* (2000). Provides guidelines for developing comprehensive plans for different emergencies and security threats to building facilities. Online at http://www.boma.org/pubs/epg.htm.

Building Owners and Managers Association International. *The Property Professional's Guide to Emergency Preparedness* (2002) is a companion to *Are Your Tenants Safe?* Addresses the emergency planning process in further detail including actions to reduce the threat from emergencies that may affect a facility. Online at http://www.boma.org/pubs/epg.htm.

Craighead, Geoff. *High-Rise Security and Fire Life Safety* (Butterworth-Heinemann, 1996). Addresses operational aspects of security and life safety for high-rise structures. Selected topics include building systems, emergency planning, security management, and security rules and procedures.

Appendix C. Glossary

access control. The functional component of security used to monitor and restrict the movement of individuals, vehicles, and material into, out of, and within secured areas.

adversary. An individual or group of individuals who may carry out spontaneous or premeditated actions against assets. Examples of adversaries include vandals, angry or deranged individuals, disgruntled employees, criminals, extremists, and terrorists.

asset. A resource that is important and of value to the needs of an individual, a business, or an organization. Asset categories include people, property, and information.

asset analysis. The process that identifies assets, estimates their value, and determines their criticality.

building hardening. The process of increasing the resistance of a building to the effects of forced entry, ballistic attacks, and bombings.

countermeasure. *See* security measure.

crime prevention through environmental design (CPTED). Design concept based on the theory that criminal and illegal behavior can be influenced by how physical environments are designed. CPTED applies *natural*, *mechanical*, and *organizational* concepts for access control, surveillance, activity support, motivation reinforcement, and territorial definition. CPTED evolved from the concept of *defensible space*.

defensible space. Public and semipublic space that can be protected in the sense that it is surveyed, demarcated, or maintained by someone. (Oscar Newman's 1973 study of the same name described the concept in the context of creating safer environments in urban public housing.)

design basis threat (DBT). The potential source of harm or loss determined to represent the highest likelihood of attack and the greatest probability of inflicting harm or loss on a client's assets.

detection. The process of discovering unlawful or undesirable behavior that may otherwise go unnoticed. Detection includes both sensing activity and signaling alarms.

emergency preparedness plan. A plan that defines goals, activities, and procedures to help businesses and organizations prepare for, respond to, and recover from the effects of disasters, accidents, and related adverse events.

hardening. Modification of a building element (e.g., wall, door, window) to make it more difficult to penetrate.

incident threshold. An indicator or set of indicators signifying an incident is imminent that requires emergency measures to avert. Potential incidents can be divided into levels (e.g., Levels I and II) to help security staff identify appropriate responses.

malevolent action. A deliberate human action with intent to harm or destroy assets.

perimeter. The outer boundary of a protected area (usually considered the first line of defense for a building or facility).

progressive collapse. A chain-reaction failure of building structural members to an extent that is disproportionate to the original localized damage. Such failure may result in upper floors of a building collapsing onto lower floors.

risk. A concept that acknowledges the uncertainty of financial loss, the variations between expected and unexpected results, or the probability that a loss will occur.

risk analysis. A process for estimating potential losses resulting from the effects of an adverse event.

safety. The protection of people and property, especially during abnormal conditions such as those resulting from fires, floods, electrical faults, toxic releases, and other adverse events. Such conditions may arise from either natural occurrences or intentional acts.

security. The protection of assets from the effects of threats. Security is achieved through a combination of physical, technological, and operational measures.

security assessment. A combination of activities that include asset, threat, vulnerability, and risk analyses, the results of which help to determine the level of protection and functional security design criteria for a property.

security measure. A physical feature, technology, or operational procedure intended to protect an asset or group of assets. (A security measure is sometimes called a *countermeasure*.)

standoff distance. The distance maintained between an exterior building wall and the potential location of an explosion.

surveillance. The functional component of security intended to provide controlled observation. Surveillance may be carried out covertly (e.g., concealed cameras) or overtly (e.g., uniformed security personnel).

territoriality. A CPTED concept delineating ownership and a distinction between private, semipublic, and public spaces. The concept is used to create environmental settings where the appearance of strangers and intruders stands out.

terrorism. The unlawful use of force or violence against persons or property to intimidate or coerce a government, a civilian population, or any segment thereof in furtherance of political or social objectives.

threat. An adverse event with the potential to harm or destroy an asset. Threats can be unintentional (natural disasters and accidents) or intentional (humanly motivated actions).

threat analysis. A process for identifying potential threats or adverse events that may be taken against an organization, and the possible outcomes and effects of such events.

TNT equivalent weight. The energetic output of an explosive compound expressed as the weight of TNT (trinitrotoluene) required to yield a similar output.

vulnerability. A physical or operational weakness in a building that can be exploited by a threat.

vulnerability analysis. A process that identifies, evaluates, and prioritizes vulnerabilities in a facility.

Illustration Credits

Index